Brief Abstract
of
Lower Norfolk County
and
Norfolk County
WILLS
1637-1710

Charles Fleming McIntosh
of Norfolk, Virginia

HERITAGE BOOKS
2009

HERITAGE BOOKS
AN IMPRINT OF HERITAGE BOOKS, INC.

Books, CDs, and more—Worldwide

For our listing of thousands of titles see our website
at
www.HeritageBooks.com

A Facsimile Reprint
Published 2009 by
HERITAGE BOOKS, INC.
Publishing Division
100 Railroad Ave. #104
Westminster, Maryland 21157

Originally published in 1914 by
The Colonial Dames of America
in the State of Virginia

— Publisher's Notice —
In reprints such as this, it is often not possible to remove blemishes from the original. We feel the contents of this book warrant its reissue despite these blemishes and hope you will agree and read it with pleasure.

International Standard Book Numbers
Paperbound: 978-1-58549-264-0
Clothbound: 978-0-7884-8149-9

PREFACE

About four or five years ago, the Abstractor of these wills was employed to examine the titles to a large number of timber tracts, situated in Norfolk County, and to carry the same back to the original grants. The first obstacle he found in his way was the lack of an Index, for the years 1637 to 1753, and it was, therefore, necessary to index deeds and wills for that period. This index required the reading, page by page, of the first nineteen volumes in the Norfolk County Clerk's Office, and formed the basis upon which the present work was made.

It was also found necessary to abstract the early wills to show an unbroken chain of title back to the grants, and, while abstracting for this purpose, it was thought wise to add such data as could be used for genealogical and historical purposes. So a full description of the tracts or plantations was made, each proper name listed, useful references to personal property, former residence when given, clues, and, in fact, all matter which attracted the Abstractor's attention or fancy.

He copied what was found, and wishes to emphasize that this Abstract is for the purpose of preservation, and is not a creation. Some of the early books are rapidly becoming useless, through decay, gross neglect and misuse, and were found in a sad and lamentable condition.

In using this Abstract, it is well to bear in mind the brief development of Norfolk County: Norfolk County was originally a part of Elizabeth City County, formed in 1634. About 1636 that portion of Elizabeth City County, lying on the south side of the James River, was formed into New Norfolk County. About 1637 New Norfolk County was divided into Upper Norfolk and Lower Norfolk Counties; Upper Norfolk County later became Nansemond County, and in 1691 Lower Norfolk was divided into Princess Anne County and Norfolk County.

In using this Abstract the reader will doubtless notice the scarcity of wills in the early period. An attempt was made to find the original wills, but no package was found prior to 1710. It is a known fact that some of these original wills were sent to James City, and probably some were sent to Williamsburg. All of these wills were burned. Oral or nuncupative wills appear in the early volumes as depositions, and were difficult to find; possibly some have been overlooked.

It is the intention of the Abstractor to continue this work from 1710 to 1800. He sincerely hopes that the present volume will be found useful to those interested in the early Colonial period.

CHARLES F. MCINTOSH.

Norfolk, Virginia. **1914**

KEY

Dotted lines indicate matter intentionally left out by the Abstractor.

Italics indicate uncertainty of spelling on the part of the Abstractor.

The testator's name in heavy type is taken from the spelling of the name, as first given, in the body of the will, and not from the signature.

When the will has been torn, decayed, or is illegible, it is so marked in parenthesis.

The Index, so far as possible, is made up from the spelling of the testator's name in the signature, and is not taken from the body of the will.

Where the exact mark of the testator or witness could not be set in type, a plus, (+), mark as used.

NOTE—In looking up names do not rely too strictly on exact spelling, our ancestors were not perfect spellers, neither were those who drew the wills, or the Clerk's who spread them. Often a name is spelled two and three different ways in the same will.

Brief Abstract

of

Lower Norfolk County and Norfolk County Wills

1637 - 1710

JOHN GOOCH of Linhaven *pishe* In ye County of new norfolke, planter . . .

Book "A," part 1, f. 54.

Dated 1 Feb. 1639. Recorded Mch. Court 1640/1.
Proved by witnesses.

. . . sett free Samill Gaskins . . .

. . . my whole estate unto my Lovinge and Trusty ffriends Tho. Bullock *Sirgin* & Tho. ffrancis Gentillman . . .

Witnesses: Robt. Gorvis Clarke &
Thomas Codd. John Gooch.

JOHN ***MAUNE*** . .
Book "A," part 3, f. 8.
Dated ——— (none) ———

Recorded. February Court 1644.

. . . to my beloved wife Isbell M*au*ne all my goods Lands . . .

. . . to my sonne John M*au*ne . . . heifer . . . ye land I doe nowe possesse when he comes to ye age of one twenty yeares . . .

. . . to my daughter Elizabeth M*aun*e one Sowe . . . at her day of marriage . . .

. . . brother John Finck shall have ye overseeing of this my will . . .

witness:—Phillip Land.
——— y Phipp John X Maune.
his marke.

(Not Proved).

RICHARD HALL of Virginia . . .
Book B, f. 96.
Dated 1 August 1648.
Recorded 16 Nov. 1648.
. . . unto Mathew Howard the elder . . .
. . . unto Ann " . . .
. . . unto Elizabeth " . . .
. . . unto Cornelius " . . .
. . . unto Mathew " the younger . . .
. . . unto Samuel " . . . . .
. . . unto Thomas Pill . . .
. . . I desire Mathew Howard ye elder my sole Executor . . .
witness: Cornelius Lloyd Richard Hall
Tho. Pill
his marke.

JNO ffORINHAUGH of Elizabeth River in Virginia, planter . . .
Book B f. 110.
Dated 7 June 1648.
Proved by both witnesses 15 June 1649.
. . . to my beloved wife Deborah fforinhaugh . . . all lands . . .
. . . wife Executrix . . .
witness: Ed. Hall, Chicurgion.
George Heigham
Jno. fforinhaugh & his Seale.

EDWARD HODGE of Virginia M^r^chant . . .
Book B, f. 119.
Dated 10 June 1649.
Proved 15 June 1649 by both witnesses.
. . . y^t^ my loving friend Mr Cornelius Lloyd doe Re^c^ all such goods servants as shallbee consigned to mee Edward Hodge this next shipping out of England . . .
. . . brother Mr. Samuell Hodg. M^r^chant . . .
. . . unto William Robinson . . .
. . . plantation in Linehaven . . .
witnesses:
M
Mathew H Howard . . . oge and his seale.
George Ridley.

SARAH JULIAN, Widd of ye County of Lower Norfolk . . .

Book B. f. 120.

Dated A° 1649.

. . . unto Sarah Kempe the daughter of George Kempe of ye same County planter . . .

The m^r^ke of Sarah Julian.

Recorded 13 May 1649.

JOHN WATKINS . . .

Book B f. 128.

Dated 26 Feb. 1648.

Proved 31 Oct. 1649 by both witnesses.

. . . wife ffrancis Watkins . . . plantation . . . untill sonne John comes fully to the age & yeares of *discerne* . . .

. . . my children . . .

. . . wife extx. . . .

. . . friends Mr. Phillipp Bennett & Mr. Edward Lloyd to bee Overseers . . .

Witnesses: Richard Owens.
The Marke M of
Mathew Read.

The marke of
John
Watking & Seale.

ANNE HAYES—(torn)— . . .

Book B. f. 145

Dated—(none)— Recorded 26 March 1650.

. . . Robt Hayes my late dec. husband . . .

. . . Nathaniel Hayes my sonne . . .

. . . Adam Hayes my sonne . . .

. . . Tho. Workman my sonne . . .

. . . Jn° Workman my sonne . . .

. . . Jane *N*edham my Bonswoman . . .

Witnesses: Jno. Hol*mes*.
Martin.
W. H. J*ermy*.

Anne Hayes & her Seale.
her marke.

JOHN BOLTON . . .

Book B. f. 149.

Dated 17 Feb. 1649.

Proved 18 June 1650.

. . . unto daughter of John Sutton dec. . . .

. . . " Ann Wesgate Daughter of Henry Wesgate . . .

. . . " John Sp*encer* . . .

. . . " my wife . . .

witnesses: Tho. Ward. The m^r^ke of
Will C*eay*. John Boulton

marke of Henry Brakes.

JOHN HATTON, in Elizabeth River in ye County of Lower Norfolke . . .

Book B. f 149. Dated 17 Feb. 1649.

Proved 18 June 1650 by both witnesses.

. . . unto Dorothy Hatton wife . . . cow I had of Mr. Tho. Browne . . . for natural life . . . then to sonne . . .

. . . all my children . . .

. . . John Hatton my eldest sonne, after decease of my said wife his Mother . . .

witnesses: John Hill. John Hatton
Tho Browne. his marke

GEORGE HORNER . . .

Book B. f. 160.

Dated 20 Aug. 1650.

Proved ———

. . . unto wife extx

. . . three children

. . . three daughters under age . . .

. . . Cosen John Holmes & Mr. L*em*uell Mason overseers.

witnesses:

Henry Brakes by mark &
Edward Gradwell by mark.

George Horner.

RICHARD ffOSTER of Elizabeth River Virginia . . .
Book B. f. 160.
Dated 31 July 1650.
. . . unto Sarah Williams . . . under sixteen . . .
. . . unto John Carraway, the said Sarah her father in lawe . . .
. . . in case the said Sarah Williams should dye before shee comes at age to receive them. That then they shall be equally devided amongst the rest of the Children of Rodger, Williams and John Carraway . . .

witnesses: Robt. Eyre. Richard Foster.
his marke
Simond S. H. Hancocke.

JOHN GILHAM . . . (Nuncupative) . . .
Book C. f. 1.
Dated ———
Recorded 15 Jan. 1651.
Mary White, aged 17 years or therabouts . . . sworne & Exam'd as a witness to ye last will & testamt of Capt. Leift John Gilham: saith That all & singler his Estate in this Country he did bequeath unto his brother in lawe Mr. Roger ffountayne, & did appoint him his sole Executo^r of his last Will & testam^t, onely did bequeath unto his Eldest sonne John Gilham his Rapier, & his usuall worne seale gould Ringe . . .

Mary White.

ROBT. POWES, (or *Powys*) of Linhaven, in Virginia Clarke . . .
Book C f. 2.
Dated 2 Dec. 1651.
Proved Dec. 1651.
. . . Daughter Mary Powys in England . . . in Case she . . And shall or do arive in Virginia . . meate Cattell Shipped home for England or Holland . .
. . . Sonne Robt^t *P*owys . . .
. . . three barrells of Indian Corne to be payd and delivered unto ye John Rich, Kingsman, within one mounth after my decease att the house of Corronell Yardly . . .

. . . *K*atherin the wife of James Phillips for teoken of my love, and for heir great payns and care in tending and looking to me in the time of my sicknesse . . .
. . . Sonne Robt Powys . . . my whole and soale Executor . . .
. . . ffrend Corronell ffrancis Yardly and . . . Maior Edward Windham Suprevizors of this my sayd will . . .

witnesses: Ed. Windham sen.
John Gilham
Ada*m* Bellamy

Robt Po*wes* Clark *wts*
Seale

EDWARD GRADWELL of ye Little Creeke in ye prish of Lynhaven Planter . . .
Book C f. 8.
Dated 3 Dec. 1651.
Proved Dec. 1651.

. . . unto Henry Brakes of ye same prish all & singler my goods & cattle . . .
. . . John Cubbic*k* shall have house & ground for himselfe & mother . . .
. . . y^t^ John Stronge servant to Henry Brakes . . .
. . . Maudlinge Kempe daughter to Mary Kempe widd. shall have a Cowe . . .

witnesses: Henry Westgate
John Spencer.
Nicholas Mason

ye marke of
Edward Gradwell.

JOHN COOKE, lately deceased & uppon his death bedd hath made his will . . . (Nuncupative) . . .
Booke C f. 9.
Dated ———
Recorded 15 Aprill 1652.

. . . unto Mary Savill . . .
. . . his mother, or his brother would come & enjoy it . . . by ye Shippinge . . .

Stephen Key
George Wright
Rich. ff*ou*nder

JOHN SIBSEY of Elizabeth River in ye County of Lower Norfolke gent . . .

Book C. f. 17.

Dated 15 July 1652.

Recorded 16 Aug. 1652.

. . . Executrix wife . . .

. . . Land Commonly called Craney Point now in ye possession of Roberte Woody to be sould for & towards ye paymt. of my debts suddenly after my decease . . .

. . . unto beloved wife All my Plate, & all my Servants & also my boate . . .

. . . unto Mary Sibsey my daughter all ye residue of my Land lyinge & beinge adioyinge unto Craney Point . . .

. . . unto Henery Wake All my right & title of that land now in ye possession of Richard Pinner . . .

. . . unto Margery W*ickstead* widd . . .

. . . unto Elizabeth daughter of ye sd. Margery W*ickstead* . . .

. . . my aforesaid daughter depte this life before Mr. Conquest her husband *s^r gent* . . . to Richard Conquest my sd. daughters husband . . .

. . . Trustinge in Almighly God y^t my sd. wife will be a mother to her . . .

. . . unto Brother in Lawe Thomas Lambert One Pistle, & my feather . . .

. . . unto William Jermy my black hilted Rapier & belt . . .

. . . servants John Paine, or David Southerly . . .

. . . Thomas Lambert & William Jermy my Supervisors

. . . Barbara ——— my now maid servant . . .

witnesses: Tho: Ivey &
Trees Mason

John Sibsey.
wt. ye Seale.

PETER BARRNES . . .

Book C f. 18.

Date 14 July 1652.

Recorded ——— 1652.

. . . my Loving Mate Richard Eastwood my sole Executor . . .

. . . unto Elizabeth Wind*e*tt the daughter of Edmond Wind*e*tt . . .

. . . unto Marry that is now servant to Mr. Thomas Wright . . .

witness: John Smith.

the marke of
Peter Barrnes.

PETER RIGLESWORTH . . .
Book C. f. 30.
Dated 2 Sept. 1652.
Recorded ——— 1652.
. . . my wife Jane Riglesworth & my two Children, Mary & Dorothy, both under 16 years of age . . .
. . . unto John Boymus, the sonne of John Boymens . . .
. . . " wife land I live on . . .
. . . servant John *Tutte* . . .
. . . " Charles Mograk— . . .
. . . appoint Charles Stevens, Robte Bowers & Robte Capps to be Ov[r]seers . . .
. . . . unto Robte Capps & Robte Springe . . . land . . .
witnesses: Robt. Springe
Even Willette
John ffinch
Proved by: Robte Springe &
John ffinch.

the marke of
Peter Riglesworth

SAMUEL CHAR*MIO*E . . .
Book C f. 36.
Dated 13 Dec. 1652.
Recorded ——— 1652.
. . . I doe putt forth my daughter Rose Char*mice* unto William Jacob duringe y[e] terme of Sixteen yeres . . .
. . . putt forth Edward Rutland to the aforesd. William Jacob the full terme of One & twenty yeres . . .
. . . plantation or ground of Edward Cooper . . .
. . . tobacco wth I sent for England by Thomas Allen,
witnesses: Tobias Mathewes
John Clarke.

ye marke of
Samuell *Jarmice*

ROBERT FOWLER . . .
Book C. p. 47.
Dated 23 Feb. 1652.
Recorded ——— 1652.
. . . unto sonne Robte. Fowler at ye age of twenty one yeres Two hundred acres of Land . . . dividend . . . I lately bought of Mr. Christopher Raynolds & my wife Mary ffowler, & his mother, his guardian . . .
. . . my kinsman George Fowler . . . bible . . .
. . . wife Mary Executrix . . .
witness: Thomas Bridge.

Robte. Fowler
wth his Seale.

DANIELL TANNER . . .

Book C f. 65.

Dated 17 Nov. 1653.

Probat ——— 1653.

. . . unto Mr. Lemuell Mason all my Estate whatsover on the South side of James River . . .

. . . unto Mrs Anne Mason, for her great paynes & care & love towards me Three Thousand pounds of tobacco, to be paid her out of my Estate in the hands of Thomas Sherley . . .

. . unto Mms. Alice Mason . . .

. . . " " Elizabeth Thelaball . . .

. . . " John Worsman . . .

. . . " James Simonds what tobacco he oweth me & forty pounds of tobacco wch. is due to me in ye hands of Jasper Hoskinson . . .

. . . unto Thomas Sherley aforesaid all the residue of my estate wch. I have in Virginia, for the use of his Child privded the Child be Christined & named Daniell . . .

. . . Mr. Lemuell Mason my Executor . . .

. . . I doe make & ordayne ye sd. Thomas Sherley & floorntyne Payne Overseers . . .

witnesses: Rich: Conquest
Robte Butler

Daniell Tanner

THOMAS GODBYE of Elizabeth River, in ye County of Lower Norfolke in Virginia, planter . . .

Book C f 76.

Dated 8 Aprill 1652.

Recorded 15 Feb. 1653.

. . . Anne my deere & Lovinge wife . . . Sole Executrix . . .

witnesses: Tho: Tooker
Lewis ffundermull.

The marke of
Thomas R. Godbye
With. his Seale.

Codicil Dated 10 Feb. 1653.

. . . bequeath to my *Wives* Sister Elizabeth Bearre . . .

witness: Rich Lee.

The marke of
Thomas Godbye.

LAWRENCE PLUMER of Lynhaven in ye County of Lower Norfolk . . .

Book C f. 98

Dated 24 Apr. 1654.

Recorded 26 Sept. 1654.

. . . wife Anne Plumer sole Executrix . . .
. . . to my Child by my said wife Ann . . .
. . . friend & brother Thomas Hall Shal be Overseere.

witnesses: Richard Smythe — Lawrence Plumer.
Roger ffountayne

JOHN CUBBIDGE . . .

Book C. f. 107.

Dated 7 Oct. 1654.

Recorded 16 Nov. 1654.

. . . unto Thomas Workeman
. . . " Stephen *Key* . . .
. . . " John Davyes . . .
. . . " Robert Russell . . .
. . . " Henry Brakes . . soale Executor . . .

witnesses: John Holmes.
John Daves & — John Cubbidge.
Robert Russell

ARNALL WILKERSON . . .

Book C. f. 112.

Dated 19 Oct. 1654.

Recorded 29 Dec. 1654.

. . . Mr. William Johnson: mchant. Taylor & now a resident ——— ye Providence of London . . .
. . . Thomas Barrett . . .
. . . George Barrett ——— is now going home in ye Shipp Providence . . .

witnesses: George Barrett — Arnall Wilkinson
Will Banne*shers* — his marke.

THOMAS WARD, . . .

Book C f. 121.

Dated 9 Dec. 1654.

Recorded 25 Jan. 1654.

. . . wife plantation . . . executrix . . .
. . . my daughter . . .
. . . Henry Holmes . . . father in law . . .
. . . my Sister Workman's sonne Thomas
. . . John Workman & Henry Holmes father in law Overseers . . .

witnesses: John Banks his mke Thomas Ward.
William Olephant his mke

THOMAS WORKMAN . . .

Book C. f. 122.

Dated 8 Nov. 1654.

Recorded 25 Jan. 1654.

. . . sonne Thomas Workman . . .
. . . brother John Workman . . . the house of Lancaster Lovett . . .
. . . unto my brother Nathniell Hayes . . .
. . . " " " Adam Hayes . . .
. . . " " " John Workman's youngest daughter . . .
. . . " " " Wards daughter . . .
. . . wife Mary Workman Executrix . . .
. . . my brother John Workman & my brother Tho. Ward to be Overseers . . .

(Not Singed).

ELLEN WHITEHURST, . . . (Memorandum) . . .

Book C. f. 122.

Dated 15 Nov. 1654.

Recorded ——— 1654.

. . . to my two daughters Ellen Whitehurst & Susan Whitehurst . . . as they shall come to age . . .

witnesses: Henry Nic*klas* the mke of
William Goldsmith. Ellen Whitehurst.
wth Seale.

THOMAS CHESEY, of Lynhaven in ye County of Lower Norfolke in Virginia . . .

Book C. f. 122.

Dated 20 Aug. 1654

Recorded 25 Jan. 1654.

. . . wife Jeane Chesey . . . sole Executrix . . .
. . . Mr. Robt. Powes & O*rsen* Hayes my Overseers . . .
. . . sonne Robt Chesey all my lands when he comes to the age of twenty one yeares . . .
. . . his mother Jeane Chesey . . .
. . . till her sonne Robt comes to Sixteene yeares of age . . .
. . . unto my Daughter in lawe Dorothy Richards . . . and her mother to have the milk & male, till her daughter comes to the age of Sixteene yeares . . .
. . . Robert Powys my Ov^r^seer . . .
. . . O*rsen* Hayes my Ov^r^seer . . .

witness: Henry Robinson. (Not Signed).

WILLIAM VINCENT, of the Country of Virginia, Merchant . . .

Book C. f. 127.

Dated 2 Nov. 1654.

Recorded 15 Feb. 1654.

. . . to Elizabeth Vincent . . . my wife One hundred pounds sterling if she be liveing to be paidd to her in England . .
. . . my Sister Mtrs. Bridgett Edmonds, and her two daughters Katherine & Elizabeth Edmonds . . .
. . . to my brother John Dep*otter* living in Amsterdam in Holland ffour hundred pounds Sterling . . .
. . . to my brothers Mr. Willm Daynes & Mr. Thomas Daynes Tenne pounds Sterling a peece . . .
. . . brother Mr. Thomas Edmonds sole Executor . . .
. . . Major Thomas Lambert and Capt. Thomas Goodrich Ovrseers . . .

THOMAS WRIGHT, of the Westerne branche of Elizabeth River in the County of Lower Norff in Virginia, planter . . .

Book C. f. 133.

Dated 10 Jan. 1654.

Recorded 15 Feb. 1654.

. . . my well beloved sonne Thomas Wright my plantation wch. I live upon at prsent provided he will come and live upon it, soe soone as he cometh into Virginia, and if he will not or if he dooth not live to enioye it, then I give & bequeath it to my well beloved sonne James Wright . . .

. . . unto my well beloved sonne Willm. Wright A tract of land being *two* hundred acres lying or bounded on a Creeke called Craney Iland Creeke . . .

. . . sonne Thomas above named . . . when he is Sixteene yeares of age . . . one chest being of Joyners worke . . . one bible . . .

. . . sonne Richard Wright . . .

. . . daughter Jane Wright . . . one golde ringe her mother gave her on her death bedd . . .

. . . daughter Christian Wright . . . one golde ringe her mother gave her . . .

. . . I desire my Six children shall have three years Schooling, and live upon my plantation . . .

. . . friends Mr. Lemuell Mason Mr. Richard Conquest Mr. William *Naskum* & Richard Starnell of the bove said County to be my Executors & Ovrseers . . .

. . . unto Thomas Warde . . . my servant at prsent . . .

witnesses: Samuel S*ond.*
John Dubar
Richard Starnell

Thomas Wright
wth Seale.

ANDREW NICHOLAS . . .

Book C. f. 157.

Dated 1 Maye 1655.

Recorded 15 Maye 1655.

. . . wife Elizabeth Nicholas . . .

. . . . to my sonne Willm. Nicholas my plantation after my wives decease . . .

. . . to my daughter Elizabeth Nicholas . . . when shee shall come to age . . .
. . . my daughter Elinor Nicholas . . . when shee shall come to age . . .

witness: Henry Nicholas
John Hebden.

Andrew Nicholas
with his Seale

Codecil . . . Calfe given by Andrew Nicholas to Eliner Nicholas the daughter of Henry Nicholas . . .
. . . Elizabeth Nicholas widd. Relict & Executive of the sd. Andrew Nicholas . . .

(Not Signed.)

WILLM MOSELEY, the elder, written in his owne hand . . .

Book C f. 166.

Dated 29 June 1655.

Recorded 15 Aug. 1655.

. . . bequeath my Soule to God that gave it, and my body to the earth to be decently buried at the discretion of my wife and Children . . .
. . . to my Cosen Willm. Cockroft . . .
. . . to my grandchilde Corker . . .
. . . unto my wife Susan Moseley . . .
. . . to my sonne Willm. Moseley Eight hundred acres of land . . . in Bartho Hodgkins Pattent . . .
. . . to my son Arthur Moseley all that tract of land wch. I bought of George Kempe . . . all that land wch. was Surveyed by Mr. Emperor when I was in England . . .

witnesses:

John Carrawaye, mke.
Abraham Thomas, mke.

Will. Moseley Senior
with A Seale.

RICHARD STARNELL of Elizab. River in the County of Lower Norfolke, *Coop* . . .

Book C f. 179.

Dated 3 Oct. 1655.

Recorded 15 Nov. 1655.

. . . my sonne Richard Sternell all my land . . . seven hundred Acres lying in ye same neck of land I live in being in two pattents. Six hundred Acres lying in a Creek in ye Southern branch of Elizab. River called ye Deep Creeke, wch pattent is in hands of Mr. Edm. Bowman . . . all my books . . . foure gunns . . . one Iron barr pistle . . .

. . . unto my daughter Elizabeth . . . one small gold ring in her possession, and one silver bodkin wch. was her mothers . . at ye age of Sixteene yeares . .

. . . unto my daughter Anne . . . at ye age of Sixteen . . .

. . . my three children equally . . .

. . . my friend Edmund Bowman to take ye care and charge of all my three Children . . .

. . . Mr. Bowman & sonne Richard Executors . . .

. . . sonne Richard . . . during his minority . . .

. . . my servant Richard Tomson . . .

. . . to Anne Mrs. Brownings maid . . .

. . . Mr. Goodrich'es

. . . Sarah Reinolds . . .

. . . Rich Bunting . . .

. . . John Hill . . . tob debt . . . for his paines in making my will and helping me to sett my house in order . . .

witnesses: Tho. Goodrich. Richard Sternell.
John Hill.

HENRY WOODHOUSE . . .

Book C f 181.
Dated 16 July 1655.
Recorded 15 Nov. 1655.

. . . unto my wife Maria Woodhouse . . .

. . . untill my sonne Henry Woodhouse shal be Twenty yeares of age . . .

. . . unto my sonne Henry Woodhouse five hundred acres of land whereon now I doe live . . .

. . . unto my sonne Horatio Woodhouse two hundred Acres of land . . . Gregorie's Creeke . . .

. . . unto my sonne John Woodhouse two hundred and Seaventy foure acres of land, lying and being at a place called the head of the Jammes. There be two shares of land Bermud*as* wch. I solde unto my brother in lawe Mr. Charles *Sothren* . . .

. . . Willm Woodhouse my sonne . . .

. . . unto my daughter Elizabeth Collins . . .

. . . wife, my friends Mr. Lemuel Mason and Thomas Allen to be Exrs . . .

witnesses: Tho: Allen　　　Hen: Woodhouse
Jeane Henley, by mke.

Proved by: Tho. Allen 15 Nov. 1655.
Jeane Henley 8 Dec. 1655.
John Martin 8 Dec. 1655.
Robt. Po*rvis* 8 Dec. 1655.

HENERY WESGATE, of ye little Creeke . . .

Book C f. 182.

Dated 24 Feb. 1654.

Recorded 17 Dec. 1655.

. . . unto my God sonne Henery Snayle . . .

. . . unto my servant Jo[n] Browne . . .

. . . unto my wife's Mother In England . . . if shee be living after my decease . . .

. . . unto my wife Ellen Westgate, and to my daughters Anne and Elizabeth Westgate, and to ye Child in her wombe if shee be wth Childe . . .

. . . But if a boy shee is now possessed to be wth. Child wth all my land either at the tearme of twenty one yeares or at the day of my wife's death . . .

. . . unto my daughters Anne and Elizabeth Westgate a hhd. of Tob. and Caske to containe three hundred and fifty pounds of tob. or there abouts . . . to buy each of them a wedding ring . . .

. . . friend John: Bridge my small gunne . . .

. . . wife Ellen Westgate sole Executrix . . .

. . . brother Roger Westgate living at ye Hagh in Holland . . .

. . . ffriends Tho. Bridge and Gyles Collins be Overseers . . .

witnesses: George Wright his mke.　　　Henery Westgate
Thomas Bridge.　　　with his Seale.

JOHN GOULDINGE. . . .

Book C. f. 187.

Dated 4 Oct. 1655.

Recorded 17 Dec. 1655.

. . . tobacco John Lownes doely receive of M[ris] Yardley, the one halfe I gave to himselfe, the other halfe to Edward Hall of Linhaven . . .

. . . unto Dorothy Lownes my *hamacke* . . .

. . . unto Cosen Dorothy Lownes Aunt one black Otto skinne . . . John Gouldinge

witness: Ja. Bankes: Dorothy Lownes.

Proved by: Thomas Goodrich last daie Dec. 1655.

HENRY SNAILE, of ye Little Creeke, Carpenter . . .

Book C. f. 203.

Dated 4 Dec. 1655.

Recorded 15 Feb. 1655.

. . . sonne Henry my plantation & all ye land at ye age of twenty one yeares and that none of his brothers & sisters shallbe put of from it untill they can shift for them selves . . .

. . . sonne Henry shall come to age . . .

. . . sonne Tho. Bennett . . .

. . . daughter Anne ye wife of Tho: Bennett . . .

. . . daughter Barberey " " Tho: Adams . . .

. . . sonne Henry Snaile sole executor . . .

witnesses: Thomas Bridge.
Ralfe Jones, by mke.

The Mke of
Henry Snaill &
his Seale.

THOMAS NEDHAM. . . .

Book C f 204.

Dated 11 Nov. 1655.

Recorded 15 Feb. 1655.

. . .

. . . unto brother Henry Nedham . . . Indian field

. . . unto brother Natha. Nedham . . .

. . . unto Edward Cooper . . .

. . . unto Tho: Allen . . . one paire of glasses . . .
. . . unto wife Elizabeth Nedham all & every . . .

witnesses: Edward Cooper, his mke.
Tho: Allen. Thomas Nedham.

Proved by: Edward Cooper, John Martin, Robt. Powes. } 8 Dec. 1655.

PETER MARKES, of ye Little Creeke . . .

Book D. p. 10.

Dated 19 Aug. 1656.

proved 15 Oct. 1656.

. . . to Anne Ashall . . .
. . . to Richard Ashall . . .
. . . to my God*after* Elizabeth Ashall . . .
. . . George Ashall my sole executor . . .

witnesses: Tho Bennett.
Rodger Hayword.

The Mke of
Peter Markes
& Seall.

COBB HOWELL . . .

Book D. p. 11.

Dated 20 Aug. 1856.

proved 15 Oct. 1856.

. . . Sarah my wel beloved wife my executrix . . .
. . . all estate in Virginia & likewise all y[t] whatsoever shall come from England . . .
. . . my father Jno. Stratton & my mother his wife . . . to act for my wife . . .

witnesses: John Bray
John Johnston.

Cob Howell.

ROBTE DAVIS (aged forty six years or there abouts) of ye County of Lower Noffolke, planter . . .

Book D. p. 346.

Dated 21 April 1662.

Recorded 18 July 1662.

. . . to be Decently buried about ye middle of my yonge Orchard . . .

. . . to Edy my Wife the thirds of my Estate . . .

. . . unto Mary the Wife of Plummer Bray Tenne pounds Sterlinge . . .

. . . unto my Godsonne Edward Cooper soone of Edward Cooper . . . when . . . twenty one yeres . . .

. . . unto John Preist M^r^chant Tenne pounds sterl & one sealed Ringe of gould mettall . . .

. . . unto Peter Malbone . . .

. . . unto Mr. Anthony Clerke of ye prish . . .

. . . unto Edward *Remmington* . . .

. . . unto John Moy . . .

. . . my wife may live uppon ny Plantation untill Richard Moy shall come to Virginia or may be found elsewhere . . .

. . . unto Rodger ffountayne for ye *use* of my God soone Robte ffountayne . . .

. . . unto Mr. Edward Hall my Caster & silver band . . .

. . . unto ye aforesd Richard Moy the whole Remainder of my Estate. Excepted one Cowe & calve usinge about the plantation of Edward Cannon . . .

. . . unto William Webb for use of his sonne Thomas Webb . . .

. . . if Richard Moy shall not be heard of to be alive within five yeres . . . then the foresd Estate given him, may be divided . . . third to John Moy & halfe *thether* third to Plummer Bray & thether halfe equally to be divided betweene Edward Cooper & Peter Malbone . . .

. . . Plummer Bray, Edward Cooper & Peter Malbone, Executors . . .

witnesses: John Robinson
Thome Brantin.

the marke of
Robte Davis.

proved 16 June in Court 1662 by both witnesses.

WILLIAM ODEON . . .

Book D. p. 368.

Dated 25 Jan. 1662.

proved 16 Feb. 1662.

. . . sonne William Odeon . . .
. . . daughter Ellen Odeon . . .
. . . sonne Richard Odeon . . . under seventeen yeres . . .
. . . unto Elizabeth Mannings Child . . .
. . . unto my servant Elizabeth Manning her tyme of servitude . . .
. . . my Lovinge friend ffrancis Sayer to be my Overseer . . .

witnesses: Richard Church
Abraham Elliott

William Odeon
wth Seale

JOHN SIDNEY Coll . . . (Nuncupative) . . .

Book D. p. 385.

Recorded 17 Oct. 1663.

. . . unto Mr. V*iress*inus Joy . . . Cosen Joy . . .
. . . daughter . . .
. . . Godaughter Kate Joy . . .

Ann Carraway aged 43 years. about
Rosammond Mullekin aged 30. years about.

MICHAELL CLARKE . . . (Nuncupative) . . .

Book D. p. 436.

Recorded 15 Feb. 1665.

. . . daughter Elizabeth . . .
. . . wife . . .

William Capps.
Darley Michaell.

WILLIAM JERMY of Lynhaven in the County of Lower Norfolk in the Country of Virginia, gent . . .

Book E f 4.

Dated 23 Aprill 1666.

Proved xv° Jan. 1666.

. . . Lemuell Mason my God sonne . . . to be disposed of by his father . . .
. . . to William Langly my God son and to Elizabeth Westgate my God Daughter . . .
. . . to my estemed friend Coll. Mason my brase pistoll . . .
. . . to my friend Mr. Thomas ffulcher my belt and the silver buckles thereunto belonging . . .
. . . to D—— John W*orland* . . .
. . . land . . . in Lynn Haven . . . to my wife Ann Jermey . . .
. . . said Ann my wife my whole and sole Executrix . . .
. . . true ffriends Coll. Mason and Capt. Tho. Futcher Overseers . . .

witnesses: Henry Woodhouse. Will Jermy
Tho: Keelinge. Seale

MARY TAYLOR . . .

Book E f. 4.
dated 25 Mch. 1666.
proved 15 Jan. 1666, by *Gulies* Miles & Geo. Wright.
. . . to my youngest daughter Hester Taylor . . .
. . . to my oldest daughter Winifred Turner . . .
. . . son John Turner Executor . . .

witness: William Miles. her
George Wright Mary Taylor
marke.

JOANE YATES . . .

Book E f 11.
Dated 22 O*ctober* 1664.
proved ————.
. . . my sonne Richard Yates and likewise my daughter ffrancis Vallentine . . . Executors . . .
. . . unto my sonne Richard Yates daughter J*one* Yates . . .
. . . to my Daughters ffrances sone George Vallentine . . . land adjoining my grandfathers land in the *merke* called Baytree hole . . .
. . . to my Grandaughter Elizabeth H*orne* . . .
. . . to my Grandsonne Thomas H*orne* . . .
. . . to my Grandaughter Hanna H*orne* . . .

. . . to my Grandaughter Elizabeth Yates . . .
. . . to my Grandaughter Mary Yates . . .
. . . to my Grandsonne Richard Yates . . .
. . . to my Grandsonne John Markeham . . .
. . . to my Grandaughter Mary ff*au*shaw . . . and not for her husband . . .
. . . to William R*etch for* . . .
. . . to my God Daughter Johanna Mortene . . .

witnesses: William Retchford. Joane Yates &
Martha *Hatton.*
John Swaine.
John E*freag.*
Wm Mortene.

CHRISTIAN FREDRICKSON . . .

Book E f 11.

Dated 11 Dec. 1662.

proved 15 Oct 1666.

. . . my wife and my sonne Frederick . . .

witnesses: Thomas Branton.
Ann Johnson.
Josias *Gewalsene.*

Christian Frederick.

THOMAS BROWNE of ye Western Branch of Elizabeth River in ye County of Lower Norfolk . . .

Book E f. 12.

Dated 22 Oct. 1666.

proved 6 Dec. 1666.

. . . my Eldest sonn Thomas Browne . . . land seated on . . .
. . . my son John Browne . . . two hundred and forty Acres of Land *A neck* . . .
. . . my sonne Brown, Henry . . . land knowne by the name of *Drum Point.* . . .
. . . my two youngest sonns Christopher Browne & William Brown all ye Land lying between *Drum point* neck & a branch called Barron point . . . at twenty-one . . .

. . . my Eldest daughter Ann ye wife of *Ric:* Cording . . .
. . . my daughter Elizabeth Browne . . .
. . . my daughter Mary . . .
witnesses: John Hatton.
Tho: Fulcher.

Thomas Browne & Seale.

ROBERT DIGBY . . .
Book E f. 13.
Dated 23 —— 1666.
proved ———.
. . . my Son John Digby . . . when . . . one and twenty yeares . . . after decease of my wife *Ann* . . .
. . . my wife and three children . . .
witnesses: William Carver.
Edward Perkins.
Elizabeth ———.

Robert Digby.

RICE JONES . . .
Book E. f. 17.
dated 25 Oct. 1666.
proved ———.
. . . wife Ann Joanes . . . all estate . . . Extx . . .
witnesses: Mary But.
Richard Poole.

Rice Jones his marke.

ROBERT PORTER . . .
Book E f 19.
dated 4 Oct. 1666.
proved 14 Apr. 1667.
. . . .Friend Jo*phall* Lewis . . .
. . . to my sonnes ——— Robert Porter or Edward Porter if either of them come into Virginia in pson . . .
witnesses: Fran. Sayer.
Tho. Sp*eks*.

Robert Porter by marke.

WILLIAM MILLS . . .

Book E f. 21.

dated 28 Mch. 1667.

proved 13 June 1667.

. . . my god son *Hoge Hayse* . . .

. . . my god daughter Hester *Holmes* . . .

. . . to Jno. C*arvers* wife . . .

. . . to Alexander *belt* . . .

. . . to John Turner . . .

. . . *Ho*ge Hayse brother . . .

witnesses: John *Neblin.*
Georg Right.

Williams Mills, by marke.

RICHARD PINNER . . .

Book E. f 22.

dated 28 Aug. 1666.

proved ——— 1667.

. . . wife & two sonnes . . .

. . . my two sonns Richard & William att sixteen yeares of age . . .

. . . unto roger Cording at 21 yeares of age . . .

. . . unto Richard Roe . . . and to his wife Ann Roe . . .

. . . unto my Cosen William Elliz. his two sonns: Philp & William . . .

. . . friends Francis Sayer, Will Elliz, Joseph Harrison, Henry Adams, to be my overseers . . .

witnesses: John Digbe.
Richard Roe.

Richard Pinner.

WILLIAM BORDAS, now Resident in Virg[a]

Book E. f 26.

dated 26 Sept. 1667.

proved 15 Oct. 1667.

. . . brother Thomas B*u*rdas . . . a parcell of goods sent from Jamaca wch is now safely arrived in England and in ye Custody of Mr. John Loving merchant living in or neere Southton who is to be heard of at A*bslon* in the Isle of Wight of his brother brother Mr. William Loving . . .

. . . at Mr. William Goldsmith's . . .
. . . at Mr. Robinson of ye Eeasterne Branch . . .
. . . in ye hands of Capt. William Carver . . .
. . . my Booke and Instruments of Navigation . . .
. . . to Ann Godby the wife of Thomas Godby . . .
. . . to Mr. Mr. Noland a booke entitled *Rubdrye's* practice of Phisicke . . .
. . . to Mr. Ivey booke . . .
. . . Ann Godby or John Porter Exors . . .
. . . John Edwards . . .
. . . children of my Brother Henry Burdas of Egl*escliffe,* in the County of Durham . . .

witnesses: Jno Edwards.
Margorie Alexander.

William B*u*rdas & Seale.

ELIZABETH BUCKMASTER . . .

Book E f 28.

dated "last day of November," 1667.

proved 16 Dec. 1667.

. . . unto Edward Poslett . . . Exor . . .
. . . my pte & share of my father's Estate late deceased . . . according to an order of Court . . .
. . . my brother Thomas . . .

witnesses: Tho. Gregory.
Jno. Edwards.
Jno. Bright

Eliz: Buckmaster by marke.

RICHARD RUSSELL, of ye Westerne branch, of Elizabeth River, in ye County of Lower Norfolk, in Virginia . . .

Book E f 29.

dated 24 July 1667.

proved 16 Dec. 1667.

. . . will in hands of Francis Sayer Void & Null . . .
. . . unto Frances Sayer . . .
. . . unto Richard Yates . . .
. . . unto Jeane King late wife unto Martin Hammon . . . and her children . . .
. . . unto *Honnor* Mariartre . . .
. . . unto Edward Mariartre . . .

. . . unto John Porter, Junr, six books his eldest child one Cowe . . .

. . . my Son William Russell . . . tobacco . . . if my son be living, & come or send for ye same . . .

. . . my wife & John Porter, the elder my Exors . . . my friend John Overseer . . .

. . . unto Katheren Green . . .

. . . unto Jno. Forbes . . .

. . . unto Jno. Whitfield . . .

. . . unto Sarah Dyer . . .

. . . unto Wm. Green his first Chuld . . . & his wife . . . & her mother . . .

. . . unto James Johnson . . . & his wife . . .

. . . unto Ann Godby . .

. . . unto Jno. Abott . . .

. . . unto Richard Lawrence . . .

. . . "And for the other pte of my Estate, I give & bequeath one pte. of itt unto Six of the poorest mens Children in Eliz. River, to pay for there schooling to read & after these six are entered, then if six more comes, I give a pte. allsoe to enter them in like manner & this I leave to ye descretion of my Exors. & further from time to time at is will reach & it will prove." . . .

. . . unto John Greene & Jno. Porter ye Elder . . .

witnesses: Frances Thelaball.
John Forbes.

Richard Russell.

proved by: Jno. Greene, Aged 58 or there about.

JAMES MULLAKIN, of ye parish of Lynn Haven . . .

Book E. f. 40.

dated 22 Aug. 1668.

proved 15 Oct. 1668.

. . . unto Richard Lee my sonn in Law when he shall attain the age of eighteen . . .

. . . unto Mary Lee a Cowe calfe in the yeare 1670 . . .

. . . unto loving wife Rosamond & to my Daughter Jane . . .

. . . friends Mr. William Moseley and Thomas Bridge Overseers . . .

witnessed: Elizabeth Goodacre.

James Mullakin, by marke.

ELIZABETH DAVIS . . .

Book E f. 47.

Book E f. 47.

dated 28 March 1669.

proved ——— Apr. 1669.

. . . unto William Barlow . . .

. . . two children Elizabeth Davis & Margaret Davis . . .

. . . my friends George fowler, John Workman & George Write . . .

witnesses: William Hattersley.
William Barlow.

Elizabeth Davis by marke.

EDWARD WARD . . .

Book E. f. 48.

dated 3 Jan. 1668.

proved 1 Apr. 1669.

. . . wife Elizabeth Ward . . .

. . . eldest daughter Frances Ward . . .

. . . youngest daughter Elizabeth Ward . . .

. . . god sonne Edward Beody . . . when he comes of age . . .

. . . Francis Woodard . . . land . . .

. . . sonne Edward Ward, comes of age . . .

witnesses: Lemuel Raymond.
Denis Dayley.

Edward Ward & Seale.

CHARLES EDGERTON . . .

Book E f. 51.

dated 27 April 1669.

proved 15 June 1669.

. . . unto Ann Snalye wch. now goeth by the name of Ann Bennett, to her foure children that is to say george, and Edward and Elizabeth and Mary my land . . . when they come to age . . .

. . . James Wishart & John Griffin Exors . . .

witnesses: George Write.
John *Wor*land.

Charles Edgerton & Seale.

JOHN TUTTJE, . . .
Book E f. 52.
dated 11 —— 1668.
proved 16 June 1669.
. . . wife . . .
. . . my daughter . . .
witnesses: Thomas Fanshaw.
Edward Browne.

John Tuttie.

THOMAS FANSHAW . . .
Book E f 54.
dated 10 Mch. 1668.
proved 16 June 1669.
. . . my sonne Thomas Fanshaw . . . infant . . .
. . . my wife Mary Fanshaw . . .
witnesses: Richard Jones, Junr
Edward Browne.

Thomas Fanshaw.

MATHEW MATHIAS . . .
Book E. f 55
dated 24 June 1669.
proved 16 Aug. 1669.
. . . wife . . .
. . . sonne John Mathias . . .
. . . three children . . .
. . . my eldest sonne & my youngest sonne all my lands . . .
. . . friends david M*orow* and Michael Macoy . . . Overseers . . .
witnesses: John Hebdon.
Ann Morrow.

EDWARD POSLETT . . . (Nuncupative) . . .
Book E. f. 63.
dated 16 Dec. 1669.
. . . wife Mary . . .
Deposition of. Margery Sherpoles. aged 43 yeares . . .
Deposition of. Mary W*edicke* aged 30 yeares . . .

RICHARD BOULING, of ye Westerne Branch of ye Eliz[a] River in ye County of Lower Norfolk . . .

Book E f. 68.

dated 14 July 1668. Computation of Church of England.

recorded 18 Jan. 1669.

. . . Eliz[a] my wife . . .

. . . Richard my sonne and my daughter Eliz[a] . . .

. . . my youngest daughter now sucking upon her mother's Brest . . .

. . . a feather bed that I sent for to England by my brother William Ellis . . .

. . . my foure youngest children (Vizt). Mary, Dorothy, Richard & Elizabeth, that now Sucks . . .

. . . Richard under twenty one . . . .

. . . eldest daughter Elizabeth . . .

. . . Elizabeth Bunting . . .

. . . neighbore Thomas Smith . . .

witnesses: Andrew Myddelton.
Crane Collins.

Richard Bouling, by marke

THOMAS BROWNE, of the Western Branch of Eliz[a] River, in the County of Lower Norfolk . . .

Book E f 73.

dated 1 Apr. 1670.

proved 11 May 1670.

. . . friend Mr. W[m] Greene . . .

. . . Michael wayborne . . .

. . . unto my Loving wife and to my daughter Ann Browne . . . under sixteen . . .

. . . wife and daughter extx . . .

. . . friends W[m] Greene & Michael wayborne, Overseers . . .

witnesses: Thomas Harding.
Thomas Gilbert.

Tho: Browne & Seale.

JNO. CUNINGHAM . . . (Nuncupative) . . .

Book E f 79.

dated 19 Oct. 1670.

sworne to: 25 Oct 1670. by Anne Rowe, aged 26 or thereabouts . . .

. . . to his mate Jno. Stenson . . .

STEPHEN MARKS . . .

Book E. f. 83.

dated 18 Nov. 1670.

proved 15 Dec. 1670.

. . . my Sone Stephen Marks all my Land that Shall bee due to mee in Nansemond after my mother in Law her decease . . . as also . . . two hundred acres of land that is bounding betweene Wm Clements one ye one Side and Mr. Stratton on ye other Side, wch. Said land John Oakes now liveth on . . . at Sixteene years of age . . .

. . . my loving wife Elinor Marks . . .

. . . my Sonne John Marks . . . land I now live on after decease of my wife . . . also . . . land Jno. Bouringe and George Wakefield boath now Live on . . . at sixteene . . .

. . . my Loving wife Elinor Marks and my foure Children as followeth: Stephen, John, Ann and Mary Marks and as they come of age . . .

. . . friends Wm Daynes and John Dallowe bee my overseers . . .

. . . wife Extx . . .

. . . I doe desire that my loving friend Jno. Dallowe may have my Sonne Jn° Marks and to take him as his owne . . .

witnesses: Robert Loveday.
George Wakefield.
Thomas Wright.

Stephen Marks & Seale.

JOHN BROWNE of Westerne Branch of Eliza. River . . .

Book E. f 87.

dated 26 Mch. 1670.

proved 15 Feb. 1670/1.

. . . unto my Brother Thomas Browne . . . materialls . . . Left mee by the Last will of my father . . .

. . . unto my Brother Henry two Cows . . .

. . . unto my Sister Ann *Southerdland* foure Cows . . . a Silver dram Cupp . . .

. . . unto my Brother Tho. Browne . . .

. . . .unto my two Brothers namely Christopher Browne and William Browne . . .

. . . my sister Ann *waite* three Cows . . .

. . . my two youngest Brothers namely Christopher and William Browne . . .
. . . my youngest sister Mary Browne . . .

witnesses: Francis W*as*ten
Thomas Gilbert.

John Browne & Seale.

HENRY BROWNE, of ye Westerne Branch of Eliz[a] River . . .

Book E f. 87.

dated 11 Apr. 1670.

proved 14 Oct. 1670/1.

. . . unto my Sister Ann Southerland my mare . . .
. . . unto Christian Wright . . .
. . . unto Tho. C*ott*on . . .
. . . unto Francis Juggins . . .
. . . unto Thomas Cording . . .
. . . unto my two brothers and two sisters, namely Ann Southerland, Christopher Browne, William Browne and Mary Browne Exequetors.

witnesses: Thomas Harding.
Francis Juggins.

Henry Browne, by marke.

ELIZABETH KEELING, of Linhaven in ye County of Lower Norfolk in ye Country of Virga . . .

Book E. f 91.

dated 30 Oct. 1670.

proved 17 Apr. 1671.

. . . brother Alexander Keeling three Thousand five hundred pounds of tobacco wch. was given to mee by my mothers deed of gift to bee paid to my Said Brother Alexander Keeling after the death of my mother according to ye tenner of the sd. deed, and in Case my sd. Brother Alexander Keeling should dye beefore hee comes to ye full age of one and twenty or wthout heyrs then ye above sd. tobacco to goe to my Brother Throwgood Keeling . . .

. . . unto god daughter Mary Okeham . . . two small gould rings . . .

. . . unto my god daughter Eliz[a] Keeling . . .
. . . unto my god daughter Eliz[a] Land . . .
. . . unto my Brother Throwgood Keeling . . . tobacco . . . wch. is due mee out of my fathers Estate . . .
. . . my father in Law Rob[t] bray my whole Exor . . .

witnesses: Joseph Ayres.
George Stevens.

Elizabeth Keeling, by marke.

EVAN WILLIAMS, of ye —— contry in ye County of Lower Norfolk, planter . . .

Book E f 94.

dated 8 Mch. 1670.

proved 17 Apr. 1671.

. . . 500 acres . . . wch I now live upon . . . unto my three daughters (viz): Eliz[a] Ellinor & Sarah Williams.
. . . friend John Edward of the Southern Branch my sole Extr . . .
. . . my Sonne in Law Robt. White house & a butt when my daughter Eliz[a] Williams comes to age, then shee to have ye sole power and managment of my Estate and
. . . to deliver to her sisters Ellinor and Mary their due proportions of my Estate when they Come of age . . .

witnesses: John Rye
Tho. gally
Mary Nichols

Evan Williams

MARY HA*VATT* . . .

Book E. f 95.

dated 3 March 1666.

proved 10 May 1671.

. . . to Mary Crafford my god daughter . . . Wm. Thomas . . . my god daughter Mary his daughter . . . shall remayne with my Cozen Okeham halfe her tyme
. . . Hester Thomas . . .

. . . Kindsman Jno Okeham all my Land wch. was given to me by my Late husband Wm Hav*ast* . . .

. . . Cosen Ann Okeham wife of my Couzen Jno. Okeham . . .

witnesses: Henry Watson.
Jno. Masters.

Mary Hav*ast.*

JAMES CRAIG, . . . (Nuncupative) . . .

Book E. f 99.

Sworn to: 15 Aug. 1671. by: Joyce Langly, aged 50 yeares or thereabouts . . .

Sworn to: 15 Aug. 1671. also my Alice Lewis, aged 30 yeares or thereabouts . . . who heard doctor grayham say . . .

. . . gives to Mrs. Francis Mason . . . Estate . . .

ARTHUR TOPPIN, of Eliz. River pish, in ye County of Lower Norfolk, in Virga. . . .

Book E f. 106.

dated 30 Oct. 1671.

proved 15 Dec. 1671.

. . . wife Ann one halfe of my Estate . . .

. . . ye other halfe I doe give & bequeath to my Child wch. Shee now goeth wth (yett unborne) . . .

. . . friend Wm. porten two books (viz) Heylands Cosmography & a Book in quarto written by Edmund gunter and also my black sword . . .

. . . to my Said wifes mother Sarah porten my sealed Ring now on my finger . . .

. . . to Warren, Jno. & Mathew godfree my wifes Brothers . . .

witness: Lemuel Phillips.

Arthur Toppin & Seale.

OSBORNE CAMARON, of Linhaven in Lower Norfolk County . . .

Book E f 108.

dated 14 Oct. 1670.

proved 15 Oct. 1671.

. . . my wife Mary Camaron . . . . Extx . . .

. . . my sonne Wm. Camaron ye Seate of land whereon I now dwell wch. Contayneth five hundred acres wch. I hould by virtue of a Patten . . .
. . . my daughter Eliz. . . .
. . . my daughter Katheren . . .
witnesses: Edward Weston
Martha *Co*seland.

Osborne Camaron, by marke

THOMAS ETHRIDGE of ye Southern Branch, of ye County of Lower Norfolk, planter . . .
Book E f. 109.
dated 9 Nov. 1671.
proved 16 Dec. 1671.
. . . unto my Eldest sonne Wm Ethridge, my plantation I now live upon . . . adjoining Jno. Brights line . . .
. . . unto my sonne Edward Ethridge ye youngest . . . land . . . betweene my sonne Williams Branch & ye pond by John Whytes house . . . about 100 acres . . .
. . . unto my sonne marmeduck Ethridge 250 Acres of land, Ye one part of 500 acres wch. my sonne John Ethridge and myselfe took . . . called by ye name of Northward necke . . .
. . . unto my wife Xtian Ethridge . . .
. . . unto my sonnes Wm, Jno. & Thomas, Marmeduck & Edward Ethridge . . .
. . . unto my daughter Ann the wife of Tho: *Nol*cott . . .
. . . unto my daughter Susan . . .
. . . my grandchild Andrew Ethredge . . .
. . . my grandchild Giles N*orc*ott . . .
. . . to Jno R*othe* . . .
witnesses: Tho: Fenford.
Jo. Edward.

Thomas Ethridge.

Codicil.
dated 17 Nov. 1671.
. . . wife Christian Ethridge dead . . .
. . . to ye three Children of ye Blanch, my grand Children . . . a Cowe a piece . . .
. . . my daughter Susanna . . .
witness: Daniel Macoy
Thomas Hetherington.

Thomas Ethridge.

ROBT. BLAKE . . .
Book E f. 123.
dated 17 May 1672.
proved 15 Aug 1672

. . . my wife may bee my Hole & sole Extx . . .
. . . to Arthur Blake my mare . . .
. . . my Children daughters . . .
. . . my Children all foure . . .
. . . my sonne Arthur my land after my wifes decease and as for ye mare wch. I give him; is in ye Roome of Some Cattle wch. I sould of his that were given him by Jno. penewell of accomack . . .

witnesses: John Pead.
John Griffins

Robt. Blake.

FRANCIS FINCH . . .
Book E f. 134.
dated 7 Nov. 1672.
proved 17 Feb. 1672.
. . . friend Henry Spratt . . all estate . . . all & Every thing belonging to mee upon Long Island wch. was given to me by Rich. brittn*aey* will as will appear by the Case by me granted . . .
witnesses: Edward Weston.
James Lewis.

Francis Finch, by marke.

GEORGE ASHALL of ye little Creek in Linhaven parish in ye County of Lower Norfolk . . .
Book E f. 134.
dated 1 Sept. 1671.
proved 17 Feb. 1672.

. . . to my Sonne Richard Ashall . . . my plantation . . . called Wolves Neck . . .
. . . untill my Sonne George Ashall comes to the age of sixteen yeares . . . plantation whereon I now live . . . butt my will is that my well beloved wife his mother Mary Ashall Enjoy the sd. plantation . . .

. . . to my Daughter Eliz[th] the wife of Tho. Reynolds . . .
. . . unto my Daughter Mary Ashall . . .
. . . unto my Daughter Susanna . . .
. . . my Sonne Richard . . . my Eldest sonne . . . wife Mary Ashall, sole Extx
. . . friend George Fouler to bee Overseer . . .

witnesses: Tho. Bridge.
Edward Bragger
George Henery.

George Ashall & Seale.

JAMES JOHNSON, of ye Westerne Branch of Eliza. River in ye County of Lower Norfolk planter . . .

Book E f. 143.

dated 8 Jan. 1672. "according to ye computation of ye Church of England."

proved 10 May 1673.

. . . my daughter Elizabeth and my daughter Jane and my daughter Mary & my wife Eliz[a] Johnson . . . cattle . . .
. . . to my daughter Catheren thirty acres of land . . .
. . . to my sonne James my best gunn and all my land for ever . . . him Sole Exequetor . . .

witnesses: Jno Greene.
Jno. Sandford.

James Johnson & Seale.

LANCASTER LOVETT of Linhaven in Lower Norfolk County in Virg[a] . . .

Book E. f. 14—.

dated 17 Oct. 1672.

proved 15 Apr. 1673.

. . . my body to be decently Interred according to ye manner & custome of ye Church of England . . .
. . . unto my sonne Lancaster Lovett three hundred acres of land being ye plantation whereon I now live from ye Iland point to ye lyne of marked trees next to ye land of Rich. poole . . .
. . . unto my Loving wife Ann Lovett . . .
. . . unto my Sonne Jno. Lovett three hundred acres of Land next ajoyning to my Sonne Lancaster . . next Jno. Martin, decd . . . next Rich. poole . . .

. . . unto my Sonne Thomas Lovett two hundred acres . . . ajoyning my sonne Jno. Lovetts . . . next Rich. poole . . . next Martin . . . next Malachy Thruston . . .

. . . unto my Sonne Randolph Lovett three hundred acres of Land Lying and being att Linhaven . . . between ye Land now in possession of George M*inchin* & Rich *bonny* . . . if he dye under age . . .

. . . give all my Stock of Cattle . . . att ye Easterne Shore wch. now are att and use ye plantation wch. Thomas Lambert now lives on . . . unto my two daughters Mary & Elizabeth Lovett . . .

to my Sonne Randolph Lovett . . . Cattle . . . att . . . plantation of Ben. Burrows

. . . Sonne Lancaster Lovett & wife Ann Lovett Sole Exors, untill ye Rest of my aforesd. Children shall bee att age, my Sonnes of twenty one yeares and my daughters Sixteene yeares . . .

. . . unto Bethsheba my daughter now wife to John ladd . . .

witnesses: Thomas Bridge, aged 57 or thereabouts, proved.
Adam Keeling
Mala Thruston

Lancaster Lovitt & Seale.

Codicil.
dated 19 Mch. 1673.
witnesses: Rich poole.
Jno. Corbett.

Lancaster Lovitt & Seale.

WM. OLIVANT . . .

Book E. f 148.
dated 18 May 1673.
proved 16 June 1673.

. . . unto Wm Holmes and Robt. Holmes sonnes unto Edward Holmes my seat of Land wch. I now live upon wch. is Called Hogg Island onely their mother is to have it for her life time . . .

. . . unto Wm Holmes and Robt. Holmes and Lemuel Holmes . . .

. . . unto Jane Holmes . . .

. . . unto Ann Poole . . .

. . . unto Jane Holmes wife unto Edward Holmes . . . her Sole Extx . . .

witnesses: Henry Holmes.
Nich^o Huggens.

Wm Olivant.

THOMAS GEE, who departed this Country of Virg^a April ye 5th 1672.

Book E. f 158.

dated 5 April 1672.

proved 21 *Aug* 1673.

. . . unto my loving wife . . . land . . . for life . . . and after her decease to my Brother James Peeters . . .

witnesses: Myles D*onnell.*
Jane Gar*iot.*

Thomas Gee.

OWEN HAYES, of ye County of Lower Norfolk . . .

Book E f 159.

dated 12 *Aug.* 1673.

proved 21 *Aug.* 1673.

. . . my sonne in law John Syllivan two hundred acres of land lying next to that tract formerly given to Edward Ward . . .

. . . I give his sonne Jno Syllivan . . .

. . . to my daughter Ann Hayes two hundred acres . . .

. . . unto Joseph Lake & Francis Woodward my horse . . . 200 acres of land I live on . . .

. . . my wife & my two daughters Isabell Lake and Ann hayse and after my wifes decease, her third *p*art to bee divided betwixt my foure daughters . . .

. . . my daughter Ann . . . comes of age . . .

witnesses: Robt. Hodge.
Wm Mercer.

Owen Hayes & Seale.

HENRY PERE . . .

Book E f 160.

dated 6 Feb. 1672/3.

proved 16 Feb. 1673.

. . . my wife Ann pere my hundred acres of land wch lyeth att ye head of Linhaven River . . .

. . . two god Children Henry Gibson and Jno. Barry . . . when of age . . .

witnesses: George fernall.
John gibson.

Henry Pere & Seale.

SARAH WILLOUGHBY of ye County of Lower Norfolk, *wid*[r] . . .
Book E f 163.
dated 15 Sept. 1673.
proved 17 Feb. 1673.
. . . to my two Children Thomas and Elizabeth Willougbye and ye two to bee sole Exors . . .
. . . Lemuel Mason, Jno. Porter *seg*[r] W[m] Por*ter* & george Newton . . . overseers . . . a morening Ring . . .
. . . to my daughter Elizabeth . . .
. . . to ye Gerle Susanna . . .
witnesses: Elizabeth Theleball.
Francis Mason.
Marg*a*ret Mason.

Sarah Willouby & Seale.

proved by M*rs*. Francis Mason & *Mrs*. Margrett Mason.

WM. DYER, of ye pish. of Linhaven, in ye County of Lower Norfolk . . .
Book E f. 166.
dated 13 Dec. 1673.
proved 15 Apr. 1674.
. . . my sonne W[m] Dyer . . . in Case that my sonne dye . . . in his minority . . . unto my loving wife Mary Dyer . . .
witnesses: W[m] Cornix.
Dennis *Da*llye.

W[m] Dyer & Seale.

JOHN GREENE of ye Westerne Branch of ye Eliz[a] River in ye County of Lower Norfolk . . .
Book E. f. 166.
dated 16 Feb. 1673.
proved 15 Apr. 1674.
. . . my loving wife Katheren greene ye land I now live on wch. I purchased of Henry Cattlin . . . life and afterwards . . . John W*hin*fell enter on ye same . . .
. . . my Couzen William Greene ye plantation . . . after ye death of Ann Kemp . . .
. . . Rich Lawrence my old *asstiate* . . .
witnesses: John ferebee.
Thos. Greene.
Jane Johnson ———.

Jn[o] Greene & Seale.

RICHARD POOLE, . . .

Book E f. 167.

dated 27 Mch. 1674.

proved 15 Apr. 1674.

. . . loving wife for life land . . . after ye deceased . . . to my daughter *Bl*andina poole and her heyrs of her body lawfully begotten . . . but in Case my Sd. Daughter *pl*andina should dye wthout issue then my land to fall to my grand child Richard Corbett. . . .

. . . unto my sonne George poole . . .

. . . my daughter Sarah Corbett . . .

. . . my grand child Mary Corbett . . .

witnesses: Robt. Bray.
Antho. Lawson.
Henry Offley.

Richard Poole & Seale.

LUCUS CA*NARADS* . . .

Book E f 167.

dated 7 June 1673.

proved 15 Apr. 1674.

. . . wife Exequtrix . . .

. . . Thomas Cannon . . . my long gun . . .

. . . Edward Cannon . . . my short gun . . .

. . . Eliz[a] Dally my god child . . .

. . . Jno. Ashworth . . .

witnesses: Jno Ashworth.
Adam Keeling.

Lucas Cana*reth*, by marke.

THOMAS P*ETTE*,

Book E. f. 168.

dated 12 Sept. 1673.

proved 16 Apr. 1674.

. . . wife Eliz[a] petty all my land . . . Extx . . .

witnesses: John Davis.
Rose Owens.

Tho: P*ette* & Seale.

GILES COLLENS, . . .

Book E f. 172.

dated 17 Aug. 1673.

proved 15 June 1674.

. . . my sonne John . . . gunn . . . choice of land . . .

. . . my daughter Judeth . . . three pewter platters . . .

. . . my sonne Henry . . .

. . . to my wife . . .

. . . my sonne Giles . . .

witnesses: John ———.
Nich° Huggens.

Giles Collins & Seale.

THOMAS BLANCH of Tanners Creek in Eliz[a] River . . .

Book E f 177.

dated 29 June 1674.

proved 15 *Feb.* 1674.

. . . my wife Elizabeth blanch . . . estate for life . . . butt after her decease to bee equally distributed to my three Children William, Mary & Tho. blanch . . .

witnesses: W[m] Chichester.
Robt. Woody.

Thomas blanch, by marke.

WM. GREENE, . . .

Book E. f 178.

dated 21 Mch. 1673.

proved 15 Feb. 1674.

. . . wife Sarah Greene . . . one third . . . extx . . .

. . . two thirds to be equally divided amongst my three daughters . . . to be made my friend Tho. Halloway segr & John Ferebee . . . Overseers . . .

. . . daughter Sarah shall be of yeares to bee possessed . . .

. . . unto Richard Philpott one young Eue . . .

witnesses: Henry Culpeper.
Jno. Whinfell.

Will Greene & Seale.

JOHN HERBERT, being in perfect health an now bound out of this Country, and nott Knowing how It may please god to dispose of mee . . .

Book E f. 185.

dated 15 Jan. 1669.

proved 16 Apr. 1675.

. . . unto my Sone Jno. Herbert my Cleare land and houseing, and as much of ye wood land adjoining to it as shall make up his Equall proportion amongst ye Rest of my wifes Sonnes. I give to ye Rest of my wifes Sonnes all ye Remaynding part of my land Equall to bee divided . . . at twenty one yeares . . .

. . . Child that my wife now goes with . . .

. . . wife Mary Herbert . . . Extx . . .

witnesses: Francis Sayer.
Mary Williams.

John *harburd* & Seale.

THOMAS MORGAN . . .

Book E f. 187.

dated 1 Jan. 1674.

proved 15 Apr. 1675 by Eliz[a] Smith & 20 May 1675 by Wm. piper.

. . . unto my well beloyed friend Mauris fitzgarralld . . . to Katherene his wife one mourning gold ring of twenty Shillings . . .

. . . to Mr. david Morgan ye like . . .

. . . to Mr. Rob[t] Horton one Ring of Same price . . .

. . . to Mr. Jno *deuester* one Ring of ye Same vallue . . .

. . . to my Brother *T*reharne Morgan, and my sister Elizabeth Willis.

witnesses W[m] Piper.
Eliz[a] Smith
John. Miles

Thomas Morgan & Seale.

EDWARD HALL . . .

Book 4 f. 5.

dated 2 Sept. 1675.

proved 15 *Oct*. 1675.

. . . my sone Humphry Hall, and my sone In Law Thorowgood Keeling to bee my hole & Sole Exequetors . . .

. . . unto my sone humphry Hall my plantation wch. I now live on and to his hyres for Ever, but if It should happen that my sone humphry Hall bee dead, or that he should dye beefore hee Comes and takes possession of ye land, that then ye land bee Equally divided between my two daughters Katheren Lemon & Luce Keeling . . .

. . . unto Tho. Harread . . .

. . . unto Tho. Benson . . .

. . . unto my grandsons Jno. Laurence and Edward Lemon, ye young mare wch. James Lemon has already in his possession . . .

. . . If my daughter in law Katheren Hall comes in a Wid[r] that then shee should live on the plantation wch. I have given my Sone Humphry Hall, soe long as shee lives a widow . . .

. . . friends Adam Keeling & Thomas Benson to see this my will well preformed . . .

witnesses:

Tho. Benson.

Jno. Benson.

Edward Hall. m[r]k. & seale.

JOHN PORTER, sigr of ye Easterne branch of Eliz[a] River in ye County of Lower Norfolk . . .

Book 4 f 7.

dated 18 Sept. 1672.

proved 15 Feb. 1675. by Rich[d] Hartwell.

. . . unto Mary my wife . . . Extx . . .

. . . unto my Brother Jn[o] Porter Jun[r] . . .

. . . unto ye sd Jno. porter Jun[r] for ye use of his Children . . .

. . . unto frances fouler ye wife of george fouler, one payre of glasses of five shillings price . . .

witnesses: John Bigge.

Rich[d] Hartwell.

Jno. Porter, segr & Seale.

JOHN WORKMAN of Lower Norfolk in Virg[a] . . .

Book 4 f 8.

dated 19 Jan. 1675.

proved 15 Feb 1675. by Sarah hattersley.

. . . unto Margrett H*adesly* wid[r] and Johanna *hadesly* her daughter all my land . . .

. . . frend Margrett ha*deserby* . . . Extx . . .

witnesses: Henry Offley.
Sarah h*adersly* John Workeman.

Codocil (Nuncupative).

Oath . . . "hee asked Jno. Workeman whether hee would nott give his Couzen Tho. Workeman or any of his Relations any thing & hee said noe, they had Enough and did nott want."

Henry Offley.

JOHN BANKS, of Little Creek . . .

Book 4 f 8.

dated 26 Jan. 1675.

proved 15 Feb. 1675.

. . . wife Eliza[th] Banks . . .

. . . to my sone Jn[o] banks, I give my house and Land . . .

. . . to my daughter Margrett . . .

. . . to my sone William . . .

. . . frends James Wishart & hugh purdy overseers . . .

witnesses: Jno. Thro*w*er.
Jno. davis.

John banks & Seale.

JOHN MURFEE . . . (Nuncupative) . . .

Book 4 f. 9.

Sworn to 16 Feb. 1675. by Henry Cruch, 24 years or thereabouts . . .

Sworn to 16 Feb 1675, by Edward Murfee, 26 years or thereabouts . . .

. . . ye middle of June Last . . . house of . . . Co*r*nellis Mahony . . .

. . . Cow to C*ar*nellis mahony . . . and Exor . . .

. . . Cow to Richard Jenings . .

. . . Cow to Edward Murfee . . .

. . . to Henry Jenings . . .

GEORGE KEMP . . .

Book 4 f 9.

dated "The 8th day of ye 12 moneth Called febuary" 1675.

proved 17 Apr. 1676.

. . . unto my Eldest sone James Kemp . . . land I now live upon . . . on ye head of ye Easterne branch of Eliz[a] River, I say after the decease of my wife Ann Kemp . . .

. . . unto my sone Jno. Kemp and Job Kemp, and my daughter Mary Williamson . . .

. . . unto my youngest daughter Eliz[a] Kemp . . .

. . . wife Ann Kemp . . . and sone James Kemp, joynt Exequetors . . .

witnesses: Isaac *H*ocker.
Abraham Wakling.

George Kemp.

THOMAS BRINSON . . .

Book 4 f. 9.

dated 27 Dec. 1675.

proved 17 Apr. 1676.

. . . my Sonnė Mathew Brinson my Land . . . Exor . . .

. . . my Sonne Jno. Brinson . . . when . . . one and twenty . . .

witnesses: Alexander Keeling.
William White.

Tho. Brinson & Seale.

WM. ANDREWS . . .

Book 4 f. 11.

dated —(torn out)—

proved 17 Apr. 1676.

. . . my deere and only daughter Winifrett Andrews . . .

. . . to my Loving frend W[m] Carver . . . my gould Ring and my gun . . . my Exequetor . . .

—(torn)—

MARY EMPEROUR, wid[r] . . .
Book 4 f. 12.
dated 20 Apr. 1676.
proved 3 July 1676.

. . . sonne Tully Emperour my Land I now live upon . . . only that part of it Comonly Called *Beare* point I give unto my loving sone William Emperour . . .

. . . to my beloved daughter Eliz[a] phillips my Ebony Cabonet, and large silk Cobert Ciphon and Childs baskett . . .

. . . to my grandaughter Mary phillips one Cow . . .

. . . to my loving sone tully Emperour one fe—— bead, and ye furniture now in ye Roome belonging to it . . .

. . . to my loving sone W[m] Emperour one feather bead now in ye *R*—— Roome, and ye furniture belonging thereto . . .

. . . to my loving sone Francis Emperour five shillings to buy him a Ring . . .

. . . to my Couzens tully, Eliz[a] & mary Robinson five shillings a peece to buy them Each a Ring . . .

. . . sone tully Emperour my Sole Exequetor . . .

witnesses: W[m] Robinson.
John Seeley.

Mary Emperour & Seale.

ROBT BUTT, sig[r] of ye Southerne branch of Eliz. River . . .
Book 4 f 13.
dated 1 Nov. 1675.
proved 3 July 1676.

. . . unto my sone Henry Butt ye neck of Land Called ye Walnutt neck and also ye s——bly neck . . .

. . . unto my sone Robert Butt the other part of ye sd oldfield . . . also . . . a pattent . . . knowne by ye name of Ralphs Ridge . . . 380 acres . . .

. . . unto my sone Tho. Butt, land called Rich neck . . .

. . . unto my sone Richard Butt neck called ——— neck . . . also . . . Long Beaches Ridg . . .

. . . unto Arthur Sayer . . .

. . . wife Jane butt Exequetrix . . .

witnesses: Jno. Edwards.
Margere Alexander als Sharp.
Rich Odien.

Robt. Butt & Seale.

JOHN WILLIAMSON, Sigr, of Lower Norfolk Tanners Creek pish in ye County of Lower Norfolk, In Virg^{a} . . .

Book 4 f 14.

dated 24 Apr. 1673.

proved 17 Apr. 1677, by Wm Cooper & Ed. Wilder.

. . . to my wife Milborough Williams . . . one third part . . .

. . . to my Sonne Jno. Williams . . . one third part . . . him to bee my Sole Exequetor . . . land he lives upon . . .

. . . to my daughter Milborough Williams . . . one third part . . .

. . . for my daughter that is marryed shee hath had her portion . . .

. . . to Charles Jones one Cow . . . when sixteen years . . .

. . . my "flying coat" to my sonne John . . .

. . . Wm. *neane* & Mr. Wm. Chichester segr to share this Estate Equally between these three . . .

witnesses: Wm Cooper.
Thos: Shanky.
Ed. Wilder.

John Williamson & Seale.

JOSEPH HURLE, sojourner in ye house of Jno. Williamson, Sig^{r} in ye County of Lower Norfolk, in Daniell Tanners Creek . . .

Book 4 f. 14.

dated 15 Jan. 1676. & 28 year of our Soverigne King Charles ye Second

proved 17 Apr. 1677.

. . . I give Katheren hone a Chestnutt mare branded on wth. an S upon ye neare buttock . . .

. . . to Theophilis hone Ju^{r} . . . a young horse of ye same mare . . .

. . . . to francis Cockett late servt. to Richard Laurence . . .

. . . unto Jno. Williamson jur. a mare . . .

. . unto Milborn Williamson a mare fole . . .

. . . unto Thomas Hone a horse . . .

. . . unto Elizabeth Ives five pounds in money to be paid upon my departure wthout Consideration of her husband timothy Ives ju^{r} . . .

. . . unto James Simonds and his wife twenty shillings . . .

. . . unto Joseph Jackson . . .

. . . unto Nicholas Williamson . . .

. . . unto Thomas Simonds . . .

. . . unto Jane Jenkins . . .

. . . unto Mary Nicholas . . . blew linen . . .

. . . unto Milsborow Williamson ye wife of Jno. Williamson . . .

. . . unto Wm Cooper twenty shillings . .

. . . my wife . . . blew linen . . .

. . . unto Joseph *hew*lin . . att goose hill . . .

. . . friend Jno. Williamson my full and whole Exequetor . . .

witnesses: James Simonds.
Thomas Simonds.

Joseph hurley & Seale.

CHRISTOPHER BROWNE of ye westerne branch of Eliz. River . . .

Book 4 f. 14.

dated 9 Jan. 1676.

proved 17 Apr 1677.

. . . buried . . . according unto ye Con*secra*tion of ye Church of England where I owen my selfe a member . . .

. . . my Sonne Thomas Browne ye plantation, and woodland groune belonging to it, that I now Live on . . .

. . . my will beloved Sone Jno. Browne ye plantation that Elcazar tart now liveth on . . .

. . . my well beloved Sone Wm Browne ye middle nick . . .

. . . to my Couzen Thomas Cording ye neck that is Called by ye name of barren point for his life and after his decease unto my Sone William Browne or ye next heyre . . .

. . . frends francis Hatton and my Loving Brother James write my overseers to look after my Estate and Children . . .

witnesses: James Brown.
Robt L*an*gley.

Xtopher Browne & Seale.

RICHARD NICHOLS . . .

Book 4 f 15.

dated 30 Aug. 1675.

proved 17 Apr 1677.

. . . buried in Christian Buriall according to ye Cannons of ye Church of England . . .

. . . my Sone Henry Nichols . . . one great pestle . . .

. . . my daughter Margrett Whitehurst . . .

. . . my daughter Mary Godfree . . .

. . . my daughter Elizabeth . . . after the decease of her mother . . . comes to age . . .

. . . my Sone Richard . . . untill hee doeth Come to age . . and a gunn muskett . . . one little pistell . . .

. . . I give Elizabeth and margrett *hand*son . . .

. . . to my Loving wife five breeders . . . Extx . . .

. . . I give Ellinor Stanley a hayfer . . .

witnesses: Tully Emperour.
Adam *doller*.

Richard Nichols & Seale.

BENJ[a] JOHNSON of ye Easterne branch of Eliz. River . . .

Book 4 f. 15.

dated "This 19th of ye 7th moneth Called Sept. 1675"

proved 17 apr. 1677 by Isaac Barrington & Alice Cartwrite.

. . to my wife deborah Johnson . . . all my land upon wc[h] I now live situate in ye Easterne branch of Eliz. River . . . shee Exequetrix . . .

. . . my gunn . . . to Wm. Handcock for making my Coffin . . .

witnesses: Richard Hayes.
Thomas B*reach*.
Alice Cartwrite.
Isaac Barrington.

Benjamin Johnson & Seale.

Sworn to before mee by Mr. Tho: B*reach*, this 11th Aug. 1675.
W[m] Robinson.

HENRY NICHOLAS, Seg^r . . .

Book 4 f. 15.

dated "The 28th day of ye 10th moneth Called decemb^r 1676."

proved 17 Apr. 1677, by Henry platt & Jno. Whitehurst.

. . . to Mary my wife her being upon ye land and ye use of ye housing during her life . . .

. . . to Henry Whitehurst ye sone of my daughter Ellinor a hayfer . . .

. . . and for ye Child of Jno. Edmonds wc^h I keept, I doe give It to my wife for its time, butt after her decease to my daughter Mary . . .

. . . to my Sone Henry Nicholas after ye decease of my wife, all my land Lying and being in ye Easterne branch of Eliz. River . . . two gunns . . .

. . . Equally divided amongst my Children . . . are ——— age . . .

witnesses: James Whitehurst.
Henry Platt.
Jno. Whitehurst.

Henry Nicholas & Seale.

THOMAS LAMBERT, of ye pish of Linhaven in ye County of Lower Norfolk . . .

Book 4 f. 16.

dated 4 Jan. 1676.

proved 17 Apr. 1677.

. . . unto Mary Johnson ye daughter of Jno. Johnson, Jn^r one two yearling hayfer . . .

. . . my loving wife Jane Lambert my Land that I bought of Wm Dyer . . . Exequetrix . . .

witnesses: Robt. Bray.
Will Cornick.

Thomas Lambert & Seale.

ABRAHAM ELLETT . . .

Book 4 f. 16.

dated 7 Feb. 1675.

proved 28 Apr. 1677, by Lazarris Jenkins.

. . . my Exequetrix Alice Elliott my well beloved wife . . .
. . . unto my daughter Jane Eliot . . .
. . . unto my daughter Alice Adams . . .
. . . unto my daughter Sarah one hundred acres of land bounding Eastward from ye plantation where I now live, and Joyning upon a Creek Called *den in ye mire* . . .
. . . my beloved wife Alice Elliott ye plantation whereon shee now liveth . . . Exequetrix . . .

witnesses: Thomas Shanks.
Lazarris Jenkins.

Abraham Elliot & Seale.

THOMAS TUCKER . . .

Book 4 f 18.

dated 4 May 1676.

proved 15 June 1677.

. . . to my Sone Thomas Tucker one hundred acres of land, that I now dwell on, onely my wife to have it as long as shee lives . . . my gun . . . and hee may have ye land to dwell on at Eighteene years of age . . .
. . . unto my Sone Edward Tucker . . . make him att age att Eighteene yeares . . .
. . . unto my Jno Tucker . . . make my Sone Jno. att age att Eighteene yeares old . . .
. . . unto my daughter Elizabeth Tucker . . . att sixteene . .
. . . wife Exequetrix . . .
. . . to my Sone Edward my Coopers tooles . . .

witnesses: Tho: L*ondes*.
Denis ashby.
Robt. Tucker.

Thomas Tucker & Seale.

MOSES LINTON . . .

proved 15 June 1677.

Book 4 f. 20.

dated 23 Nov. 1676.

. . . unto my sone Moses Linton . . . my whole dividend of Land . . . (my wife Enjoying her thirds during her life) . . . butt if ye Child my wife now goes with prove to bee a sonne then he to have halfe my Said Land . . . my sonne bee of age and Inheritt att sixteene years old . . .

. . . wife Exequetrix . . .

witnesses: Jno. Edwards.
Jno pearse.

Moses Linton Jnr & Seale.

NICHOLAS ROBINSON of ye Southerne Branch of Eliz. River in Virga, planter.

Book 4 f. 22.

dated 28 Jan. 1666. "Compution of ye Church of England."

proved 15 Aug. 1677, by Jno. Edwards & Marmaduck Warington.

. . . wife Ann Robinson . . . Estate . . . for Life . . . and after her decease . . . to fall to my loving daughter Ānnis Robinson now ye wife of Wm E*ndri*dg and her Children . . .

witnesses: Jo. Edwards.
Marneduck Warrington.
Wm. *Ethri*dg.

Nicholas Robinson & Seale.

JOHN *BOURI*NG . . .

Book 4 f 22.

dated 31 Jan. 1673.

. . . unto my two Sonnes being Edmond & John bouring all my Land being six hundred acres of land and to be equally divided betweene them when they shall come of age . . .

witnesses: Wm Hatfield.
hugh hoskings.

Jno. bouring

Deposition of hugh hoskings, aged 34 yeares or thereabouts 17 June 1677.

Adam Keeling. hugh hoskins & Seale.

ELIZ[th] COKEE, Widow . . .

Book 4 f 30.

dated 3 Feb. 1676.

proved 7 March 1677/8.

. . . unto my sonne Jn° Cokee my Land & Cattle . . .
. . . calfe att Jn° grigmans . . .

. . . hayfer att Thomas Londes . . .

. . . hayfer att Thomas *Costers*

. . . one great Chest wth a lock and key to it and ye pattent of my Land In itt . . .

. . . Richard b*acon* to bee my Lawfull Exequetor . . . and to have possession of my Child . . . untill hee Cometh to ye age of Eighteene yeares, and after that time my brother Jno. Jollif together wth. Jno grigman to have ye oversight of him and his Estate untill hee Cometh of age of one and twenty . . .

witnesses: Jno. Jollif.
Jno. grigman.

Eliz[th] Cokee.

JOHN PEAD . . .

Book 4 f 30.

dated 4 Feb. 1677/8.

proved 15 apr. 1678.

. . . unto my wife and Children making my wife Sole Exequetrix . . .

. . . unto my sonne W[m] pead his first Choice of his part of my land . . .

. . . my sonne Jn° pead should have the other part . . .

. . . my two sonnes W[m] & John having Cattle already of their owne should have none of my cattle, butt that they bee divided beetweene my wife and the other Children.

witnesses: Jno. griffin
James Peeters.

Jno. pead.

. . . my neighbour Jno. griffin . . . Overseer . . .

Seale.

GEORGE LAWSON, Jur. of ye Easterne Branch of Elizabeth River in ye County of Lower Norfolk . . .

Book 4 f 34.

dated 6 Oct. 1676.

proved 15 Aug. 1678, by Richard Hays.

. . . unto Mary my wife all my Estate . . . as Long as shee livith . . . and Extx . . .

. . . unto Thomas Lawson & Mary Lawson and Margrett Lawson, sonne and daughters unto Mr. Anthony Lawson ye one halfe of my Estate . . . unto Thomas Lawson one quarter, and unto Mary Lawson one quarter and unto Margrett Lawson ye one halfe . . .

. . . unto Edward Moseley one mare & foale . . .

witnesses: Richard Hays.
Thos. Bre*och*.

George Lawson & Seale.

TRUSTRAM MASON of ye County of Lower Norfolk in ye Collony of Virg[a]

Book 4 f 34.

dated 8 Feb. 1666.

proved 15 Aug. 1678, by Geo: I*v*ey.

. . . I ordaine that daneill L*eni*er Sonne to my beloved wife barbery Trustram . . .

. . . unto my Children Eliz[th] Mason & Thos. Mason

. . . wife Barbray Mason . . . Extx . . .

witnesses: George Ivey.
peleg d*uns*ton

Trustram Mason & Seale.

WM. PORTEN, of Eliz[th] River pish. in ye Country of Lower Norfolk send greeting . . . (Will?) . . .

Book 4 f 35.

dated 23th Sept. 1675.

Ack 15th Aug. 1678.

. . . for ye love and affection wch. I doe beare towards my will beloved wife Sarah and her Children doe freely give absolutely and Clearely give and grant . . .

. . . one large wrought Silver Ladle Cup, one Silver tumbler, all her rings . . . Shee ye sd. Sarah may Lawfully Dispose of her Children Either by deede of guife *nun*cupative will, or written will, or any other ways . . .

witnesses: Charles Egerton.
Mathew godfree.

Wm Porten & Seale.

"Nott wht stanting what is above written It is my meaning will and Intent, In Case I dye wth out a will that this shall noe ways Cutt of or debarr my wife from her due share . . . and further I doe declare that It is nott my Intent or will, that my Brother or any friend I have in England Shaull have to doe wth my Estate heere after my decease." . . .

dated 22 May 1676.
witnesses: francis Baker.
Jno. pattman

Wm Porten.

ack. 15 Augt 1678.

SARAH PORTEN. . . .

Book 4 f 35.
dated 28 Sept. 1675.
ack in Court 15 Aug. 1678.

. . . doe make and ordaine this my Last will and testamnt first I bequeath my Soule to God . . .
. . . my loving husband . . .
. . . unto my Sonne Mathew Godfree . . .
. . . unto my Sonne Jno. godfree . . .
. . . unto my Sonne Warner godfree . . .
. . . unto my daughter Sarah Malbone . . . rings . . . to her owne dispose and nott to be Intermingled wth her husbands Estate nor hee to have any thing to doe wth It
. . . my daughter Ann Egerton one Silver tumbler . . .

witnesses: Geo. Newton.
francis Newton.

Sarah Porten.

. . . what tob. I have given to my daughter Ann Egerton, I doe now Revoke and give ye Same to my sd. Sonne mathew godfree, and shee onely to have ye Silver tumbler . . .

dated 22 May 1676.
witnesses: francis Baker
Jno. patman.

Sarah Porten.

ack. 15 Augt 1678.

HENRY OFFLEY, . . .

Book 4 f. 36.

dated 20 June 1678.

proved 16 Aug. 1678.

. . . appoint my Loving friend Anthony Lawson of Eliz[th] River my Lawfull Exequetor . . .
. . . my goods and Chattles w[ch] doe[th] belong or may any *wais* acrew or apertaine unto mee in this Country of Virg[a] to him ye said Anth[o] Lawson . . .

witnesses:

Edward Moseley.
Joseph p*etty*.

Henry Offley & Seale.

FRANCIS ALDRIDGE of Linhaven in Ye County of Lower Norfolk . . .

Book 4 f 38.

dated 15 Oct. 1678.

proved 15 Oct. 1678.

. . . unto my Loving wife my plantation that I now live upon wth all houseing & Cleared ground thereunto belonging to her ye sd. Jane Aldridge . . .
. . . unto Thomas Brinson ye Sone of Rob[t] Brinson . . .
. . . wife Jane Aldridge Exequetrix . . .

witnesses: Robt. Bray.
Thorowgood Keeling.

francis Aldridge

ANN KEMP . . .

Book 4 f. 41.

dated 9 Oct. 1677.

proved 15 Jan. 1678/9.

. . . unto my sonne in law Job: Kempe . . .
. . . unto my son in law John Kempe . . .
. . . unto my daughter in Law Mary Williamson . . . and to her sonne Richard Williamson . . .
. . . unto my daughter in Law Eliz[th] Kemp . . .
. . . unto my friend Mary Hocker . . .

. . . unto my sonne Jameses sonne George Kemp . . .
. . . my daughters Ann Kemp & Mary Williamson . . .
. . . unto my sonne In Law James Kemp . . . Exequetrix . . .

witnesses: Wm Hancock.
Jno. Evans.

Ann Kempe & Seale

THOMAS AXWELL . . .

Book 4 f. 41.

dated 1 Dec. 1678.

proved 15 Jan. 1678/9 by Mr. Wm *Narne* & Jno Sanford.

. . . unto my frend Joseph Whitson . . .
. . . unto Thomas Whitson . . .
. . . unto Xtopher Bustians Sonne and daughter . . .
. . . unto Geo. Vallentine . . .
. . . unto Joseph Whitson Jn^r^ . . .
. . . unto John Wallis . . . after ye decease of my wife Marg*rett* . . . that William my wife's sonne . . .
. . . oweing to mee from Mr. Thomas mathews . . .
. . . wife Margrett Axwell my Sole Exequetrix . . .

witnesses: Francis Sayer.
William *Nar*ne.
Jno. Sanford.

Tho. Axwell & Seale.

MORRIS F*ITS*GARRALL . . .

Book 4 f 42

dated 1 Jan. *1678*.

proved 16 Jan 1678/9.

. . . Christian burreil according to the Cannons of the Church of England . . .
. . . my deare wife Katheren my Sole Exequetrix . . .
. . . my Sonne keepe wth his mother untill hee shall come to age . . .

witnesses: Richard waterman.
Adam doller.

Morris f*itsgerrall* & Seale.

KATHEREN F*IT*SGARRALL . . .

Book 4. f. 42.

dated 9 Jan. 1678/9.

proved 16 Jan. 1678/9.

. . . to Jane Snaile a serge petticoat . . .
. . . I doe give unto Richard founder my husbands Coasting Coat . . .
. . . unto Eliz. founder . . .
. . . unto my Servt. Richard Waterman all his time of service by the Request of my husband upon his death bed . . .
. . . unto my Sonne in Law Henry f*its*garrall my plantation . . .
. . . I doe desire that Capt. Anthony Lawson may take all the Estate into his Custody till my Sone In Law come to age of Eighteene yeares

witnesses: Jacob Johnson.
Mary grady.

Katheren f*it*garrall & Seale.

ROBT. LOVEDAY of ye County of Lower Norfolk . . .

Book 4 f. 45.

dated 1 Jan. 1678.

proved 28 Mch. 1678/9, by Richd Smith.

. . . unto my Loving wife Sarah Loveday all my plantation and all my Estate during her Life . . .
. . . unto my daughter Dorothy after the decease of my wife one hundred acres of Land and foure head of Cattle . . .
. . . unto my daughter mary . . . Exequetrix . . .

witnesses: Jno. Sandford.
Richd Smith.

Robt. Loveday & Seale.

"We whose names are under written doe Constitute our Loving frend W^{m} daines Seg^{r} or atturney to prove ye Last will of Robt Loveday as witnesse our hands this 12th of March *1678*."

Sarah Loveday.
Mary Loveday.

witnesses: Edward *W*orley.
Richard Ca*rr*ey.

NICHOLAS WILLIAMS . . .

Book 4 f. 46.

dated 9 Apr. 1679.

proved 20 May 1679.

. . . "to bee buried att my father In Laws; Thomas Si*monss,* and by brother James, and my brother francis baker, and my brother Thomas, and my brother James I make them my full and whole Exequetors, two sones & two daughters I leave to them, and my daughter francke unto my brother francis baker, and my gunn I give to my Brother Thomas" . . .

. . . Estate . . . to bee divided Equall amongst them my Children when that they Come of age . . .

witnesses: Jno. Adams.
Jno. Bouring.

Nich. Williams & Seale.

JNO, M*CEE*LLALLEN . . .

Book 4 f. 46.

dated 27 Jan. 1678/9.

proved 20 May 1679.

. . . unto my Sonne John . . . cows . . .

. . . unto my daughter mary . . . hayfer . . .

. . . Rest of my Estate . . . divided betweene my wife and my two Children . . .

. . . make my wife Jane my Sole Exequetrix . . .

. . . friends Jacob Johnson & Mr. Anthony Lawson . . . oversight of my Children . . .

witnesses: Joseph pittss.
James *Slavin.*

Jno. *Mceellallen.*

ROBT. SPRING . . .

Book 4 f. 47.

dated 16 Mch. 1678/9.

proved 20 May 1679.

. . . unto my sonnes moses and Aaron . . . plantation that I now live upon being two hundred acres . . . after ye decease of my well beloved wife Anis Spring . . .

. . . my mail Servant Jane Williams . . .

. . . when Aaron Spring comes to ye age of twenty one . . .

. . . my Sonne Robert Spring . . . when hee comes to to twenty one yeares of age . . .
. . . unto John grigman . . .
. . . unto Edward Outlaw . . .

witnesses: John Spring
Edward Outlaw

Robert Spring.

THOMAS *HOW* (or *STOW*) . . .

Book 4 f. 47.
dated 20 Apr. 1679.
proved 20 May 1679, by Thomas & Eliz[th] greene.

. . . unto Henry greene and Ann greene . . .
. . . unto Henry greene my Gun, & foure hundred and fifty pounds of tob. that he owes unto mee, and my Adz . . . five and twenty pounds of lead . . my tooles . . . tob due unto me from W[m] *mem*ox . . . polk due unto mee from Thomas *wors*ley, and att humphrey Stephens . . . and att Richard phillpotts . . . att henry pullens . . .
. . . unto Jno. Gammon . . . bill due me from Richard Bacon . . .
. . . unto Crany Collins . . .
. . . unto W[m] *an*is

witnesses: Tho: greene.
Eliz. greene.
Mathew gage.

Thomas How (or Stow).

ROBERT WHITEH*E*RST . . .

Book 4 f. 47.
dated 15 Mch. 1678/9.
proved 20 May 1679.

. . . Buried according to ye Cannons of ye Church of England . . .
. . . unto my wife Ellenior Whitehorst, her being pon ye plantation during her life . . .
. . . unto my Children all ye Rest of my Catle . . . come to age . . .
. . . two sones . . . come to age . . .
. . . unto my sone Henry Whiteh*er*st the plantation w[ch] I now live upon . . .

. . . unto my sone Robt. Whiteh*e*rst my part of Land att ye Three R*unns* when it is divided . . .

. . . unto Isaac Barringtons two boys w[ch] now lives wth mee . . .

. . . my Loving Brother Jno. Whiteh*e*rst . . . see that my Children may nott bee abused . . .

. . . wife Exequetrix . . .

witnesses: Jno: Whitehurst.
Ed: R*aven*ing.

Robt. Whiteh*er*st.

HENRY STRAT*O*N . . .

Book 4 f. 48.

dated 28 Mch. 1679.

proved 20 May 1679.

. . . bequeath all my Land to Ruth Woodhouse and Eliz[a] Woodhouse ye daughters of Jn[o] Woodhouse . . .

. . . to Daniell fresell . . .

. . . to Henry *lat*ny towards puting him to schoole . . .

. . . unto Mary B*ence* . . .

. . . to Jno. Woodhouse . . . Remaynder . . . to pay debts . . .

witnesses: Charles Henley.
Jno. gesborne.

Henry Strat*o*n.

JAMES KENDELL . . .

Book 4 f. 48.

dated 12 Apr. 1679.

proved 20 May 1679 by Tho: Creed & francis plomer.

. . . unto francis plumer one gune . . .

. . . unto Edward ye sonne of Edward Ould . . .

. . . unto Mary ye daughter of Lewis *purvine* . . .

. . . unto Tho: Creed . . .

. . . unto Rauland *Lully* and Robert Brinson . . .

. . . unto Alexand. Keeling five pewter dishes and six plates and one tankard . . .

. . . unto Jno. Woodhouse all my Estate Lands and buildings . . . Exequetors . . .

witnesses: Tho: Creed.
francis plomer.
Alexand[r] Keeling.

James Kend*a*ll & Seale.

RICHARD YATES of Eliz. River in ye County of Lower Norfolk in Virg[a] Shipwrite . . .

Booke 4 f. 50.

dated 22 Nov. 1678.

proved 21 May 1679.

. . . unto my loving wife Jane Yates all my Estate . . . during her natural life Excepting one gun now in the possession of my Sonne In Law Jno. Whiden . . . Likewise one gun that was my Sonne Richard Yates Late dec[d] I give unto my unto my grandson Richard Etheridge . . .
. . . and for my three daughters (viz) Jane, Elizabeth & Mary Yates . . .
. . . my grandson Jno. Whidon . . .
. . . my grand daughter Jane Whidon . . .
. . . my two grand daughters (viz) Eliz. Etheridge and Mary Leak . . .
. . . my daughter faith yates, the youngest . . .
. . . my land in deepe Creek now in ye possession and occupation of francis Leak and marneduck Etheridge . . . equall division . . . unto ye sd. Leak and ye sd. Etheridge (my Sonnes in Law) during their and my daughters their wifes Life . . . then to descent to next hyer of ye bodyes of my Said daughters Elizabeth and Mary their wives . . .

witnesses: Jno. Edwards.
Edward Etheridg.

Richard Yates & Seale.

PAUL TRIGGS . . .

Book 4 f. 50.

dated 9 Mch. 1677.

proved ——— ———

. . . my loving wife Eliz[th] triggs all ye necestaryes wth in my house secondly I doe give & beequeath to my Loving wife above named all my hoggs Except foure Sows my Children Each of them one . . .
. . . to my Sonne Henry triggs seaven head of Catle . . .
. . . to my Sonne Thomas Triggs five head of Catle . . .
. . . to my daughter Elizabeth triggs five head of catle . . .
. . . to my daughter Mary triggs five head of Catle . . .
. . . wife my whole Exequetrix . . .

. . . I desire Jacob Johnson & morris *fit*garrall to have an oversight of my Children . . .

. . . my Children may Enjoy their Estates att sixteene yeares of age . . .

witnesses: James Lewis.
John Webster

Paul trigs.

JNO. HERBERT . . .

Book 4 f. 50.

dated ——— 1679.

proved 21 May 1679, by francis Lake and Henry Lake.

. . . my deare sonne Jno. Herbert halfe my land, and if ye other bee—Boy to have ye other halfe, and if nott John Herbert —— have it all, and also a gunn & a Cutlas . . .

. . . wife all my whole Estate as Long as shee lives a wid^{w} and after shee marryed ye Estate Is to be Equall divided amongst his two Children & ye wid^{r} and if his two Children dyes then I doe give it to Richard flewellen and Edward flewellen . . .

. . . desire that my Sone Jno. may bee att age att Eighteene years . . . and if the other be a boy to be att age att Eighteene yeares . . . if it bee a girle shee is to bee att age att Sixteene . . .

. . . I doe Impower my brother Tho. Willoughbye to see that my Children are nott wronged.

witnesses: Thomas Willoughby.
fra. Lake.

Jno. Herbert wth a Seale.

RICHARD TAYLOR . . .

Book 4 f. 51.

dated 29 Mch. 1679.

proved 21 May 1679.

. . . unto my wife Margrett taylor . . .

. . . my sonne John . . . plantation I now live one . . .

. . . my daughter Margrett . . .

. . . my sone Richard . . .

. . . my daughter Suzan . . .

. . . my godson Richard Hodges . . .

. . . my god daughter Elizabeth davis . .

. . . sons to live with wife untill twenty-one . . .

. . . to my Sone John two guns, my old gun and ye gun I bought of Jno. fallock and my Son Richard Richard one Muskett w[ch] I bought about of ye Rose.

witnesses: Rodger Hodges.
Ellinor Owens.

Richard taylor.

ROBT. SMITH . . .

Book 4 f. 51.

dated 8 Feb. 1678/9.

proved ——— ———

. . . In ye next place I doe make *Nech*[u] Huge*n*s my hole and Sole Exeq[ur] . . .

. . . tob . . . due unto mee from Henry Holmes and that I beequeath unto him to make my coffin . . .

witnesses: Thomas *le*therington Jn[r].
William Burrough.

Robert Smith.

WM. CAMERELL . . .

Book 4 f. 53.

dated 28 Jan. 1678.

proved 15 Aug. 1679.

. . . my whole Estate Consisting of five hundred acres of land . . .

. . . four hundred acres to my sister Elizabeth . . .

. . . one hundred acres to my sister Katheren . . . adjoining to ye plantation that Edward Baxter Liveth upon . . .

. . . my father In Law Owen grady bee full Exequetor & possessor thereof untill such time as my aforesd. Sisters Elizabeth and Katheren bee past their minority, and that they shall Cohabite and dwell wth him . . .

. . . desire that Capt. Anth[o] Lawson and Mr. Robt. Hodge my faithful frends take charge of ye oversight of these my Sisters . . .

witnesses: ——— porter.
William Emperour.

W[m] Camarell & Seale.

THOROWGOOD KEELING of ye pish. of Linhaven in ye County of Lower Norfolk . . .

Book 4 f. 54.
dated 31 Mch. 1679.
proved 15 Aug. 1679.

. . . to my eldest daughter Lucy ye plantation whereon I Live after my wifes decease . . .

. . . unto my youngest daughter Ann Keeling one hundred acres of land Lying in ye woods neare Ren*atus* Land wch. I bought of Jesper land . . . att ye age of Sixteene . . .

. . . to Lucy att Sixteene . . .

. . . Lucy and Ann Keeling . . . all that is in ye hands of my father Bray due to mee after my mothers decease . . .

. . . wife Lucy Keeling all ye Rest . . . Sole Exequetrix . . .

. . . & Impower my Loving frends my Brother Henry Woodhouse & Wm Cornick to see ye pformance of this my last will.

witnesses: Edward Raulings.
Wm Cornick.

Thorowgood Keeling & Seale.

FRANCIS WOODWARD of Lower Norfolk Virga . . .

Book 4 f. 55.
dated 21 Apr. 1679.
proved 15 Aug. 1679.

. . . I frances wooddard . . .

. . . my body to Receive Xtian buriell in ye orchard wth my wife . . .

. . . to my two sonnes Jno. and henry wooddard all that tract of Land, that I bought of Be*nony* Burrough . . .

. . . to my daughter Mary Woodard . . .

. . . to my daughter Eliz. Woodard . . .

. . . apoint nicholas *wes*ley & Benj. granger my Sole Exequetors . . . and care of my Children untill they Come to age . . .

. . . to pay unto Joseph Lake . . .

. . . my daughter mary woodary to be kept by Joseph Lake and *his* wife untill . . . Sixteene or marryed . . .

witnesses: Joseph Lake.
Wm Newport.

francis woodard & Seale.

MARGRETT TAYLOR . . .

Book 4 f. 56.

dated 5 Apr. 1679.

proved 15 Aug. 1679.

. . . unto my foure small Children . . . my sone John to have his choice . . .

. . . I desire my brother Roger Hodges may have my daughter Margarett and my brother Thomas maning my daughter Suzanna, and Wm Owens my sone Richard . . .

. . . Brothers Roger Hodges and Jno. maning, and Thomas maning and my loving frend Wm Owens to bee my overseers . . .

. . . my Sone Thomas, after this years nursing to bee att ye disposition of my overseers . . .

witnesses: Rodger Hodges.
Richard Harris.

Maargrett taylor.

THOMAS MOSIER, Carpenter . . .

Book 4 f. 56.

dated 24 May 1679.

proved 15 Aug. 1679.

. . . unto mary Chichester during ye time of her life . . . then to bee equally divided between Wm Chichester and Suzanna Carmady . . .

witnesses: francis Hatton.
Wm Bennett.

Tho: Moyser.

MICHAELL LAURENCE . . .

Book 4 f. 58.

dated 16 March 1678/9.

proved 16 Aug. 1679.

. . . unto my wife margare Laurence, all my Estate . . . during her life . . . her Exequetrix . . .

. . . two daughters Eliz. Holmes & hester Guy . . .

. . . grand children Henry Holmes & James Guy . . .

. . . ye Rest of my grandchildren . . .

. . . that John Bouskine may live in my house . . .

. . . unto Moses Bous*kine* one Cow . . . att little Creek . . . when he is free . . .

. . . appoint Coll. Lem. mason, Wm *Nearne,* Thomas mason & Wm Langley overseers.

witnesses: Lemuel Mason.
W^{m} *N*arne.

Michaell Laurence & Seale.

FRANCES FOULER . . .

Book 4 f. 58.

dated 26 Jan. 1678.

proved 16 Aug. 1679, by Jno. Davis & *Rich. drout.*

. . . my late decd. husband Geo. fouler did formerly sell unto Wm Handcock, a pcell of land given by my father Coll. Jno. Sidney unto my eldest daughter Pembrook fouler, and shee ye sd. pembr*oc*k nott yett being Recompences by her Said father for ye Same . . .

. . . my other two Children George fouler and sidney fouler . . .

. . . appoint Coll. Lemuell mason & my brother Jno por*ter* Joynt Exequetors . . .

. . . daughter pembro*o*ke, and my Sone Geo. fouler shall bee att ye Charge of bringing up their sister Sidney fouler . . .

witnesses:
John davis.
R*eoh*^{a} dr*out.*
Robt fouler.

ffrances fouler & Seale.

MARY FENWICK, ye wife of Tho: fenwick . . . (Nuncupative)—

Book 4 f. 59.

dated 24 May 1679.

recorded 16 Aug 1679.

The deposition of James Porter aged 22 years or thereabouts . . . says hee the sd. deponent wrott ye will and testament of mary fenwick, ye wife of Tho: fenwick . . . att ye late dwelling house of george fouler on little Creek . . . her will was that her husband Thomas fenwick Should enjoy her Lands as long as Shee lived this in ye will Exprest during his naturall life and after ye death of her husband, and after ye Decease . . . to John Porter Jun[r] and to his hyers for Ever . . .

witnesses: Lemuel Mason. James Porter, Ju[r]

Interogatorys putt to W[m] Browne . . .
dated 16 Aug. 1679 . . .

JAMES MATHEWS . . .

Book 4 f. 59.
dated 27 Mch. 1679.
proved 16 Aug. 1679.

. . . unto my wife Ellinor the Land whereon I live . . .
. . . to my daughter Ellinor Mathews . . .
. . . if . . . my wife shall happen to bee to bee with Child and have a sonne then I bequeath the aforesaid land to him and his hyres for ever . . .
. . . Ann I*tson* and he Sister mary Itson . . . .
. . . unto Ann I*tson*, one prcell of Land Commonly Called by ye name of ye blanch pine swamp Ridge . . . when they Come to the age of Sixteene . . .

witnesses: Henry Butt.
Joseph weldbone.

James Mathews & Seale.

JOHN POORE of ye pish of Linhaven in ye County of Lower Norfolk . . .

Book 4 f. 63.
dated 22 July 1678.
proved 15 Oct 1679. by Edward Cooper & W[m] Cornix.

. . . unto my Sonne in Law Edward Cooper for ye use of his first born Child a yearling hayfer . . .
. . . unto Rob[t] brinsons daughter Susanna . . .
. . . to my loving wife Eliz[th] . . . Sole Exequetrix . . .

witnesses: Thomas Jones.
Edward Cooper.

John poore & Seale.

JOHN JOHNSON of Linhaven in ye County of Lower Norfolk . . .

Book 4 f. 63.

dated this last day of March 1679.

proved 15 Aug. 1679, by Edward Rawlings.

" 18 Aug. 1679, by trustram may*o*.

. . . to my loving wife Ann Johnson all my Lands during her life, and I give and bequeath to my Loving Children, one thousand pounds of tob. a piece . . .

. . . wife Exequetrix . . .

witnesses: Trustram may*o*.
Edward Rawlings.

John Johnson & Seale.

MARTIN JOYCE of ye Westerne branch of Eliz[th] River in ye County of Lower norfolk planter

Book 4 f. 64.

dated 23 June 1677.

proved 15 Feb. 1679.

. . . I give my plantation wth ye 200 acres of Land unto my wife Judeth Joyce her life, and afterwards to bee Equally divided beetwixt my three Children viz: Jn[o] Joyce, Eliz[th] Joyce and Judeth Joyce . . . butt In Case of Eyther of their mortalityes beefore hee or shee shall Come att age or man or womans Estate . . .

. . . when my Children shall attayne to ye age of Sixteene . . .

witnesses: John ferebee.
Eliz. ferebee.

Martin Joyce & Seale.

JOHN SALLMON . . .

Book 4 f. 65.

dated 22 March 1678/9.

proved 15 Oct. 1679.

. . . unto my daughter Susanna . . .
. . . unto my daughter Eliz. . . .
. . . unto my daughter Mary . . .

. . . to my Sone John ye one halfe of my Land . . .
. . . to my Sone William ye other halfe . . .
. . . unto my wife Eliz. . . . Sole Exequetrix . . .
. . . appoint Capt. Thomas Ivy & francis Ship overseers . . .

witnesses: Warren Godfree.
Rich[d] Williams.

John Salmon.

GEORGE CREMOR of ye County of Lower Norfolk . . .
Book 4 f 67.
dated 21 June 1679.
proved 16 Oct. 1679.

. . . unto my Eldest sone James Cremor . . . one halfe ye Carpenters tooles . . . ye age of one and twenty yeares . . .
. . . to my youngest sone Jno. Cremor four head of female catle . . . & ye other halfe of my Carpenters tooles when he shall accomplish ye age of one & twenty . . .
. . . unto Ann Cremor my wife . . . Sole Exequetrix . . .
. . . my trusty frends W[m] Chichester & Jno. Williams and Samuel Milicent . . . Overseers . . .

witnesses: Edward *Hews.*
Andrew Anderson.

George Cremor & Seale.

THOMAS FENFORD of Eliz. River in Virg[a] Cooper . . .
Book 4 f. 67.
dated 23 Sept. 1675.
proved 13 Nov. 1679. by Jno. Edwards & Herbert Jones.

. . . to my Sonne Thomas . . . all my Land & houseing In gen. Included in my pattent . . .
. . . to my daughters . . .
. . . during his mothers life . . .
. . . Sonne Thomas (when hee is thereof Capable) bee bound out aprentice to ye trade of a Cooper . . .
. . . wife Sarah fenford . . . my Sole Exequetrix . . .

witnesses: Jo. Edwards.
Rich[d] Marks.

Thomas fenford & Seale.

MARY FENICK . . .

Book 4 f 68.

dated 28 Jan 1678/9.

proved 16 Aug. last (1679). by Mr. James Porter & Mr. W[m] browne.

. . . unto my husband Thomas fenwick . . . Land . . . during his naturall life and after ye decrease of my said husband to John Porter Ju[r] . . .

witnesses: James Porter.
William browne.

Mary fenwick & Seale.

EMANUELL OLIVER . . .

Book 4 f. 69.

dated 10 July 1676.

proved 15 Dec. 1679.

. . . "being in pfect health and memory, butt being prest for to goe against ye Indians, doe make this my Last will and testam[t] . . .

. . . to my god sonne Oliver Andre my mare . . .

. . . unto francis Andre . . .

. . . unto Oliver *auere* my god sonne . . .

. . . and bequeath my Brother Jn[o] Andre all ye Rest of my Catle . . . one att Thomas Smithers . . . another att henry Snayles . . .

. . . my brother Jn[o] Andre to bee my Lawfull atturney till I Returne againe, and If Itt please god that I never Returne againe then my brother to bee my hole & Sole Exequetor . . .

witnesses: John Turner.
daniell Stringer.

Emanuel Oliver.

JAMES WISHART Living att Ye little Creeke. In ye County of Lower Norfolk . . .

Book 4 f. 71.

dated 1 Oct. 1674.

proved 1 Mch. 1679/80.

. . . unto my wife Eliz. Wishart ye third part of my plantation that I now Live on . . . during ye time of her naturall life . . .

. . . to my sone James Wishart my plantation whereon I now live together wth two hundred acres of land Lying att Giles Branch . . . hee shall bee full Eighteene yeares of age . . .

. . . unto my daughter Joyce Wishart three thousand pounds of good tob . . . a serge petticoat and wescoat wch belonged to her mother . . . (shee haveing her Choice *next* after my wife) . . .

. . . unto my Sone Jno. Wishert my plantation att Sowell's point contayning one hundred and fifty acres or thereabouts . . . when hee is full Sixteene yeares of age . . .

. . . unto my sonne William Wishart, my plantation att ye little Creek wch I bought of W^m^ R*ich*eson Conteyning two hundred acres of land or thereabut . . . when hee shall bee full Eighteene yeares old . . .

. . . for use of my son Thomas Wishart . . . when hee shall bee full Eighteene yeares old . . .

. . . my daughter francis wishart . . . when shee shall be Sixteene yeares old . . .

. . . unto James banks my god sonne . . . to be delivered unto him when he is free . . .

. . . appraised by Jacob Johnson, Sam Roberts, Simon Handcock and James Peeters . . .

. . . my two Loving frends and brothers in Law Exequetors . . .

. . . frends Coll. Lemuell mason, Mr. George Newton, Wm Narne & Wm Hunter as overseers . . .

witnesses: Wm Hunter.
William Narne.

James Wishart & Seale.

SIMON PEETERS . . .

Book 4 f. 72.

dated 4 May 1678.

proved 1 Mch. 1679/80 by Andrew Basha*w*.

. . . to my Sonne James twelve pence . . .
. . . to my daughter Alice twelve pence . . .
. . . to my daughter Ann twelve pence . . .
. . . to my daughter Sarah two Cows . . .
. . . to my sonne Simon a Cow & a gun . . .

. . . to my sonne Jacob a Cow & a gun . . .
. . . to my daughter margere a cow . . .
. . . to my daughter Rebecca a Cow . . .
. . . my wife . . . ye Children of my & her body . . .

witnesses: Andrew Bashaw.
daniell Lenard.

Simon peeters.

EDMIND C*REACK*ON.

Book 4 f. 80.
dated 28 Mch. 1678/9.
proved 16 Aug. 1680.

. . . unto my sone John Creackman *one* Dividend or seat of Land being the plantation I now live uppon being in or by the mouth of Deeap Creek in the Southerne Branch of Elizabeth River . . .

. . . when my youngest sone Edmon Creackmon shall Come to ye age of twenty one yeares then my sone Jno. to pay unto his Brother Edmon Creackmon or his order two thousand pounds of tobacco and Caske Convenient in this Country . . .

. . . unto my sone Edward my seate of land, Lying Southerly from Richard Jones Sen[r] . . . when his Brother Edmon shall come to age . . . one thousand pounds of tobacco . . .

. . . unto my daughter Elizabeth foure head of Cattles . . .

. . . unto my wife Jane . . . two thirds . . life . . .

witnesses: Robert Burges.
John prescott.

E.Creekmon and Seale

HENRY NEWELL of blackwater In Coratock . . .

Book 4 f. 84.
dated 5 Dec. 1677.
proved 15 Oct. 1680.

. . . unto my young sone Henry Newell on Cow . . .

. . . my wife should give my Eldest sone Henry newell one Cow when hee is free . . .

witnesses: Henry Simonds.
Ed Car*ter*.

henry Newell by mke.

RENAT*RIS* LAND of Linhaven pish, in Lower Norfolk County in Virg[a] . . .

Book 4 f. 96.

dated 1 Oct. 1680.

proved 10 May 1681. by Geo. Walker.

. . . to my Eldest Sonne Rona*tus* Land ye Rest of my plantation, that Is now In ye ocupation of David Whitford att ye age of Nineteene yeares . . . a gould ring wth a signe of a deaths head upon it . . .

. . . unto my second sone Edward Land and my third sone Rob[t] Land, my plantation I now live upon . . . a payre of silver *Cod piste* buttons, and a sett of Silver buttons for shirt collar & wrist . . .

. . . unto my sonne Robert Land . . . a silver hatt band . . .

. . . unto my Eldest daughter Elizabeth Land . . . a Small dimond Ring . . .

. . . unto my daughter Ann Land . . .

. . . unto my wife frances Land . . .

. . . my sonne Renat*ris* Land, and my brother francis Land my Exequetors . . .

witnesses: W[m] We*bb*.
Geo. Walker.

Renat*res* *Land* & Seale.

JOHN WHITE . . .

Book 4 f. 98.

dated 9 Feb. 1680.

proved 11 May 1681.

. . . Sone in Law James S*her*wood all my Land . . .
. . . unto Jno. *sew*ell a Cow . . .
. . . unto Mary *sew*ell a Cow . . .
. . . unto James ye Sone of James Sherwood . . .
. . . unto Jno. *Ceu*ell my great gun . . .
. . . unto Edward Atwood seg[r] . . .
. . . James Sherwood my sole Exequetor . . .

witnesses: Alexand[r] Keeling
Jno Corperhew.

John White & Seale.

JOHN JACOB of Eliz. River . . .

Book 4 f. 100.

dated 2 Feb. 1680.

proved 12 May 1681.

. . . to Ann godby my Chest and all that It Contayned In it w[ch] Is now att Maj. francis Sayers within ye Southern branch of Eliz. River . . .

. . . unto Thomas Wood Living in ye upper pish of ye Isle of Wieght County . . . and his sonne George . . .

. . . Ann godby my Sole Exequetrix . . .

witnesses: John *trauer.*
John portlocke.

John Jacobs & Seale.

ELIZ. BLANCH of ye County of Lower Norfolk, wid[r] . . .

Book 4 f. 100.

dated 17 Aug. 1680.

ack. 15 June 1681.

. . . unto Thomas *Ivy* ye sone of George *Ivy* a tract or dividend of Land Contayning one hundred & forty acres of Land Lying and being In daniell tanners Creek, bounded on ye East side w[th] ye land of Robt. Woody as by ye patent apeareth att p[r]sent seated by my selfe . . .

. . . ye Rest . . . unto ye Children of ye above mentioned Geo. *Ivy* (viz.) Alexander, Samuell, George and Thomas *Ivy* brothers and to Eliz. *Ivy* their sister . . .

. . . George *Ivy* . . . Sole Exequetor . . .

witnesses: Hannah *Ivy*.
Tho: bridge.

Elizabeth Blanch & Seale.

ROBT. BRAY of Lower Norfolk County in Virg[a] being Sonne of Edward bray decd. Late of big*lswade* In bedfordshere in England . . .

Book 4 f 101.

dated 24 Apr. 1681.

proved 15 June 1681.

. . . . unto my two Couzens Edward & Jno. bray Sonnes of my Brother Jn° bray of Biglswade, aforesd fifty pounds Sterling money . . .

. . . . unto Mary Okeham my negro man named Guy . . . after ye decease of my wife Ann Bray . . .

. . . . unto Jno. Okeham negroes . . .

. . . . unto William Okeham my two negroes . . . if Either ye sd. Mary, John or William Okeham should dye under age . . .

. . . . unto my Brother plomer bray and his heyrs ye plantation Lately bought of Richard Carver . . .

. . . . to Alexander Keeling ye whole debt hee Oweth mee . . .

. . . . unto J*u*ell martin a large Silver tankerd wch was formerly his fathers, one good gun, and one horse . . .

. . . . unto my brother in Law Thomas Tomkings of bigleswade . . . and to my kinsman Jno. Boodington of ye same place . . .

. . . . unto my frend Anth° Lawson my gray horse watt, my plate hilted sword and belt . . . my large plate punch boule . . .

. . . . my aforesd. two Couzens Edward & Jn° bray . . . ye some of fifty pounds Sterling *mone;* to bee sent home for England Either by bills Exchange or In Ready money . . .

. . . . Ann Bray my wife Exequetrix . . .

. . . . unto each of Anth° Lawson Children two plate spoons . . .

. . . . my loving brother plomer bray & my frend anth° Lawson to be overseers . . .

witnesses: Wm Hunter.

Jno. Corperhew.

Robt Bray & Seale.

MATHEW BRINSON of ye pish. of Linhaven in ye County of Lower Norfolk . . .

Book 4 f. 101.

dated 12 June 1681.

ack. 15 June 1681.

. . . . bequeath unto Thomas Rus*s*ell Ju^{nr} ye Sone of Thomas Rus*s*ell of ye fresh ponds in ye pish of Linhaven in ye County aforesd, after myne and my wifes decease I doe wil and bequeath unto him my plantation whereon I now live being a divedent of one hundred acres . . . Adjoyning to ye land of John Axt*el* . . .

. . . And in Case that ye sd. Thomas Rus*t*ell should dye beefore me ye sd. mathew brinson and Eliz. my wife . . . then . . . unto his sister Mary Rus*t*ell ye daughter of ye afsd. Thomas Rus*s*ell seg^r . . .

. . . Thomas Rus*s*ell Ju^nr shall have Liberty to seat . . att ye age of one & twenty yeares . . .

witnesses: Jno. Brinson.
William Cornick.

Mathew Brinson & Seale.

Linhaven, June 14th 1681.

. . . unto my beloved brother Jno. Brinson of ye aforesd. pish. and County, one hundred acres of Land . . . In dam neck Joyning upon ye land of Jno. S*ue*llivant . . .

. . . brother Jno. brinson my full sole and Lawfull Exequetor . . .

witnesses: George M*inc*hen.
Tho: p*itts*.

Mathew Brinson & Seale.

ROGER FELWOOD . . . (Nuncupative) . . .

Book 4 f 104.

. . . The dep^o of W^m Co*n*ell aged 22 yeares or thereabouts . . . say^th that being prsent In *Comp*^a wth Roger felwood made his verbal will . . .

. . . unto Richard Burton all that hee had In ye Ship wages and Cloaths and goods onely to make ye Ships Comp. ———, and five shillings that hee owed his Landlady in England, and further nott.

. . . and I Ric*h*^e young sayth same. W^m Co*n*ell.

Sworne to in Court 15 Aug. 1681 by ye sd. young & Co*n*ell.

ROBERT HODGE . . .

Book 4 f. 106.

dated 10 Sept. 1681.

proved 18 Oct. 1681, "by ye oaths of all ye Evidences."

. . . buried with Christian burial according to ye discretion of my Executrix & my two friends Anthony Lawson & Bennoni Burroughs . . . in ye southside of ye Chancell in Linhaven Church . . .

. . . . unto my God son Anthony Lawson ye son of Anthony Lawson . . . when ye sd. Anthony is seaven years of age . . . .

. . . . unto my God son Anthony Ivy . . .

. . . . & to each Godson & God Daughter —— I have in Virginia besides one bible & two Sermon Books . . .

. . . . unto my Eldest Brother Alex: Hodge & unto my Brothers Jno. & Thomas Hodge & to each of their wives one mourning Ring of twenty shillings ster^{l} . . .

. . . . unto my Brother in law peter Shepheard & unto my Sister Mary his wife to each of them one Ring of twenty shilling Ster^{l} price . . .

. . . . unto Jno. *Tottle* of Plym^{o} one Ring of twenty shillings ster^{l} price, if he bee living at my Decease . . .

. . . . unto Malachi peale one ring . . .

. . . . unto Bennoni Burroughs one Ring . . .

. . . . unto Anthony Lawson one Ring . . .

. . . . unto each of my Bro: Jno Hodges Children five pounds ster^{l}: a peece . . .

. . . . unto my God son peter ye son of my Brother in Law peter Shepheard of Modbury ten pounds ster^{l} . . .

. . . . unto Dorothy Rowell that was my servant two thousand pounds of tobacco & Caske . . .

. . . . unto my friend Bennoni Burroughs & his heirs for Ever all my halfe of ye Tract of Land, patten'd in ye name of Anthony Lawson & my Selfe, wch Land is Called by ye name of Chester—fforrest . . . my great *K*earsey Coat lined with red serge & ten yards of Docoles Linnen out of my great Chest in ye Store . . .

. . . . unto my friend Anthony Lawson five pounds Ster^{l} money . . .

. . . . unto my ffeather in Law Coll. Lemuel Mason, my plush Saddle & furniture . . . my ffeather in law Mason & his wife to Each of them one Ring of twenty shillings price.

. . . . my dear & loving wife Alice Hodge to be my law full Executrix, & whereas it is supposed y^{t} she my said wife is with Child . . . .

. . . . Remayning part of my Estate . . . (if male) . . . equally diveded between ye mother & my sonne . . . & y^{t} like wife he be possest of ye other halfe of my Land after ye decease of his mother my now wife. But if . . . a female . . . an equall half of all my Land. But if . . . neither . . . and comes to age, Then I doe make & ordayne Robert Hodge ye Son of my Brother Jno. Hodge of Dartsmouth, to be my lawfull heir to all my Lands; & in Case he dies in his minority, then peter ye son of my Brother in Law peter Shepheard of Modbury, to be my lawfull heir and if ye said peter Shepheard should die, then Jno Hodge ye son of my Brother Jno. Hodge of Dartmo to be my lawfull heir . . .

. . . friends Anthony Lawson & Bennoni Borroughs to be overseers . . .

. . . my Brother Jno Hodge . . . his son Robert . . .

. . . my Eldest Brothers Children . . .

. . . to my Sister Mary Shepheard in Molbury . . .

. . . forty shillings to be paid to ye poore of ye pish of Modbury, & a Marble stone to be sent in heere to be laid upon my Grave.

witnesses:

David Whitford.
Pat. Angus.
Anthony Lawson.
Ben Burrough.

Rob Hodge & Seale.

JNO. MOORE . . . (Nuncupative) . . .

Book 4 f. 108.

. . The depo of Ann Wilder aged 55 years or thereabouts . . .

In July Last Shee being att ye house of Mr. Jno Moore . . .

. . . taking Mris Sarah Rasby by ye hand, take notice said hee I doe take her for my wife and said ye sd. Jno Moore, whether I marry her or nott, If I dye to-moorow, I give her all I have, and this Is my Last will . . .

Sworn In Court 19 Oct. 1681.

Ann Wilder.

Ann grant aged 30 years or thereabout . . . same . . .
Ann Grant, by mke.

WM. LEVINGSTON of Lower Norfolk County in Virga . . .

Book 4 f. 113.

dated 27 June 1681.

proved 16 Dec. 1681.

. . . unto my sonne Wm Levingston sonn of Eliz. Smith now wife to Richd Smith Living on ye Easterne Shore of Linhaven in ye County of Lower Norfolk two negroes . . . twenty pounds sterling money to bee paid him out of that money wch Mr. david Whitford oweth mee . . . when . . . 18 yeares old . . .

. . . my wife Katheren Lovingston . . . Exequetrix . . .

. . . unto my frend Adam Keeling twenty shillings Sterling money to bee laid out in a Ring to wear in Remembrance of mee . . .

. . . my two frends Mr. david whitford and Adam Keeling overseers . . .

witnesses: Wm Hunter.
Adam Keeling.

Wm Levingston & Seale.

ROBT. HATTON . . .

Book 4 f. 114.

dated 2 Feb. 1675.

proved 16 Feb. 1681.

. . . to my Sone Robt. all my Land . . . Comes to ye age of twenty one . . . after his mothers decease . . .

. . . unto my sonne Robert 3 Cowes . . . Comes to ye age of one and twenty years . . .

. . . two fouling pieces . . .

. . . to my daughter Eliz Hatton . . . when shee comes to ye age of sixteene years . . .

. . . unto my daughter Elizabeth . . .

. . . unto my Loving wife Eliz. Hatton . . . Exequetrix . . .

. . . apoint my Loving brothers Capt. Jno. Hatton & francis Hatton to bee overseers . . .

witnesses: Eleazer tart.
Geo. Horne.

Robt. Hatton & Seale.

ANNE MORTON, widow . . .

Book 4 f. 114.

dated 26 March 1679.

proved 10 May 1682.

. . . my Son Wm Morton, may administer on my husband's & my Estate, & satisfie all his fathers due Debts . . . all lands houses . . . untill he shall be twenty one years of age . . . take advice, & be advised by Jno. Prescott . . .

witnesses:

Herbert Griffyth.

Thomas Branton, by mke.

Anne Morton & Seale.

MICHAELL MACOY . . .

Book 4 f. 119.

dated 8 Feb. 1680.

proved 11 May 1682.

. . . unto my son Michaell Macoy my now dwelling house & ye plantation & ye halfe of ye Codd plantation . . .
. . . give James Macoy my son ye plantation called ye poplar neck & halfe of ye Codd Plantation . . .
. . . unto my son Mitchaell Macoy one Cow . . .
. . . unto my son James Macoy one Cow . . .
. . . give Hannah Macoy one Cow . .
. . . give Anne Macoy one Cow . . .
. . . give Mary Macoy one heifer . . .
. . . ye boyes & girls be free at ye age of sixteen yeares . . .
. . . leave my son James Macoy wth my father David Murrah for ye time of his servitude . . .
. . . leave Anne Macoy to my Sister Ellinor Sholand for ye time of her servitude . . .
. . . leave all ye rest of my Children to my loving wife Anne Macoy . . . my Exequetrix . . .

witnesses: Richard Hill.

David Murray.

Anne Murray. by mke.

Michaell Macoy & Seale.
his marke.

RICHARD BACHELOR of Lower Norfolk County *in* ye Southerne branch of Eliz. River . . .

Book 4 f. 128.

dated 12 Mch. 1680/1.

proved 17 Oct. 1682. by Charles Shaw & biggs

. . . . to my Eldest Sone John Bacheler one hundred acres of Land . . . I now live on . . . my Divedend of four hundred acres . . . att his full age of twenty one years by my Exequetrix . . .

. . . . unto my Sone Joseph one hundred acres joyning . . . att his Respective age . . .

. . . . unto my Sone Richard one hundred acres of Land Joyning . . . att his Respective age . . .

. . . . to my Sone Edward one hundred acres of Land Joyning . . . att his Respective age . . .

. . . . wife Ann have free Liberty to live in ye mannor house ——— to her own use during her naturall life . . .

. . . . to my daughter Alice a Cow . . .

. . . . to my daughter E*d*y a Cow . . .

. . . . to Charles Shaw one p*ell* of Land Lying on ye north Side of ye Run . . . three hundred acres . . . part of my grand pattent . . .

. . . . unto mathew Caswell . . . three hundred acres of Land I Sould him freely from me my hyers &c. . . .

. . . . wife Ann Bachelor . . . Sole Exequetrix . . .

witnesses: francis Sayer.
Thomas Bigg. by mke.
Charles Shaw, by mke.

Richard Bacheler & Seale.

Dep° of Jno. ferebee aged 40 years or thereabouts . . .
. . . . unto mathew Casewell . . . 300 acres of Land I Sold him freely from mee my heyres &c. . . .

Sworne to in Court 17 Oct. 1682.

Jno. ferebee.

ROBERT BARLEY of ye County of Lower norfolk . . .

Book 4 f. 129.

dated 4 Oct. 1682.

proved 16 Dec. 1682.

. . . . to Mr. Geo. Newton of ye County of Lower Norfolk as aforesaid all my estate . . .

. . . To Thomas godby of Eliz. River in ye County aforesd my Still . . . att Mr. Geo. Newtons plantation in ye Southerne branch w[ch] was formerly Capt. W[m] Carvers ma*rianor* . . .

. . . my deare frend Mr. Geo. newton . . . my Exeq . . .

witnesses: Jno. Edwards.
W[m] Stafford.
Robt. Barley.

RICHARD JONES, Seg[r] of ye Southerne branch of Eliz. River in ye County of Lower Norfolk . . .

Book 4 f. 130.
dated 28 Nov. 1682.
proved *20* Jan. 1682/3. by Rich[d] Overington & Tim[o] I*ves* seg[r].

. . . unto my sone Rich[d] Jones Ju[r] . . . my sealed Ring . . .

. . . unto francis White my serv[t] woman her freedome . . .

. . . my Loving wife mary Jones during her naturall life . . .

. . . my Loving frends Alexand[r] foreman and W[m] Maund bee my Sole Exequetors . . .

witnesses: francis Sayer.
Rich[d] O*ver*ington.
Tim[o] Ives. seg[r].
Rich[d] Jones seg[r] & Seale.

WM. CARNEY, sig[r] . . .

Book 4 f. 149.
dated 19 Oct. 1681.
proved 15 Oct. 1683.

. . . wife Abigaill Carney all that plantation whereon I now live during during ye time & terme of her naturall life, and after her decease to my three sonnes (viz). James, Richard & david Carney . . .

. . . to my daughter mary Carney . . .

. . . my Sone Jno. Carney . . .

witnesses: W[m] Bathurst.
Robt. Jordan.
William Carney & Seale.

JNO. ADAMS . . .
Book 4 f. 149.
dated 7 Nov. 1679.
proved 15 Oct. 1683.

. . . to my Loving wife my plantation that I now live upon Induring her life, and att her decease to bee equally divided for my three Children, my wife Alice Adams . . .

. . . to my three sonnes . . . their mother . . . as they come to age . . .

. . . the Rest of my Stock and moveable I give my wife, a Cutles to my sone John, and a gun for my Sone Richard.

witnesses: Robt. Arden.
James Jackson.

Jn° Adams & Seale.

ADAM KEELING of County of Lower Norfolk, Gent. . . .
Book 4 f. 155.
dated 25 Apr. 1683.
proved 17 Dec. 1683, by Jno. Sanford, fra. Sayer & Tho. Hodges.

. . . to my loving wife Ann Keelinge that plantation I now live & Inhabit upon . . . for . . . life and after . . . unto my Sone Thomas Keelinge . . . timber . . . from London bridge Land for his use . . .

. . . unto my Sone Jno. Keeling that plantation or tract of Land hee now liveth on being about foureteen hundred acres, formerly beelonging unto my father in Law Jno. Martin . . . when hee attains ye age of twenty years . . . provided (he) . . . give . . . for . . . deed In Law made out unto his Brother Adam Keeling . . . for . . . all that divident or tract of Land being about two thousand acres Lately pattented in the name & to the use of my said Sone Jno. Keeling being that land that now my mother lives on and called London bridge . . .

. . . unto my above mentioned Sone Thomas Keelinge that prcell of Land Commonly known by ye name of dudlies (and Joyning upon that belonging to my Brother Alexand^{r} Keeling) . . . beinge neeare foure hundred acre . . .

. . . unto my daughter Eliz. Keeling a prcell. of land about three or foure hundred acres by mee Entered wth Rights towards ye Southward neere Matchepongo, and doe desire ye Same bee surveyed and pattented in my said daughter Elizabeths name . . .

. . . unto my daughter Ann Keelinge a certaine tract of land Joyning unto Rudee Comonly knowne by ye name of Black walnutt Ridge and lately bought of Anth° Lawson being about twelve hundred acres . . .

. . . to my sone Adam Keeling . . .

. . . my above named Children . . . as they attaine Each of them to ye age twenty one years . . . daughters att ye age of sixteene years or day of marriage . . .

. . . one whole years schooling Edward Bouring . . . a Cow . . . when hee comes to age of twenty one years . . .

. . . wife Ann Keeling my whole and Sole Exequetrix . . .

. . . my Brother In Law, Lt Coll. Antho. Lawson & my frend Mala. thruston overseers . . . unto Each . . . twenty five Shillings Sterling Each to buy Each of them a Ring to weare In Remembrance of mee . . .

witnesses: Jno. ferebee.
Jno. Sandford.
francis Sayer.
Tho. Hodgis.

Adam Keeling & Seale.

Postcript 4th of July 1683.
witnesses: Tho. gordone.
Jno. R*eche*son.
Mala. Thruston.

Adam Keeling & Seale.

WM. MOORE . . . (Nuncupative) . . .

Book 4 f. 155.

The Dep° of Wm frost aged 30 years or thereabouts . . . sayeth that on tuesday ye 6th of Novembr *1683* I was prsent . . . give It proportionably to my wife and daughter . . .

. . . desire Mr. Hodgis & Cpt Hatton may take an Inventory of my Estate, and that I may have a decent buriall, and as to my accounts ye Court will judge & further sayth nott.

Sworne to in Court 17 Dec. 1683.

Wm frost.

Sworne to in Court 17 Dec. 1683.
. . . aged 34 years . . . Lewis C*oner*.

Sworne to in Court 17 Dec. 1683.
. . . aged 24 years . . . Tho. Sayer.

Teste: Henry Mason dep. Cl. Cur.

***JAS.* PORTER** . . .
Book 4 f. 156.
dated 8 June 1683.

proved 17 Dec. 1683.

"The onely sovereigne wife god who hath onely power of Life and death *doe*th by ye voice of his *Red* Call mee to f*ix* my thoughts and desires upon ye time of my disolution for w[ch] Cause —— —— of ye —— —— forlorne and —— —— sones of Adam I beetake my selft to ye Satisfactory and blessed meritts of his deere and onely Sone Christ jesus Renouncing all selfe Righteousnesse, I alonely Relye on his for Salvation, and thoughe hee hath gratiously Convinced mee that my sins are out of measure Sinfull and for multitude Innumerable yett hath hee spoken peace to my soule, and given mee ashurance of Remission and ye Lively hoope of a Blessed and joyfull Resurection att ye last day; . . .

. . . I declare that Contract of marriage wth my wife Mary to bee null & void . . .

. . . to my two youngest Children frances and florentins, all and whole young and old my stock of Catle . . . come to age . . .

. . . Mr. Thomas Ivy my father In Law . . .

. . . to be delivered to ye Custody of Mr. Malachy Thruston, and his wife . . .

. . . to my youngest Sone florentins . . .

. . . horse bought last yeare of Henry Smith . . .

. . . ye turkey Carpett, wth my deske, a share of my books Lay[d] by for him . . .

. . . I give to my my daughter Jane and my daughter Thruston . . .

. . . to my good and kind neighbour daniel frisel my wearing chooths . . . a p[r] of new french fall shoes . .

. . . to Rob[t] Rayne for diging my grave . . .

. . . Sone in Law Mr. Mala Thruston Sole and full Executor . . . . .

. . . frends dinah poole and Lemuell phillips to ye Education of my Sone florentins . . .

. . . written wth my own hand . . .

witnesses: daniell frisell.
Robt Rene.

Jas. Porter & Seale.

ELIZABETH NICHOLAS . . .

Book 4 f. 169.

dated 6 Dec. 1681.

proved 16 June 1684, by Edward Moseley & Wm Handcock.

. . . unto my son William Nicholas . . .

. . . unto my Grand Child Andrew Nicholas the son of Wm Nicholas . . .

. . . my daughter Elizabeth Etheridge . . .

. . . unto my Daughtr Eliza far—d . . . unto my Daughr Sarah Moo*ne* . . .

. . . unto my Daughtr Elenor nicholas to be my Executrix . . .

. . . Due to mee from Henry Widd*eike* . . .

witnesses: Edward Moseley.
Wm Hancock.
Daniell Duglas, by marke.

Elizabeth Nicholas & Seale.
by marke.

WILLIAM GOODAKER . . .

Book 4 f. 170.

dated 13 Feb. 1683.

proved 16 June 1684.

. . . to my Cosen Joseph Goodaker . . . when . . . twenty one . . .

. . . to my Cosen Jno. Goodaker . . . when . . . twenty one . . .

. . . to my Cosen William Goodaker . . . land . . . when twenty one . . .

. . . to my Cosen Robert Goodaker . . . when hee shall come to age . . .

. . . unto my Cosen Sarah Smith wife to Robert Smith . . .

. . . unto my very loving brother Thomas Goodaker . . . Executor . . .

witnesses: Robert Barttee.
Beno Borroughs.

William Goodaker & Seale.

JOHN *LAUARRANCE* att Virginia I ye County of Lower Norfolke, In Little Creek at ye house of nich. hagging . . .

Book 4 f. 182.

dated 26 Sept. 1684.

proved 15 Oct. 1684.

. . . Declare that Jam the Eldest Lawfull Sone of Jn° & Dorithy Larrence and was borne & baptized att ye Wormly b*err*y house in ye pish of Wormly in harford shere and J*am* now p*osest* of sixteen —— seitueate July pish of s. giles in ye fieles in Church Lane, wch I was Resolved to to give to Cary Larrance the Eldest sone of Andrew Larrance, my Brother Son . . .

. . . I thought fit to Come to Virg^a to a sister wch. I had liveing there, expecting to find Comfort by her, but not finding that Entertaynin wch. I did expect, I did not tarry Long wth: her, but went and Lived In mary Land three yeares, where I preached the gospell to ye Compfort of many thousands, but Could not bee Endured by ye Romand Catholicks, and after wards I was peswaded to gooe for Carolina, wch. pswassons I did Imbrace and to that Effort I tooke a boate att potomack River on perpose to *Tra*nsport my selfe to Carolina and Coming to point Comfort I did meet wth. a good frend abord a shipe bound for that same place, where I was bound . . . and meeting wth thy good friend by name M^rs mary beason wid^r . . . she did lay mee pon her one bed and In her one Cabin and did attend upon mee boath night and Day for five moneths to ye Admin —— of all ye people that heard or knew of it & being aged three score & fifteen yeares . . . and I doe hereby Leave to here and to her aforesaid all my Jewells, Rings, gould Silver and all whatsoe —— I have . . . ye afores^d Mrs Mary Benson Wd^r and her aforsaide to up lift and Receave Seaven yeares Rent of ye sd Six tenam^t: *coll* 36 £ Sterling p yeare allowing 50 £ Sterling wch I Recd. by mee, and it is to be deducted out of ye afordsd. —— years Rent . . .

witnesses: Jacob Johnson.
Jno. *C—e.*
Geo. smart.

John Larance & Seale.

THOMAS VIZ^{t} IVY of Eliz. River in Lower Norfolk County in ye Colony of Virg^{a} . . .

Book 4 f. 185.

dated 21 Sept. 1684.

proved 17 Oct. 1684.

. . . to my Loving Son Thomas Ivy all my Land Excepting this here after given to my other two Sons *Luidford* and Anthony Ivy . . .

. . . unto my second son Ludford and to my son Anthony Ivy foure hundred acres of Land being on ye ould markt plaines it being one hundred acres bought of Bennony Borroughs and ye Resedue to be made up out of ye grand pattent whereon I now dwell . . . my son Anthony shall have y^{t} part of ye Land which hath a house upon it . . . and ye other part being Chinkapine ridge to my son Ludford . . . If either . . . dye under age of Eighteen years . . . I will my son Lemuel Ivy . . .

. . . my Loving wife Alice Ivy . . .

. . . to my Daughter Agnes . . .

. . . to my Daughter Katherine *taylor* . . .

. . . to my two youngest Daughtest frances and Elizabeth . . .

. . . unto my friend John Porter Junr . . .

. . . friends Lt Coll. Anthony Lawson, Capt. Plumer Bray and John Porter Seg^{r} . . .

. . . Anthony Lawson.
James Kempe.
Edw. Moseley.

Tho: Vis. Ivy & Seale.

WILLIAM WHITE . . .

Book 4 f. 187.

dated 21 Aug. 1683.

proved 17 Nov. 1684.

. . . unto my Sone Joseph White after ye decease of my wife Eighty Eight acres of Land . . .

. . . unto my Daughter Janne White all ye Cattle of her marke . . .

. . . my daughter Susanna White . . .

witnesses: Robert Lane.
Elizabeth Lane. by mke.

William White, by marke.

THOMAS CANNON of ye parish of Linhaven in ye County of Lower Norfolk . . .

Book 4 f. 191.

dated 18 Jan. 1684.

proved 16 Feb. 1684.

. . . unto my Eldest son Edward Cannon ye plantation whereon I now live . . . after my wifes decease, but if my said wife Elizabeth shall live untill my said son Edward shall attaine unto ye age of twenty one . . . my wife his mother . . . my divident of Land of two hundred and fivety acres Lying in ye swamp Adjoyning unto my father Cornickes Land . . . provided that my brother Edward Cannon . . .

. . . unto my two youngest sons Thomas Cannon and John Cannon my Divident of Land Called green land being three hundred acres . . . to Each of them A Cow . . . age of sixteene yeares . . .

. . . unto my Daughter Sarah Cannon . . . ataine unto ye age of twelve yeares ould . . .

. . . my brother in law Simon Cornick . . .

witnesses: Edward Cannon.
Wm Cornick, Segr.
Simond Cornick.

Thomas Cannon & Seale

ELIZABETH CANNON wife and Executrix of my late decd. husband Thomas Cannon . . .

Book 4 f. 191.

dated 30 Jan. 1684.

proved by Wm. Cornick Junr and Simon Cornick.

. . . my yongest son John . . .

. . . my two Eldest sons Edward Cannon and Thomas Cannon . . .

. . . unto my son John Cannon my Indian boy peter by name when he shall ataine unto ye age of sixteene . . .

. . . unto my daughter Sarah . . . five Rings and one Silver bodkin and a Silver whisell ye Rings two gold hoope rings and two Silver Rings and a small stone ring . . .

. . . unto my sister barbara Cornick my midell most gold ring . . .

. . . my father William Cornick and my mother in law Sarah Cab*eito* and my Brother in Law Edward Cannon . . . my Executors . . .

witnesses: William Cornick Junr.
Simond Cornick.
Ann Corpric.

Elizabeth Cannon & Seale.

DARMAN MACKEEL, . . .

Book 4 f. 193.
dated 23 Feb. 1683/4.
proved 16 Feb. 1684/5. by Mr Ben^o Burroughs & Wm Burroughs.

. . . to my Eldest son *Dan*iell mackeel . . . when he shall come to lawful age . . . all my Lands . . .
. . . to my son John mackeel . . . when he shall come to lawfull age . . .
. . . to my son Anthony Mackeel . . . when he Comes to Lawfull age . . .
. . . to my son Thomas mackeel . . . .
. . . to my daughter margritt . . .
. . . my five Children . . .
. . . wife Ann mackeel . . . Executrix . . .
. . . friends Coll. Anthony Lawson and Bennony Burroughs to be my overseers . . .

witnesses: Wm Burroughs.
Ben^o Burroughs.
Mary Burroughs.

Darman Mackeel & Seale.

JOHN NORMAN . . .

Book 4 f. 195.
dated 3 Nov. 1684.
proved 18 Mch. 1684/5.

. . . unto Ann Keeling . . the Daughter of Alexander Keeling when shee comes to the age of sixteene . . .
. . . unto Edward Cannon all ye Rest . . . Soule Executor . . .

witnesses: Robert Lane.
Richard Hill S^en.

John Norman.

HENRY HOLLSTEAD . . .

Book 4 f. 200.

dated 12 Mch. 1684.

proved 15 May. 1685.

. . . to my Symond Hallstead my manor plantation . . . it being that part or parcell of Land that I bought of Wm Whitehurst . . .

. . . to my son Henry Hollstead one hundred acres of land Lying next to my manor plantation . . . Catle to be delivered at the Deed of his father . . .

. . . to my son John Hollstead one hundred acres . . . when he comes to age . . .

. . . to Ann Hollstead daughter . . .

. . . my loving wife & son Simond Hallstead Exors . . .

. . . my two sons Henry and John Hollstead two yeares skooling . . .

. . . my daughter Ann hollstead . . .

witnesses: Richard Whitehurst.
Robert Butt.

Henry Hollstead by marke

THOMAS PITTS . . .

Book 4 f. 200.

dated 7 Jan. 1684/5.

proved 15 May 1685.

. . . my Lawfull wife Elizabeth pitts Executrix . . .

. . . my son John Pitts to be the Lawfull heire of all my Land . . .

. . . my daughter Jeane pitts . . .

. . my daughter Sarah Brooke . . .

witnesses: James Lamont.
Robert Hannah.

Tho. Pitts & Seale.

THOMAS MORRIS . . .

Book 4 f. 205.

dated 8 Feb. 1684.

proved 15 July 1685. by Chamberlin and Sheene.

. . . morris Stubes Should have ye plantation y^t^ I live on to ye halfe way tree and my Sonn Jozia*h* have ye other halfe . . .

. . . If Joziah morris Shall die before moris Stubes comes to age then y[e] late tract of land to fall to him . . .

. . . that John Jones shall have one Cow and Calfe . . .

. . . that Edward Jones Should have all my Worldly Estate in his Custody . . .

. . . till morris Stubbs comes to bee nineteen yeares of Eage . . .

. . . that Richard Bonney and Edward Jones shall see all things performed . . .

witnesses: Daniell Sheane.
Elizabeth Lane. by marke.

Thomas Morris & Seale, by marke.

. . . I will and ad unto y[e] forsaid will:

. . . Edward Jones . . .

. . . morris Stubes . . .

. . . Josias Morris . . .

dated 1 Oct. 1684.

witnesses: Jermyen Sheen.
Thomas Chamberlin.

Thomas Morris, by marke.

THOMAS HAYES of the pish of Linhaven . . .

Book 4 f 207.

dated 1 Sept. 1684.

proved 16 Sept. 1685.

. . . unto my Loving Wife Isabella Hayes all my Estate . . .

. . . my Land I now live upon which I bought of M[r] Bennoy Burroughs and W[m] Smith be Sold by my Lo: wife and my Lo: freind W[m] Robinson for and towards the paymt. of my just debts . . .

. . . wife . . . Soal Execuetrix . . .

witnesses: Geo. Smith.
Ben[o] Burroughs.
Tully Robinson.

Thomas Hayes & seal.

WM. RODGERS of ye Easterne branch of Eliz. River in the County of Lower Norfolk . . .
Book 4 f. 212.
dated 16 Aug. 1684.
proved 16 Nov. 1685.

. . . unto my Loving wife Ann Rogers and Shee to bee my Sole Exeq^{t}x . . .

Warren Godfrey.
Stepen Pew.
Jo: Edwards.

Wm Rogers & Seale.

ADAM THOROGOOD of Linhaven in the County of Lower Norfollke in Virginia, Gent . . .
Book 4 f. 217.
dated "last day of October 1679."
proved 1 feb. 1685/6 by Mr. Mala Thruston & Jno Thorowgood.

. . . unto my Loving wife francis Thorowgood all that p^{r}se. of my plantation whereon I now live to the full qunity of Six hundred Acres to bee lying most Convenient to my house I now live in and att her owne Choice and discrecon . . . during her naturall life and after her decease to goe unto my son Argoll Thorowgood and to his heires forever.

I give and bequeath all the rest of my lands where soever itt Lyeth, into my five sones (vix^{t}) Argoll, John, Adam, Francis and Robert Thorowgood to bee equally devided betwixt them att the will and discretion of my Loving wife . . . when my son Argoll Shall come to the Age of one and twenty yeares, and to take his first Choice, and soe Each of my Said sons to make Choice of his part thereof as hee Shall Come to the aforesaid Age of one and twenty yeares, the Elder to have the priority . . .

. . . in case . . . wife Shall dye before such devision bee made then . . . it bee devided . . . by my loving friends Coll Lemuell Mason, Maj^{r} Anthony Lawson. Malachy Thruston and Mr. William Porten or Either three of them . . . who shall have the Charge or guardianship of my Children for and towards the bringing up and Educating my Said Sons to Reading wrigth- and Arithmetick, and what other Education Shee or they Shall see fitt & Convenient, to bestowe upon them . . .

. . . my Executrix . . . doe Cause five Gold Signett Rings with my Coate of Armes, Cutt in Each of them to bee sent for att the full vallue of five & twenty Shillings, Each Ring and those to bee given to Each of my Said five Sons one; allsoe fower other deaths head Gold Rings of the value of fifteene Shillings prize Each, to bee delivered one of them to Each of my foure friends heare after apoynted my overseers . . .

. . . my Tenant Robert Smith . . .

. . . unto my daughter Rose Thorowgood one negro Child called Mary . . .

. . . the Rest . . . to bee Equally devided betwixt my Said Loving wife and all my Said Six Children, and to bee delivered unto as they shall come to theire respective Ages . . .

. . . my well beloved Wife Francis thorowgood my whole and Sole Exequetrix . . .

. . . my Loving friends Coll: Lemuel Mason, Major Anthony Lawson, Malachi Thruston & Mr. William Porten overseers . . .

. . . my Execuetrix after my decease Cause my body to bee Interred in the Church of Linhaven in the grave of my father and that shee Cause a toombe stone of Marble to be sent for with the Coate Armes of Sir. George Yardley and my selfe and the same Inscription as upon the broaken tomb, and the same to bee layd over my Grave and the other over the grave of my mother upon brick . . .

witnesses: Alexandr Murten.
John Thorowgood.
Mala Thruston.

Adam Thorowgood & Seale.

NARTHANIL BRANKER of the County of Lower Norfolke . . .

Book 4 f. 218.
dated 10 Oct. 1685.
proved 1 Feb. 1685/6.

. . . unto a kinsman of Mr Robt. draper desed. whose name was mistaken In his the Some of thirty pounds Str. to bee payd. to his use forthwith In London . . .

. . . unto Edward Littleton Esqr and two his Lady and two his two dafters: and to Mr. John b*rounc*lye his wife and to my brother and sister G*eniliam,* to Each of them one Ring of twenty five shillings price . . .

. . . unto Coll. Lemuel Mason one Ring of five pounds price . . .

. . . unto my Sonn Edward branker Six men negroes . . . four women negroes . . . three boys . . . and y[e] moyety of what Estate I have, Ither heer In Virginia, or in any other parts of ye Kings Dominion . . . when . . . he shall Come to the age of twenty yeares . . .

. . . unto my Sonn narthanill Branker three men negroes . . . foure women negroes . . . one girl . . . five boys . . . and the other moyety of all my Estate . . . at the Age of twenty yeares . . .

. . . that for the faythfullnes of my negro man trumpo and his wife hannah . . . that hee may bee keep at the Roupers trade and have freemans alowance . . .

. . . my two Sonnes . . . my whole and Sole Executors . . .

. . . apoynt Mr. John br*own*ley of barbadoes to bee guardian to the Same . . .

. . . Mr[s] Mary Chichester Widdow . . . twenty pounds St[r] for the Same . . .

. . . Lemuel Mason Esq[r], Edward Littleton Esq[r], and the Afoersd. Mr. John bronely to be overseers . . .

witnesses: Mary Chichester.
Ann Bennets marke.
W[m] Chichester.

Nar[th] Branker and Seale.

RICHARD KING of Lower Norfolke . . .
Book 4 f. 229.
dated 14 *Oct.* 1685.
proved 1 June 1686.

. . . to Richard Stone . . . at ye Age of Sixteen . . .

. . . to William Barington . . . when hee Comes to the age Eighteen . . .

. . . to Eliz. Jones . . . at ye age of fourteen . . .

. . . my Lo: wife Elizabeth King all my whole Estate . . . doe make her whole Execuetrix . . .

. . . Ann Lenton and ye heyers of her body . . .

witnesses: Tho. Cocke.
Tho. Moar.
doroth[e] Morrah.

Richard King & Seal.

WILLIAM DAFFNELL . . . (Nuncupative) . . .
Book 4 f. 230.

The Deposition of John R*os*iter adged 55 years or thereabouts

. . . being att ye house of William d*a*ffnell . . .
. . . to my sonn William a younge horse . . .
. . . to Edward out Lawis daughter Sarah a Lambe & to Mary *Ives Folley* a Lambe . . . and to my daughter Sarah a sadle ——— . . .
. . . my wife . . . my children . . .

Sworne to in Court p[r] June 1686.

John Rositer.

Sworne to in Court p[r] June 1686.

Dorothy Stanley.

. . . aged twenty years . . .
. . . to Sarah outlaw one lamb . . .
. . . to Mary my dafter Child Called mary one lambe . . .
. . . to my daughter Sarah *pu*cknell one Sadle . . .

Thomas Jones.

RICHARD HILL . . .

Book 4 f. 236.

dated 28 Sept. 1685.

proved 17 July 1686. by Mr. Richard Church.

. . . to Mr. Lemuel Mason Jun[r] . . . at Mr. Thomas cockes . . .
. . . to John G*ascatt* my hand vice . . .
. . . to my brother in law J*eronia* Beack . . .
. . . wife Jeane hill . . .

witnesses: John goscott.
Rich[d] Church.
Briget hallsted.

Richard Hill & Seale.

JOHN AXSTELL in ye County of Lower Norfolke . . .

Book 4 f. 248.

dated 30 June 1686.

proved 29 *Aug*. 1686 by Jno. Benson & Jno. Whiton.

. . . wife Deborah Axstell . . . Executrix . . .
. . . my Eldest Sonn Jno. Axstell halfe of my land he haveing the manor house . . . two hundred acres . . .
. . . sonn Jno. Axstell . . . his brother Thomas . . . his brother Samuell . . .
. . . unto my sonn Thomas Axstell the other halfe . . . two hundred acres . . . called Hocker ridge . . .
. . . my Sonn Samuell Axstell . . .
. . . my daughter Ruth . . .

witnesses: John Benson.
Ruth Axstell.
John Wittinghall.

Jno. Axstell & Seale.

RICHARD SAVELL . . .

Book 4 f. 249.

dated 7 Oct. 1686.

proved 30 Nov. 1686.

. . . wife mary savell . . . for life . . . unto tobytha wright . . . her sister Katherene Wright . . .
. . . my frend Wm Wright to be my Sole Exec . . .

witnesses: James Wright.
Slick Sander paterson.

Richard Savell & Seale.

RICHARD HARGROVE, Senior . . .

Book 5 f 1.

dated 21 Nov. 1686.

proved 17 Jan. 1686/7.

. . . to my sonn Richard Hargrove . . .
. . . to my Sonn Benjamin Hargrove . . .
. . . to my Daughter Margreatt Roberts one Sermon booke being doct. prestons workes . . .
. . . to my Sonn In Law Mr. Arthur Moseley all ye remaining part of my personal Estate . . . Executor . . .

witnesses: Edward Mosely.
Wm Hancock.

Richard Hargrave & Seale.

THOMAS BRIDGE . . . Little Creake . . . Virginia . . .

Book 5 f 1.

dated 13 Jan. 1685.

proved 17 Jan 1686/7.

. . . Eight hundred pounds of good Sound tob° bee Shippt and sent to my kinsman John Ree*ne* for London . . . my brother Jacob Bridge . . .

. . . my *b*ever hatt that was my Bro Charles . . . to Lemuel phillips. . . .

. . . my loving wife Hester Bridge shal bee my Sole Executrix . . . to whome I give & Bequeath my whole Estate . . .

witnesses: John Wi*blin*.
Simon franklin.

Thomas Bridge & Seale.

HENRY WOODHOUSE of the p^r^rish of Linhaven in the County of Lower Norfolk in virginia . . .

Book 5 f. 5.

dated 29 Jan. 1686.

proved 21 Feb. 1686/7.

. . . unto my Eldest son Henry Woodhouse my plantation whereon I now live being a devident of five hundred acres of Land . . .

. . . unto my second son horacio woodhouse that devidt. of land comonly Called by the name of Moyes land adioning to my owen land . . . moyes neck . . .

. . . unto my son John woodhouse my divedent of Land Lying and adioning to Richard bonnyes land whereon Richards debbs dwelleth . . .

. . . unto my two Sones horacio & John my divident of land that I bought of Mr. William Basnett sen^er^ Lying in the woods by John si*v*ells land . . . Equally . . .

. . . my son Henry woodhouse Executor . . .

. . . my children . . . horacio, John, Elizabeth and luce, my two sons bee at age . . . att Eighteen yeares ould and my too daughters att sixteen yeares ould . . .

. . . my daughter mary the wife of william more . . .

. . . my daughter Sarah the wife of Caton more . . . money due me from Mr. Thomas mumford . . .

. . . my too youngest Daughters Elizabeth and luce . . .
. . . my Sole Executor . . . shall bring up all my younger Children in the feare of god and to learne them to read and to wright . . .
. . . too largest Silver Tankerds . . . .
. . . my son Henry Woodhouse my Executor shall . . . plant an orchard of six hundred aple trees upon my son horacioes plantation and keepe the same sufficiently fenced . . .

witnesses: William Cornick.
T Finckley.
John Woodhouse.
Mala Thruston.

Henry Woodhouse & Seale.

ALLEXSANDER ROSE . . .

Book 5 f. 6.

dated 19 Jan. 1686/7.

proved 21 Feb. 1686/7.

. . . to my John rose halfe my Land . . .
. . . my wife Martha Rose to have hur thurds of the manor plantation during hur Life . . .
. . . my son John Rose . . .
. . . to my son Allexsander rose the ovor part of my land beginning at the River side . . .
. . . my fouwer dafters . . .
. . . my dafter Ann rose . . . when shee comes to age . . .
. . . my dafter Isble rose . . .
. . . my dafter Ann rose two my loving friend Robert butt and to his tuishion . . .
. . . friend Robert Butt takes Jane his Custody . . .

witnesses: Peeter Cartright.
Guorg bain.

Allexsander Rose & Seale.

THOMAS GODBY of Elizabeth River . . .

Book 5 f. 6.

dated 28 Sept. 1671.

proved 21 Feb. 1686/7.

. . . unto Ann my deare and Loving wife all my Lands & tennyments which I nowe possess att the head of a branch that comes out of the Southerne branch of Elizabeth River in the County of Lower Norfolk in Virginia . . . my Executrix . . .

witnesses: Francis Sayer.
Richard Whitbe.

Thomas godby & Seale.

SAMUELL WALSTEN of Lower Norfolke in ye Collony of Virginia. . . .

Book 5 f 6.

dated 28 Jan. 1686/7.

proved 21 Feb. 1686/7. Proved by the Oath of Wm Cuthrill Mr. david Whitford being dead.

. . . to my Brother Henry Walston . . .

. . . due to me p^r^ bill from Mr. Johnsandford . . .

. . . foure hundred pounds of to^bo^ due to me from William more & two hundred pounds tob^o^ due to me from Mr. Anbray and a Caster hatt due to me by Allexsander Keeling . . . one p^r^ of french falls shoes due to me by Jno. Keeling . . .

witnesses: David Whiteford.
William *Catterell*.

Samuel Walston & Seale.

WILLIAM COCKRUFT of the Easterne branch in Elizabeth River planter . . .

Book 5 f. 7.

dated 20 Jan. 1686.

proved 21 Feb. 1686/7, by William Mosely & Jno Wild Bore.

. . . unto my Loving son Wm Cockruft my plantation I now live on . . . wch. I bought of my Cos. Wm Mosely decd.

. . . after ye death of my now wife . . .

. . . unto m loving sons J*ehue* & Tho. Cockruft all my land wch I have Lying & being one the West side of the Broade Creeke being by pattent five hundred and ten acres one hundred acres there of being Sold by me unto Edw. Weston . . .

. . . In Case either of my above three sons should dye . . . then . . . to my youngest son John Cockruft . . .

. . . all my five Children viz[t] Sarah: William, Jehue, Thomas & Jno. Cockruft . . . as they come to age . . .

. . . . wife Sarah Cockruft . . . Executrix . . .

. . . my Lo: bro: In Law W[m] handcock & my Lo: friend Lem: philieps to be overseers . . .

Jno Willbor.
Jno. Willbro.
Simon franklin.

Will. Cockruft & Seale

DAVID WHITFORD . . . (Nuncupative) . . .

Book 5 f. 7.

The Deposition of Robert Hannay aged thirty yeares or thereabouts . . . being at the house of James Lemons watching wth Mr. David Whitford in the time of his last sickness whereof hee died . . .

. . . the deceased whitford said I give all to James . . . James Lemont . . .

Robert hanay.

Richard Cox 26 yeares or thereabouts . . . the same . . .

Richard Cox.

Sworn to by Rich[d] Cox & Rob[t] Hanah . . .
21 Feb. 1686/7.

ROBERT SMITH of Linhaven in the County of Lower Norfolk . . .

Book 5 f. 11.

dated 28 Jan. 1686/7.

proved 15 Mch. 1686/7.

. . . unto my daughter Elizabeth the plantation whereon Job Gaskin liveth being one hundred acres . . .

. . . unto my son Richard the plantation whereon I now live being one hundred and fifty acres . . . the plantation whereon Thomas English now liveth called possum quarter . . .

. . . unto my daughter margret two hundred and twenty five acres of Land Lying on the horse bridge run . . .
. . . unto my Brother in Law Robert Goodaker . . .
. . . my deere and loving wife Sarah . . .

witnesses: ffrancis Land.
Wm barsley.
Pat Angus.

Robert Smith & Seale.

JAMES MULLIKEN . . .
Book 5 f. 11.
dated 7 Mch. 1686/7.
proved 15 Mch. 1686/7.
. . . unto Job Kemp . . .
. . . unto John Kemp . . . & to his wife . . .
. . . unto Thomas and David Scott . . . Execgrs . . .

witnesses: Robert pe*tie*.
Wm Edwards.

James Mulligan.

HENRY SPRATT . . .
Book 5 f. 12.
dated 26 Feb. 1686/7.
proved 15 Mch. 1686/7 by Mr. Wm Dundas, Mr. Jno Thorowgood & henry Chapman.
. . . wife Isabella Spratt and my five children that plantation called nawnoys Creek . . .
. . . to Henry Spratt my Eldest sonne my plantation whereon I now live . . .
. . . my youngest daughter Isabella Spratt . . .
. . . my plantation wch goes by the name of bear quarter, and all my land att the head of Linhaven river bee Sold . . .
. . . desire Capt. William Robinson & Lt Coll. Antho Lawson overseers . . .

witnesses: Tho: Cock.
Jno. Thorowgood.
Henry Chapman.
Wm Dundas.

henry Spratt segr & seale.

JOHN WEB*LIN* . . .
Book 5 f. 12.
dated 22 Feb. 1686/7.
proved 15 Mch. 1686/7.
. . . unto my daughter in Law Ester *micle*ton . . .
. . . unto my son in Law henry midleton . . . if he continues with my wife untill hee bee att age . . .
. . . my gun to Elizabeth midelton if shee stayes untill shee be att age . . .
. . . my dearly beloved wife Anna weblin . . . Extx . . .
. . . to my son John . . .
. . . to my son George, and if henry please to make use of the p[r]cell of land bequeath unto George, hee may untill the said George is att age . . .
witnesses: Jno. owens.
Simon franklin.
hester bridge. John Weblin.

WILLIAM LOWRRY of the Kingdome of Scotland . . .
Book 5 f. 12.
dated 23 Jan. 1686/7.
proved 15 Mch. 1686/7 by yorley Lourrey & Jane ray.
. . . wife Jenit *anderson* and all my Children nowe surviving . . .
. . . to my Eldest Son James . . . if he apeare in the Contry . . .
. . . ordaine Mr. Thomas Scott. Mr francis *Makemie* my Executors . . .
. . . y*atxo*by lourry . . .
witnesses: Francis Sayer.
Jane Ray.
yoxel y*lowrie*.
William Lourry & Seale.

RICHARD CO*O*CK seni[r] . . .
Book 5 f. 13.
dated 23 Feb. 1686.
proved 15 Mch. 1686/7 by Robt. Hanah & dominick monyerd.

. . . wife hanah cooke one hundred acres of Land situated in little creeke that was formerly the plantation of Robert hannay . . . my Executr . . .

. . . me the said Richard Cooke . . .

witnesses: Robert hanny.
Dominyue monignand.
James fishgarall.

Richard Cooke & Seale by marke.

JOSHUA CORNEWELL, Lower Norfolk in Virginia Little Creeke . . .

Book 5 f 14.
dated 3 Feb. 1686.
proved 16 Mch. 1686/7. by Richard drout.
" 17 May 1686/7. by Abigail Caisen.

. . . to my Eldest daughter rebecka . . . my Land . . . to her sister my youngest daughter mary . . . att age . . .

. . . apoynt John wiblin to bee my Executor . . .

witnesses: Richard Drought.
Abigail Caisen.

Joshua Cornwell & Seale.

JOHN GILCRIST . . . of Lower Norfolke in the Collony of Virga Gentleman . . .

Book 5 f. 15.
dated 27 Jan 1686/7.
proved 16 Mch 1686/7 by Pr Smith & Jnoo Edwards.

. . . appoynt William Craford Gentman & hugh Cambell Gentman my whole & Sole Executors . . .

. . . Agnes Gilcrist my wife, robust and John Gilcrist my Children . . .

. . . unto poore of the Church three thousand pounds of tobacco . . .

. . . "I desire to bee Buried att the Church in Tanners Creeke and that my Execueters, Expend for the dovinge thereof *fives* pounds sterling or twelve hundred pounds of tobacco" . . .

. . . unto my sd. Executo^rs two morneing rings Each ring to bee in vallue twenty one Shillings & to Mr. George Craford one of ten shillings value & to Mr. Thomas Scott one of five shillings to Coll. Millioner one of ten Shillings . . .

. . . I Give unto the writer heare of John Edwards one ring value ten Shillings . . .

. . . Mr Geo. Newton bills wch I have against him of nynteen hundred & Six thousand be given up unto him hee giving unto my Executo^rs — generill release in full . . . also . . . one ring value ten shillings . . .

. . . unto Sarah peters my best feather bed . . . my best *tankad* . . .

. . . unto Sam Roberts my Gun . . .

. . . unto Mr. George Craford my Sword belt sadle & furniture . . .

witnesses: Peter Smith.
Danull*un* Goring.
Jno. Edwards.

Je^oilcrist & Seale.

CASON MORE of Lower Norfolke County in Virg^a planter . . .

Book 5 f. 15.

dated 24 Jan. 1686/7.

proved 17 Mch. 1686/7.

. . . my Eldest son cason more the plantation I now Live on which which I bought of William Grinto wth three hundred & thirty acres of Land adjoyning to ye plantation . . . a tract of Land Called Long ridge wch I bought of Francis Jones containing one hundred thirty seven acres of Land . . . one Entrie of a hundred & odd acres Joyning to ye sd ridge . . .

. . .to my Son Henry More . . . three hundred and thirty acres of Land Joyning upon his brother . . . ye equall halfe of the Same patten . . . I bought of William Grinto & Richard Bony . . . a plantation in the woods called little bear quarter adyoning upon a plantation of Mr Henry Spratts . . .

. . . to my daughter Sarah more a plantation in ye Woods wch I bought of John James contaying three hundred and fifty acres . . .

. . . unto my brother Thomas more a p^r^cell of land contening one hundred acres Commonly called tem*pemans* ridge which I bought of Joseph deserne and is prt. of John James patten . . .

. . . my three children Cason, Henry & Sarah more . . .

. . . my father Edmond More . . .

. . . my brother Wm More and my Bro. in Law Henry Wood house . . . care of Children . . .

. . . wife Executrix . . .

witnesses: F. Finckley.
Adam hayes.

Cason more & Seale.

JOHN B*RU*KS . . .

Book 5 f. 19.

dated 7 Mch. 1686.

proved 17 May 1687. by Rich^d^ boney & Jane Etterington.

. . . unto my sons Jno. Bruks and Jobe bruks and my Land . . . my wife to have her life time upon It . . .

. . . unto my daughter Sarah Bruks one Cow . . .

. . . unto my daughter Grace Bruks one Cow . . .

. . . unto Thomas Ward one heifer . . .

. . . wife J*a*ne Bruks . . . Executer . . .

witnesses: J*ea*ne hetherington
Thomas Ward.
Richd Boney.

John Bruks & Seale.

ROBERT ROUSE. of ye county of Lower Norfolk . . .

Book 5 f. 19.

dated 23 April 1687.

proved 17 May 1687 by Mag^r^ Jno. Nichols & Jno Weston.

. . . all that my plantation & Land wth the appurtenances now in the tenure of Elinor cranberry wch I have in reversion I give unto my Brother in Law Jno Hodges to him & his heires forever & I *defaul* . . . my Brother in Law Thomas hodges have the Same . . .

. . . a Couple of pewter dishes . . . unto my kinswoman Mary hollowell . . . at her day of marrage or when she doth attaine to the age of Sixteene . . .

. . . paire of Serge breeches & a Serge westcote I give unto Tho *A*ldridge . . .

witnesses: John Ferebee.
Jno. Nichols.
Jno. Weston.

Robt Rowse & Seale.

RICHARD LAURENCE of the Westerne branch of Elizabeth River in the County of Lower Norfolk . . .

Book 5 f. 20.

dated 6 Feb. 1681.

proved 17 May 1687, by Geo. Horne.

. . . unto Richard & d*any* Carney being my god sons . . .
. . . unto Katherin Greene one *Camlett* coate . . .
. . . unto John Wh*ei*fell Juno^r one Cow Calfe . . .
. . . friend John Wh*in*fell Seno^r . . .
. . . Executrix . . .

witnesses: Jno Griffith.
George Horne.

Richard Laurence & Seale.

EDWARD RALLINGS of the parrish of Lynhaven and in the County of Lower Norfolke planter . . .

Book 5 f. 20.

dated 6 Feb. 1686.

proved 17 May 1687. by Ed. Cooper & Jno. Cooper—*hav.*

. . . wife Jane Rollings the Said plantation which I live upon . . . Executor . . .

. . . unto John Cooper the Sonne of Edward Cooper . . . one Cowe Calfe . . .

witnesses: John C*orphere*.
Edward Cooper.
Edward Brighouse.

Edward Rallings & Seale.

WILLIAM SHR*EE*FES of the County of Lower Norfolk and of the p^rrish. of Linheaven . . .

Book 5 f. 20.

dated "March or Aprill last."

proved 17 May 1687 by all Evidences to be the act & dead of Wm Shri*ff*^e.

. . . . wife . . . all that hee hath in the world . . . Executo^r of Land . . . the first Child that my wife bares of her body shall bee are of my Land . . .

witnesses: Charles har*tle*.
Richard L*ues*
John Gisborne.

William Shri*ll*es.

THOMAS SMITHERS . . .

Book 5 f 21.

dated 1 Dec. 1682.

proved 6 Apr. 1687 att a County att James Citty by oath of John Squire.

. . . to my Cosen Thomas Ewell a young filly . . .

. . . Joseph pitts . . .

. . . unto my Cosen Thomas Ewell after the decease of my wife the land which I now live on . . .

. . . unto my Cosen Sarah Ewell two heifers . . . when she comes to age of sixteen . . .

. . . Cosen Thomas Ewell when he comes to age . . . of Eighteen . . . .

. . . wife Ann my Exequetrix . . .

witnesses: John Squire.
Joseph Pitts.

Thomas Smithers & seale.

WILLIAM BROCKE Seno[r] of ye parrish of Linheaven and in the County of Lower Norfolk planter . . .

Book 5 f. 21.

dated 13 Feb. 1686.

proved 17 May 1687 by Sarah prince & Eliz[a] Barnes.

. . . my Sonne Thomas Brocke that plantation which I doe live upon and my best bed with Curtaines and vallions . . . Executo[r] . . .

. . . my Sonne William Brock . . . the plantation w[ch] hee doth live upon Containing one hundred acres of Land . . .

. . . unto William Brocke the Sonne of John Brocke one heifer . . .

witnesses: Eliz[a]beth Barnes.
Sarah Prince.
Edward Brigthouse.

William Brock & Seal.

DENIS DOLLEY of Linheaven p^r^ish & in ye County of Lower Norfolke planter . . .

Book 5 f. 21.

dated 23 Feb. 1686.

proved 17 May 1687 by John poole & Ed. Cannon.

. . . unto Sarah Dolley now the wife of Edward Cannon one hundred and fifty acres of Land Joyning upon Mr. plumer bray . . . want of any heires . . . the to returne to my Sonne John dolley . . .

. . . unto my daughter Eliz[a]beth dolley one hundred and fifty acres of land called poupeler Ridge possom Ridge & Beech Ridge all lying and Joining together . . .

. . . unto Mary Brocke my Grand daughter one Cowe & a Calfe . . .

. . . unto my god Sonne denis Capps one heifer . . .

. . . As for the plantation which I Live upon and all other parte and p[r]ll thereof as by pattent doth beare mention only three hundred acres as before mentioned to bee Excepted . . . unto Margrett dolley my Loveing wife . . . Seaven hundred acres . . . after her decease . . . reterne unto my Sonne John dolley . . .

. . . wife Executo[r] . . .

witnesses: Edward Cannon.
John poole.
Edward Brighthouse.

Denis Dolley & Seale.

M[r] WILLIAM BASSETT Seno[r] of Lower Norfolk County p[r]ish of Linheaven . . .

Book 5 f. 22.

dated 25 March 1687.

proved 17 May 1687.

. . . unto my Sonne W[m] Bassnett all my Land to have only the use during his life & after his decease unto his heires for Ever . . . my gold Ring . . . negro man due to me by Adam haies . . .

. . . unto Charles hartly one Cow Calfe . . .

. . . unto Every one of my Servants whytt & negro one Cow Calfe a peace . . .

. . . unto my three Children to say William bassett & Jane tull wife of Tho. tull & Mary Grandy wife of Thomas Grandy . . . share & share Like . . .

. . . my Sonne William Bassnett shall be Executr . . .

witnesses: James Sharood.
John poole.
James Daug.

Wm Bassnett & Seale.

THOMAS HOLLEWELL Senor of Lower Norfolk County . . .

Book 5 f. 22.
dated 13 Mch. 1686/7.
proved 17 May 1687.

. . . unto my Sonne Henry Hallewell all the Land hee now—Liveth one & that hee has Cleared and builte upon & all a long to the heather Egde of the thickett next to his cleare ground called ye great thicket and Soe along to the Corner of the Swampe . . . taking in Chinckapin Ridge . . . in defaulte of such heires . . . to the next Brother . . .

. . . wife alce Hollewell my plantation I nowe liveth one . . . During hurr naturall life & after . . . unto my two Sonnes Edmond hollewell & John hollewell . . . Edmond to have ye furst choyce . . .

. . . unto my Sonn Thomas one Cow . . .

. . . my five Sonnes & three daughters heare named to Say Henry Joseph Benjamin Edmond & John & my daughter Sarah Hawood & Elizabeth & alce . . . them that are heare named . . .

. . . wife Executrix & my Sonn Henry Executor . . .

witnesses: Robt Bowers.
Henry Bowles.
Tho Hodgis.

Thomas hollewell & Seale.

WILLIAM HANDCOCKE of ye Easterne Branch of Elizabest River in Lower Norfolke County . . .

Book 5 f. 23.
dated 14 Apr. 1687.
proved 17 May, 1687.

. . . unto my Eldest Sone Simon Hancocke ye plantation I nowe live on being Bounded with a small C^{r} ye mouth of wch runs in a little below the Chapell and runeth up nigh my dwelling house & bounded E^{ly} with an old trench on ye N^{w} on a C^{r} form^{r}ly Cald. hoskins Cr. and n^{ly} on a branch cald. deepe branch . . .

. . . unto my sone Wm Hancocke all ye Land that I have lying on ye Sr Side of the above sd small Cr. being where ye chapel now stands, bounded on . . . John Caraway . . .

. . . unto my Sone Samuell Hancock a p^{r}all of Land lying on ye N^{w} Side of ye head of ye aforesd. hoskins Cr. bounded on Wm Cockruft Edw. Moseley & Lt. Coll. Antho. Lawson and along from my line to an rige over ye Swamp along to white pine Swamp & ye path that leads from my house to Linhaven Church . . .

. . . unto my Sone John Hancock ye remanid^{r} of my Land . . .

. . . unto my daughter Mary Hancock all her mothers wareing cloths . . . a warming pan . . . nott to bee Delivered my daughter untill my mothers decease . . .

. . . unto my daughter frances Hancocke . . .

. . . unto my loveing mother Sarah piggott all my stock of hogs . . . what woole my flocke of Sheep Shall P^{r}oduce fro: yeare to yeare . . .

. . . unto my kinsman Wm Moseley libertie to live on any parte of my land untill the heire thereof shall come of age . . .

. . . unto my two youngest Sons Edw. & Geo. Hancock all ye remaing part of my p^{r}sonall Estate . . .

. . . my sd. Love mother my whole & Sole Executrix . . .

. . . my love freinds Mr. Arth. Moseley, Bartho. Williamson, John Caraway and Edw. Moseley to apoint a time meete & take an Exact Inventorie . . . & likewise that they lay out & marke ye lands given unto my Sons according to my will . . .

witnesses: Anthony Lawson.
John Caraway.
Barth^{o} Williamson.
Edw. Moseley.

Will Hancocke & Seale.

. . . Aprill ye Last day 1687 wee whose names are heere und^{r}written have meett Layd outt and marked ye Lands of Simon Wm Samuell & John Hancock according to ye Last will and testamet. of William Hancock decd . . .

Ath: Moseley.
Barth^{o} Williamson.
John Caraway.
Edw: Moseley.

JOSEPH LAKE of the p^r^ish. of Linheaven and County of Lower Norfolk . . .

Book 5 f. 23.
dated 6 Jan. 1686/7.
proved 17 May 1687.

. . . to my daughter Annie Lake all my land . . .
. . . my wife Elizabeth and my sd. daughter Annie when she Shall attain . . . Sixteen yeares . . .
. . . wife Executrix . . .
. . . land on ye fresh ponds wch I have sould to Anthony barnes . . . one hundred and seaventy acres . . .
. . . my father in Law Jno. Corprew . . .
. . . if my daughter Annie shall die wth out issue of her own body . . . then . . . prsonall in that case to bee Given and disposed of for the good & relife of the poor in ye p^r^ish of Linheaven . . .
. . . my father in Law Jno Corperew & my Loveing friend francis Land to be overseers . . .

witnesses: Wm Newport.
Adam ferguson.
Pat: Angus.

Joseph Lake & Seale.

RICHARD CHAMBERS . . .

Book 5 f. 26.
dated 3 Jan. 1686.
proved 18 May 1687 by Jno. Sandford &
16 July 1687 by Michaell way*burne*.

. . . D*onity* Chambers my beloved wife . . . lands . . . Executrix . . .

witnesses: Thomas ffergasson.
Brigett ffergasson.
John Sandford.
Mychael wybord.

Richard Chambers & Seale.

CHARLES GRANDY . . .

Book 5 f. 27.
dated 14 Feb. 1686.
proved 15 July 1687 by W^m^ *twyst* & Godin ost.

. . . wife Executrix . . . all my whole Estate both real & p^r^sonall during her naturall life and after . . . all my Lands lying on ye nor*th* Side of muddy creeke Joyning tanners Creeke being to ye number of Seventy & five acres to my sons William & Jno. to bee Equally diveded . . .

. . . my other Lands Joyning to Mr. ffulchers in chis*pinctp* bay to my sons Charles & Thomas to bee Equally diveded . . . being to ye number acres ninety & Seven . . .

. . . to my Godson Godin host a cow calfe . . .

. . . to my daughter Mary Hattersly a read cow . . .

witnesses: Godwin Host.
Pall Hattersley.
Wm Twyst.

Charles Grandy & Seale.

WILLIAM MAMAKEN of the Western branch of Eliz. River in ye County of Lower Norfolk planter . . .

Book 5 f. 28.

dated 9 Mch 1686/7.

proved 15 July 1687 by Hester hitchcock.

. . . margaret mamaken wife . . . Executrix . . . Lands . . .

witnesses: Ester Hitchcocke.
Dorothy Nicholls.

Wm Mamak*es* & Seale.

WILLIAM DEANES, sen^r^ of ye County of Lower Norfolk in Virginia . . .

Book 5 f. 30.

dated 9 Feb. 1686/7.

proved 15 July 1687 by Capt. Hatton & Mr. Luke haueild & Jno. Graham.

. . . to my sonn William Deanes a parcell af Land Lying & Joyning unto a noather p^r^cell of one hundred acres wch I formerly gave him . . .

. . . to my daughter mary H*af*der all that p^r^cell of Land which I now Dwell on . . .

. . . my Loveing wife Ann Deanes my Lawfull Exeq^r^ . . .

witnesses: John Hatton.
Luke H*aueild.*
Jno. Graham.

William Deanes & Seale.

EDWARD WILDER . . .

book 5 f. 38.

dated ——— 1686.

proved 15 Sept. 1687 by Sam Roberts and his wife.

. . . Sonne Mikell Wilder and my Deare wife Ann Wilder Executr^{x}o . . .

. . . unto my Sonne Mickell Wilder ye plantation houses Land orchards . . . after the Death of his mother . . . but if *the* Said Mickell dye without heire, then the Said Land to fall to his brother Henry Wilder . . .

. . . unto my Sonn Henry wilder one tracke of wood Land Conteining one hundred and nine acres of Land lying betweene ye maner plantation of Edward Wilder and James Thelaball which If the Said Henry dy without heire that It may returne to his brother Michell Wilder or his heires.

witnesses: Samuell Roberts.
John *whettinh*all.
Margaret Roberts.

Edward Wilder & Seale.

THOMAS HUGHLEY . . .

Book 5 f. 45.

dated ——— ———

proved 15 Nov. 1687.

. . . *Sole to God* . . .
. . . unto henry Booles my mare & bridle & sadle . . .
. . . unto John Johnson Junr one two yeare ould Heifer . . .
. . . unto Wm Johnson one two yeare old heifer . . .
. . . unto my Cozin Eleazer tarte one Blacke Steere . . . att Tho: Wards . . .
. . . Cozin Eleazar tart my plantation being three hundred acres of Land to him & his heires . . . Executor . . .

witnesses: Aaron Spring.
John Johnson.
Wm Johnson.
Henry Booles.

Thomas hughby

DANIELL DUGLASS of ye Easterne branch of Elizabeth River . . .

Book 5 f. 46.

dated 14 Aug. 1676.

proved 16 Nov. 1687 by Capt. Robinson, Mr Cocke & Jno. Brown.

. . . my wife Bridget Douglas all my Land . . . During her naturall life and after . . . to bee Equally diveded between John br*an*ton and ffrances the wife of Beiamin Bransgrove . . .

. . . John Porter of the Easterne branch of Elizabeth River . . . Custody . . . him ye Said Branton . . . come to age . . .

. . . I Doe appoint foure men of the neighbourhood namely William Robinson, George Lawson, William Handcock & John Porter to take an Inventory . . . or any three . . .

. . . wife Executrix . . .

witnesses: Wm Robinson.
John Dolley.
Tho: Cocke.
Jno. Browne.

Daniell Duglas & Seale.

This 15 Day of June 1687 I Daniell Duglas . . . Doe ratify & Confirme ye will made one the other Side Dated 14th day of August 1676 Exsepting these p^rtic*ler* Legises . . .

. . . unto my ffriend Robet *peatre* my now riding horse . . .

. . . unto John Branton . . . my wearing Cloathes . . .

. . . Executrix named one the other Side . . .

witnesses: Tho: Cocke.
Jno. Browne.
Jno. Mathias

proved 16 Nov. 1687 by Mr. Tho Cocke & Jno Brown.

---

ffRANCIS NASH . . .

Book 5 f. 53.

dated 16 Mch. 1686.

proved 16 Feb. 1687/8. by Rich. bacon & Robt. bowers.

. . . wife Martha my whole Exec^r . . .

. . . unto my daughter Sarah a Cow & Calfe . . .

. . . unto my Son Jno one Cow & Calfe . . . att ye age of Seventen . . .

. . . unto my Daughter Francis one fether bed . . . one chest . . .

. . . unto my Daughter Elizabeth one bead . . .

. . . unto my daughter Elizabeth . . . one Chest & three pewter Dishes and three plates & three poringers . . .

. . . to young Thomas maning . . . Cow . . .

. . . my stock of hoggs Cattle and Sheep to bee Equally Divided amoung my yongest Chilldren . . .

. . . my Loving ffriends Robert bowers and Jno Bowers to oversee . . .

witnesses: Rich[d] Bacon.
Robt. bowres.
John bowres.

ffrancis Nash.

THOMAS GOODAKER of Linhaven in Lower Norfolke County . . .

Book 5 f. 61.

dated *24* Feb. 1687/8.

proved 15 Mch. 1687/8.

. . . to my youngest son Thomas Goodaker my Land and plantation whereon Mr. *John* Godand now Lives . . . if . . . Dye under age . . . then . . . to my Eldest Son Joseph Goodaker . . .

. . . unto my sd. Son Thomas . . . my Great Chest . . . Great table . . . six Joynt Stoules . . . two pewter dishes . . . my Small gun . . . when . . . twenty yeares . . .

. . . unto my Son William goodaker . . . two pewter dishes . . . my new Chest . . . pestell and Gun . . . when twenty one . . .

. . . to my Son John Goodaker one flock beed . . . one pewter tankard & one pewter dish and a gun . . . when twenty one . . .

. . . to my Son Robert Goodaker one thousand pounds of tobacco in the hands of my Son in Law Henry wallston . . . one great pewter dish . . . one ould Chest & a gun . . . when . . . twenty one . . .

. . . ordaine my Son in Law Henry wallston . . . Exc[r] . . .

witnesses: Ben[o] Borrough.
ffrancis Land.
Thomas tu*r*ton.

Thomas Goodaker and Seale.

JNº POWELL of Lower Norfolke County . . .

Book 5 f. 66

dated 19 Dec. 1687.

proved 15 May 1688.

. . . unto my Sonn Lemuell powell all my Land . . .
. . . my Daughters . . .
. . . to my Daughter Mary one Redd heifer . . .
. . . to my Cossen Richard powell one Gun . . .
. . . to my Cossen Jnº powell one muskett . . .
. . . my Daughter Sussan powell . . .
. . . my Daughter Dorcas powell two Ewes . . .
. . . my Daughter Kathern powell two Ewes . . .
. . . my Cossen Elizabeth powell two Ewes . . .
. . . my Brother William powell two Karssy Coates
. . . my Daughter Sarah powell two Ewes . . .
. . . unto William Ellis two pear of breches . . .
. . . wife Sussan powell all the ress of my Cattle and Sheep and hoggs and horse . . . Executrix . . .

witnesses: Tho: Hodgis.
Jnº wayte.
Tho: fergason.

Jnº powell & Seale.

FRANCIS HATTON of the westerne branch of Eliz. River in the County of Lower Norfolk planter . . .

Book 5 f. 67.

dated 27 Dec. 1687. Church of England Compe.

proved 16 July 1688.

. . . unto my brother Jnº hatton one bras pestal . . .
. . . unto my Cosen Thomas Sayer one Castor hatt one large Coate . . .
. . . unto my Cosen Jnº Dean . . . heifer . . .
. . . unto my Cosen Jnº Wright one pestol . . .
. . . unto Sarah my wife . . . Rest . . . Executrix . . .

witnesses: Abraham Bruce.
James Wright.
Richᵈ Lawrence.

ffrancis Hatton & Seale.

WILLIAM CLEMENS *live*ing in ye western branch of Eliz. River In the County of Lower Norfolk planter . . .

Book 5 f 67.

dated 13 Dec. 1687.

proved 16 July 1688 by Thomas Aldridge & Henry Jeneing.

. . . unto my grand Sonn William powell my plantation where I now live after the decease of Mary my now wife . . .

. . . unto my ten Grand Children the Children of my daughter Susana powell the now wife of John powell Six head of Catle Equally to be Devided amongst them when they shall Come to the age of twenty & one yeares . . .

. . . unto my grandaughter Elizabeth powell foure pewter dishes and three pewter plates and one Chest when she shall come to age of twenty . . .

. . . unto my grand son Richard p*owell* one Chest . . .

. . . unto Richard *Cyech* my wifes Grandsonn my hors and one Ewe when . . . twenty one . . .

. . . Mary my now wife all the Remaing . . .

witnesses: Tho. Aldridge.
Henry Genings.
Richard Larrance.

Wm Clemens & Seale.

JN^o BUSTIAN . . .

Book 5 f 68.

dated ——— 1687/8

proved 16 July 1688.

. . . my wife to bee my whole Executo^r . . .

. . . my two sons Christopher bustian and John Bustian all my tract of Land . . . one hundred and fifty acres . . .

. . . the Child with my wife goeth now with . . .

. . . my Daughter francis bustian one heifer . . .

. . . my wife Margrett bustian . . . the Rest . . .

witnesses: John Ives
Wm Ives.

Jno Bustian & Seale.

PATRICK GYE . . .

Book 5 f. 70.

dated 27 Nov. 1687.

proved 16 July 1688 by Nich° Hugans & peter poyner.

. . . my Son James gie my Long gun . . . when he comes to age . . .

. . . unto my Son John gie one hundred and tenn acres of Land lying and being in Crab Creek and Joyning upon peter poyner the sd. land to begin att Coll. Mason Road and soe *run* to the Littell m*irtell* branch next to my ould plantation . . . when he comes to age . . .

. . . my Son pattrick gye my manor plantation Lying and being in Creek above said . . . when he shall come to age

. . . to my daughter Margry two large pewter dishes . . . one gould ring . . . when she shall come to age . . .

. . . to my daughter Elizabeth two pewter dishes . . . when she Shall come to age . . .

. . . wife hester gie all the Rest . . . Exetrix . . .

. . . friends Nicholas hugans and James peeters may bee overseers . . .

witnesses: Wm Vaughan.
Nicholas Hugkins.
Peter poyner.

Patrick Gie & Seale.

MARGRET BUSTIAN . . .

Book 5 f. 75.

dated ——— ———

proved 18 Sept. 1688.

. . . whole Estate to be Equally Devided between my three Children for there maintaining and bringing up to Schooling . . .

. . . bed . . . to my Daughter and the two guns to my two Sons . . . and my two Sons to bee free when they Come to bee . . . Eighteen yeares of age . . . daughter to bee free att Sixten . . .

. . . my sistr francis Scott to bee my whole Exeq^r . . .

witnesses: Henry Fleetwood.
Elizabeth Williams.

Margrett Bustian.

ALEXANDER FOREMAN . . . (Nuncupative) . . .

Book 5. f. 84.

The Verball will of Alexander foreman Decd. Imprmis hee Did Give and Bequeath to his son John foreman three breeding Cowes one Gun & one table . . .

. . . to Each of his two daughters vizt. Dorethy and Elizabeth foreman three breeding Cowes . . .

. . . Left his Son to his grandfather Alexander foreman with him to bee brought up . . . Left his Daughter Elizabeth to his brother Richard foreman with him to bee brought up till shee Comes to age all which was Spoken in the p^r^sence of us.

Allexand^r^ foreman
Richard foreman.

Sworne to In Court 16th November 1688.

GEORGE IVY of the County of Lower norfolke planter . . .

Book 5 f. 86.

dated 6 Mch. 1685/6.

proved 17 Jan. 1688/9. by W^m^ & Tho. Langley.

. . . buried att the Discretion of my beloved wife and Executrix . . .

. . . wife Hannah Ivy my plantation or tract of Land whereon I now Live being about one hundred and forty Six acres of Land During her Life and after her Deceis to my Eldest Son Alexander Ivy . . . if it Shall please God to Call him out of this world before hee Come to age without issue male then the next brother to Succeid & Soe Consequently to the forth brother or more if ther Shall bee any——

. . . unto my Son George Ivy that tract of Land Commonly Called Crouches old field being one hundred acres . . . Comes to age . . .

. . . unto my Son Samuell Ivy that nick of Land Called Cedars Nick being one hundred acres of Land . . . Soe Soone as hee is of age . . .

. . . unto my Son Thomas Ivy fifty acres of Land joyning next to Coll. Lemuel Mason Land neare to the mouth of the broad nick . . . soe Soon as hee is of age . . .

. . . to my Son John Ivy one hundred acres of Land by and in the Deep nick . . . soe soon as he is of age . . .

. . . unto my son Joseph Ivy fiftie acres of Land Commonly Called the Cods by and betwixt Deep *neck* and the old field Commonly Called Crouches old field . . . soe soon as hee is of age . . .

. . . unto my Daughter Elizabeth one Ewe . . .

. . . unto my youngest Daughter Hanah Ivy one Ewe . . .

. . . Children Shall bee of age att Sixteen yeares . . .

. . . my daughters . . .

. . . wife hannah Ivy . . . Executrix . . .

. . . William & Thomas Langlyes my near neighbours bee . . . overseers . . .

witnesses: Daniell Gorring.
George Smart.
Wm Langley.
Tho: Langley.
June ye 21: 1688.

George Ivy & Seale.

ALEXANDER BELL of the Little Creeke in Linheaven p^rish . . .

Book 5 f. 89.

dated 1 Dec. 1688.

proved 17 Jan. 1688/9.

. . . unto John terner one Cow . . . when he shall come of age . . .

. . . to winford terner one Cow . . . att Sixteene yeares . . .

. . . unto Mary terner my feather bed . . . Brass Kettle and pewter bason *one* tankard . . .

. . . unto Thomas ternner one Chest . . .

. . . unto Mary Wishard one Cow . . .

. . . unto Jacob Johnson all my Smithes tools . . .

. . . unto William perdy one heifer . . .

. . . unto Winford Davis all the Rest of my Cattle . . .

. . . unto Thomas Davis all the Rest of my Estate . . .

. . . Jacob Johnson bee Exec^r . . .

. . . unto Wm Browne two barrells of Corne . . .

witnesses: James Wishart.
Jno hambelton, his marke.

Alexander Bell & Seale.

WILLIAM VAUGHAN . . .

Book 5 f. 89.

dated 8 March 1687/8.

proved 16 Jan. 1688.

. . . wife Elizabeth that plantation whereon I now live being one hundred acres and was formerly belonging to her father Hugh purdy Decd. for . . . life and after her Decease I Give and bequeath the same unto my Son John Vaughan . . . and In Case my said Son John Shall attaine to the age of twenty one years his said mother Liveing then Shee his mother to assigne him part of the Said Land to Settle on at her Discretion if hee Desire it. . . .

. . . unto my Sonn William vaughan one hundred and twenty acres or thereabout adjoyning to his Bro° Johns Land over a branch next the Land of John Elder . . .

. . . by mee taken upp to bee added to the pattent of hugh purdyes abovesaid the Said one hundred and twenty acres I give to my Said Son Jno. vaughan . . .

. . . to my Daughter Sarah vaughan one Good fether bed and furniture to bee Delivered her att the age of Sixteen yeares . . .

. . . wife Elizabeth Vaughan . . . the Rest of my p^r^sónall Estate . . . Executrix . . .

witnesses: Malla thruston.
Wm Bradford.
Hugh Purdy.

William Vaughan & Seale.

ANTHONY HATCH of the province of north Carolina in the County of arbermarle . . .

Book 5 f. 90.

dated 10 Dec. 1688.

proved 17 Jan 1688/9 by Mr. Wm Cornick and Martin Cornick.

. . . my wife Elizabeth and my Son Anthony hatch . . .
. . . wife Elizabeth hatch Execortrix . . .

witnesses: Wm Cornick.
Martin Cornick.
francis Morse.

Anthony Hatch & Seale.

SARAH PIGGOTT of the p^r^ish of Linheaven . . .
Book 5 f. 99.
dated 1 Aprill 1689.
proved 15 May 1689.

. . . . unto my Grand Daughter Susanah moseley, a fether bed . . . with all the furniture thereunto belonging foure pewter dishes . . . two Ewes one Chest one negro woman . . . one large table Cloath & halfe a Dozen of ozenbrigs napkins . . . a heifer . . . a paire of good Sheets foure breeding Sowes & a horse Called Sparke . . .

. . . . unto my grand Daughters Mary & Susan Moseley all my wearing Clothes . . .

. . . . unto my Grand Son George Hancock y[e] Son of Wm. Hancocke . . . one Ewe . . . when he comes to age . . .

. . . . unto my Grand Son Edward Hancocke . . . one Ewe . . . when he Comes to age . . .

. . . . unto my Son Simon Hancocke Children Every one of them a Lamb to bee *D D* them when they are weanable of this p[r]sent y[rs] Stocke . . .

. . . . unto my grand Daughter ffrances Hancocke a yeares Schooling . . .

. . . . unto my Grand Son W[m] Moseley & to his heires as many feathers as will fill a bed . . .

. . . . unto my Grand Son Edward Moseley one Ewe & Doe make him overseer on y[e] plantation until my Grand Son Simon Hancocke y[e] Son of W[m] Hancocke Comes to age & that hee keepe my three grand Children vizt: Simon, Samuel and George Hancocke the Sons of W[m] Hancocke until they shall all come to age according to their fathers will . . .

. . . . the Stock w[ch] was my Sons W[m] Hancockes . . .

. . . . my grand Son Edward Hancocke Should live with his unckle Simon Hancocke & that my Son Simon Should have his proportion of the Cloth . . .

. . . . my foure Grand Sons Vizt: Simon, Samuell Edward and George Hancocke the Sons of W[m] Hancocke unto Every one of them a yeares Scholing . . . and yt. my grand Son Ed[w] Moseley if hee thinks fitt to Give them their Scholling to be paid out of my Estate as aforesd. . . .

. . . . all the Remaining part of my Estate to be Equally Divided beetween my two Sons Rob[t] and Simon Hancocke . . . my Executors . . .

. . . my Loving friend Jno. Carraway & my Loveing Son Simon Hancocke . . . overseers . . .

witnesses: Edward Moseley.
Jno. Moseley.

Sarah Piggott & Seale.

ALICE NEWMAN . . .

Book 5 f. 99.

dated 15 Mch. 1688.

proved 15 May 1689.

. . . to William Adams one Cow . . . two platers . . . a Ringe to be Delivered by John Warden when he Cometh to age . . .

. . . unto Alice Wardin a feather bed . . .

. . . to James Wardin one heifer . . .

. . . to John Wardin my plantation and halfe the Land belonging to It & the other halfe to James Wardin . . .

. . . unto my Daughter Alice br*u*nt twelve po*unds* . . .

. . . unto James Wardin 50 acres of the Land that was the Docto^rs. and the Rest to William Adams. . .

. . . William Adams may bee with John wardin till he Cometh to age and if that Thomas B*r*u*ntt* will have him y^t ye Sd brunt pay for his keeping

witnesses: Wm. Cooper Senr.
Jno Cooper.
Jno. Pearse.

Alice Newman & Seale.

JNO. FRISSELL . . .

Book 5 f. 99.

dated 6 ——— 1688.

proved 15 May 1689.

. . . to my Son John frissill the Land that I now Live on after the Decease of his mother . . .

. . . to my Son Daniell frisell a cow . . .

. . . to my Son francis frisell one Cow . . .

. . . these my Children . . . for their use untill they Come to the age of Sixteen

. . . my Son Jno fresill to bee att age att Sixteen . . .

. . . unto my Lawfull Wife francis the plantation that I now Live upon During her Life time Shee nott hindering my Son Jn° to build and Cleare on the other Side of the Swamp . . .

. . . to my Son Daniell frissell that hundred acres of Land that Is Due to mee by obligation from Mathew Brinson . . .

. . . Wm Caps and Adam hayes bee overseers of my Childrens Estate that Ba*ses*ed . . .

witnesses: Robert Hannay.
Jacob Taylor.
Rose Taylor

Jn° Frisell & Seale.

MORGGON MOORE of the County of Lower Norfolk in Virginia . . .

Book 5 f. 113.

dated 7 May 1689.

proved 17 Sept. 1689.

. . . unto my Sone Thomas Moore and my Sone Morgan Moore my plantation I now Live upon to bee Equally Devided betwixt them when my Sone Morgan Moore is att aghteene yeares of age . . . If . . . Dies before hee Comes . . . Eighteen . . . my Sone William Shall have his part . . .

. . . unto my Loveing wife Alice Moore my house I now Dwele in and to Live upon my plantation Soe Long as Shee Shall keep her Selfe a widow . . .

. . . my Son Jacob Moore to Mr. Thomas C*reck* till hee Come to twenty yeares . . . provided hee Doe Learne him to right and Read . . .

. . . my Sone William Moore to Wiliam Nichollson the Cooper till hee Comes to twenty . . . to Learne to bee a Cooper . . .

. . . my Sone Thomas to bee my whole Exector . . .

witnesses: Jeremiah Bock.
Jno. Mathias.
David Morrah.

Morgan Moore & Seale.

HUGH WILLSON . . .
Book 5 f. 126.
dated 16 Dec. 1689.
proved 18 Mch. 1689 by Henry Fitsgarrell.

. . . my Loveing friend J*a*b Johnson my hole and Sole Executo^r . . .

witnesses: Henry Fitsgerall.
Jno. *motlen.*

Hugh Willson, his marke.

"See March Court 1690/1 for further proof of this will."

SIDNEY FOWLER of Linhaven In Lower Norfolke County In Virginia . . .
Book 5 f. 126.
dated 27 Feb. 1689.
proved 27 Feb. 1689.

. . . my Child have all y^t Estate I am to have but In Case my Said Child Should Dye within a yeare then my Desire is that the Estate to goe to my Brother George Fowle^r; if my Child Live my Will is the father of my Deare Childe have the Bringing up of my Child . . .

witnesses: Eliz^a Phillips.
Argall Thorowgood.

Sidney Fowler, her marke

JONATHAN MARTIN . . .
Book 5 f. 139.
dated 5 Aprill 1690.
proved 15 Sept. 1690.

. . . my plantation whereon I now Dwell bee sold and my horse bee Sould alsoe by my Execq^r to pay my Debts. 2^{ly} my Land att the head of Collonies branch I give unto my wife During her naturall Life and after her Deth unto my son Johnathan Martin . . .

. . . Movable Estate and Cattle and Sheepe bee Equally Devided betweene my Wife and Son . . . att the age of Sixteen yeares . . . son . . . Sole Execq^r . . .

. . . my Loveing friend Jacob Johnson oveʳseare . . .
. . . appoint Simon hancock and James Wishart to Devid my Estate . . .

witnesses: Jnᵒ mun*crust.*
James Wishart.

Johnathan Martin, his marke

SAMUELL B*ALL*, cle*r.* in the County of Lower Norfolke in Virginia . . .

Book 5 f. 143.

dated 13 Oct. 1690.

proved 17 Nov. 1690 by Mr. tho: Scott &
16 Feb. *1691* by Law. Sawyer.

. . . to my wife and Children as Shee Shall minds to order unto them . . .

. . . the ordering of all things to this End I intrust to the Care of my trusty and well beloved Executoʳs, Mr. Peter Smith of Elizᵃ *twone* Mr. John porter Junʳ & Mʳ Jno Sandford of Linhaven . . . they make themselves full satisfaction for all trouble . . . in being as helpefull to my wife and Children as they Can & in *S*ending to them what they Can make for them . . .

. . . my Sd. Executoʳˢ . . . Each of them a booke as they Shall Choose for their reading . . .

witnesses: Tho: Scott.
Law: Sawyer.

Samuell B*ass* & Seale.

THOMAS S*KE V*INGTON

Book 5 f. 147

dated 16 Jan. 1690/91.

proved 16 Feb. 1690/1.

. . . unto hester Becher I Doe give one Black maire . . . heifer being marked of John Brinson marke . . .

. . . unto the two children . . . wᵗʰ'all her Stock belonging unto her and her Children . . .

. . . now appoint Mʳ John Sanford and Coll. Anthony Lawson my hole Execqʳ onᵉ my hole Estate boath heare & in England and Elsewhere . . .

. . . my Sister Elizabeth in England for I doe Give all unto her . . .

. . . & to hester Beacher I Doe Give what provision is now provided in my house and Corne, but her husband beacher never to have any thing to Doe heare . . .

. . . my Shue buckells . . .

. . . to Mr. thruston my horse Called Jack . . .

. . . to Mr. Sandford my Brass kettle . . .

. . . to tho: Web my Gun . . .

witnesses: Edward Norwood.
Edmond Bery.

Thomas Skevengton.

WILLIAM POPE . . .

Book 5 f. 150.

dated 17 Feb. 1689.

proved 16 Mch. 1690/1.

. . . 3ly as to my p^r^sonall Estate I Doe give it to Edward old Sene^r^ . . . Execto^r^ . . .

witnesses: Robert Hanny.
Elizabeth thomas.

Wm Pope & Seale.

WILLIAM REAVEN of the County of Lower Norfolke, In the Collony of Virginia . . .

Book 5 f. 151.

dated 4 Nov. 1690.

proved 16 Mch. 1690/1. by Wm Bateman.
18 Mch 1690/1. by Jno Jenett.

. . . wife Eleno^r^ Reaven my whole and Sole Exect^r^ . . .

. . . unto my Son William Reaven the Land ——— is due mee by Condition out of the Land whereon I now Live . . .

. . . my Land Called mount pleasant I give unto my Execu trix . . .

. . . as for my Cattle whereas I formerly gave unto my Daughter Elizabeth and my Daughter Jeane and my Son William Each of them a Cow Calve . . . untill they Come to the age of twelve . . .

. . . my Daughter Eleno^r^ I give one yearling heifer . . . untill Shee Comes to the age of twelve . . .

. . . the Child my wife goeth with att this Instance . . .

witnesses: Jno Jennitt.
Wm Bateman.

Wm Reaven & Seale.

JOHN *F*ALKE . . .

Book 5 f. 154.

dated 13 Jan. 1690.

proved 16 June 1691.

. . . my Loveing wife Ann *F*alke and the Rest of my good friends . . .

. . . wife Ann falke the third part of my whole Estate . . . the rest to bee Equally Devided beetween my small Children my Dafter Sarah holloway having her Share already . . .

. . . friends Roger Hodgis and Thomas Mercer to bee my full and whole Exeq^{r} . . . to sell my vessell . . .

witnesses: Wm Maund.
Jno Maning.

John *ff*alk.

WM. POWELL of the Southern branch of Eliz. River in the County of Lower Norfolke . . .

Book 5 f. 154.

dated 1*8* June 1690.

proved 17 June 1691.

. . . my wife Anne Powwell . . . my Execu^{r} . . .

. . . to my Eldest Daughter Mary powell the plantation I Live on with its fifty acres of Land as allso fifty acres of Land out of the one hundred & fifty acres that I bought of Mr Newton and that lying on the nearer Side Joyning on my father Williams his Line . . .

. . . unto my Daughter Ann powell one hundred acres of Land Called by the name of the Broad neck being the Remanderng part of the Said one hundred and fifty acres . . .

. . . unto my Daughters Elizabeth, Sarah and Keziah white back Stately and their Calves . . .

. . . my wife being att p^{r}sent with Child . . .

. . . if my Said wife Should remaine a widdow Sixteene yeares and the said nege^{r} man faithfully Serve Soe Long my will is that hee bee then free . . .

witnesses: Jno Ferebee.
Thomas Mercer.

William Powell & Seale.

JOHN GOOSCOTT of Elizabeth River p^r^ish in the County of Lower Norfolke . . .

Book 5 f. 155.

dated 15 Mch. 1688/9.

proved 16 June 1691 by Mr David Scott and Mary Crutchett.
16 July 1691 by Wm Chichester.

. . . my Loving Wife Bridgett the plantation whereon I now Live that I bought of Mr. Thomas Willoughby . . . During her naturall Life . . . after . . . fall and Descend to George Mason Sonn of Coll. Lemuell Mason . . .

. . . my will is that the Sloope I now am In and bound to ante*gee* In if I neavo^r^ Returne . . . unto Coll. Lemuell Mason and to Thomas Mason his Sonn . . .

. . . Coll. Lemuell Mason and his Sonn Thomas Mason procure a gold ring of twenty Shillings price which I Give and bequeath to Lemuell Mason Junr . . .

. . . if I nevo^r^ Returne for Virginia from the voiage I now am going to antegoe that my man thomas that is with mee bee free and have a Sute of Clothes now in my Chest in Virginia . . .

. . . unto Every one of my wifes Children begotten on her body to Every one twelve pence apeace . . .

. . . Coll. Lemuel Mason my whole and Sole Execq^r^ . . .

witnesses: David Scott.
Wm Chichester.
Mary C*rut*shett. her marke.

Jno *gooscott* & Seale.

The Dep^o^ of Mary Crutchett aged 32 yeares or thereabouts . . . Sayth that Just upon Jno. G*a*scotts going on his voyage to antego being att the house of Coll. Lemuel Mason Shee was Called to bee an Evidence . . .

Sworne to In Court 16 June 1691.

Mary Crutchett.

JOHN RAYNER . . .

Book 5 f. 159.

dated 31 Mch. 1691.

proved 15 July 1691.

. . . unto my Son John Rayne^r^ this plantation that I now Live upon . . . being fifty acres . . . att the age of Eighteene . . .

. . . unto my Son Richard Rayner my uper plantation Likewise being fifty acres . . . att the age of Eighteene . . .

. . . wife Ann Rayner . . . Exeq[r] . . .

witnesses: Thomas Willson.
Aaron Spring.

John Rayner and Seale.

FRANCIS FLEETWOOD . . . (Nuncupative) . . .

Book 5 f. 162.

The Dep[o] of John Ives aged thirty nine or their abouts . . . Saith . . . being in y[e] ——— of francis fleetwood att the house of Jno. Bustin Decd other Company . . . william paton Jzack freeman and Mary Chamberlin . . . Did give his whole Estate . . . to his Son Henry fleetwood . . . nurse Mary Giles . . . 19 July 1689 . . . William payton aged 57 . . . same.

John Ives
William Payton.

RICHARD JONES of Eliz. River p[r]ish. in ye County of Norfolke, Marono[r] . . .

Book 5 f. 164.

dated 18 Sep. 1691.

proved 15 Jan. 1691/2 by tho. Sayer

16 Jan. 1691/2 by Walter Coniers.

. . . bee Desently buried intered Layd. by the two bodyes of my two wifes allready Decesed . . .

. . . unto my Loving friend M[r] Malacy thruston . . . one neck of Land comonly Called the Brisshie Neck Containeing by Estimation one hundred acres . . . bounded upon William Newmans Line on the*one* Side and with a branch one the other Sid Comonly Called the Mudy Branch . . .

. . . unto my Daughter and onely Child hester Jones all the Residue of my Lands . . . p[r]vided Shee Continues Duttifull and Remaines and abid with me her aged father . . .

. . . unto Eliz. Branton the wife of tho. Branton three Ewes . . .

. . . friend francis Sayer three young steeres . . .

. . . francis Sayer and Mr Malacy thruston my whole and Sole Executo^{r}s . . .

witnesses: Walter Cono^{r}.
Thomas Sayer.
Elizabeth oden.

Richard Jones & Seale.

WALTER BARTON . . .

Book 5 f. 164.
dated 7 Nov. 1691.
proved 15 Jan. 1691/2.

. . . Executor^{r} to pay as Due to Mr William *Guardian* Liveing in Scots Walk London the Just Quantity of five thousand pounds of tobac^{o} alsoe to pay unto Mr James Lemon . . . Liveth in francious Street London . . .

. . . unto James peeters my watch my voyelin with the Case . . .

. . . to Elizabeth peter one Stond gould Ringe . .

. . . to Sarvants of James peters five Shillings to Each . . .

. . . to thomas Spratt one peace of Silver Sheu buckells to my Servant Anthony Jackson a broad Cloath Coat one Stript wascoate one Read wascoat . . .

. . . the rest of my Estate . . . to my two breathren John and Thomas Barton . . .

. . . friend James peeters to bee my full and whole Executo^{r} . . .

witnesses: Edward Waston.
Beniamen hargrave.

Walter Barton & Seale.

NICHOLLAS HUGINS . . .

Book 5 f. 165.
dated 4 Dec. 1691.
proved 16 Jan. 1691/2.

. . . wife Alice Hugins my . . . whole Executrix . . . after her Decease I Give . . . my Land to my two Grand Children John Jameson an *Joanah* Colings John Jameson to have my two Dwelling houses . . .

and Joanah Collings that part of my Land where my Son In Law Alexander Jameson now Lives . . . Land being att Ready . . .

. . . to the Rest of my Daughters Mary Jamesons, Children . . . to Couzen philip Hugins . . .

witnesses: Arthur Blacke.
Thomas parsons.

Nichollas Hugings and Seale.

WILLIAM HOOKEY of the towne of *throop* in the Kingdom of England Chicrigon . . .

Book 5 f. 168.

dated 29 Jan. 1691/2.

proved 15 Mch. 1691/2. by Major Francis Sayer & James Carter.

. . . wife Sarah hookey all my p^r^sonall Estate that I nowe am posesed with in the Kingdom of England . . . Soe Long as Shee Remaines . . . widow but In Case my Said wife Doe marry that then my above said Estate . . . bee Equally Devided beetweene my Said wife and Children . . .

. . . Estate . . . in Virginia . . . with a Compytent Satisfaction alowed to John *Mac*erell whoom I ordaine my Exeuitto^r^ in trust . . . my Estate bee then . . . transported into the Kingdom of England . . . and Delivered to my Said Wife Sarah Hookey all Dangers and Resques Excepted . . .

. . . my Loving Son James Hookey bee my whole . . . Execto^r^ . . .

witnesses: Francis Sayer.
Thomas Wallis.
James Carter.

William Hookey & Seale.

JOHN WHITHURST . . . Norfolk County . . .

Book 5 f. 169.

dated 15 Nov. 1691.

proved 15 Mch. 1691/2 by Henry Nicholas & Edward tranter.
16 Mch. 1691/2 by Wm Linton.

. . . to my two Sons John Whitehurst and Henry Whitehurst my part of the Land Lying att the three Runs . . .

. . . unto my Son Henry the Land that was formerly William Rogers . . .
. . . unto my Son John the plantation wc^h^ I now Live one . . . after the Decease of my wife and if the said John Live to bee att the age of Sixteen then to have halfe the plantation and Orchard and the Bigest Roome in the house . . .
. . . to my foure Children three maires now runing in ye woods to Run for their good tel they Come at age . . .
. . . my Sons Shall bee at age at Sixteene . . .
. . . to my two Dafters . . .
. . . my Son John my Sword and Carbine belt . . .
. . . my Dafter Elizabeth . . .
. . . my wife Mary Whitehurst . . . Executo^r^ . . .

witnesses: Henry Nicholas.
Edward tranter.
William Linton.
James Whithurst.

John Whithurst.
marke.

RICHARD EASTWOOD Senr . . .

Book 5 f. 170.

dated 12 Jan. 1691.

proved 16 Mch. 1691/2.

. . . unto my Sonne Richard Eastwood my plantation and all the Devident of Land belonging to it which I Now Jnjoy and which I bought of John Wattford . . . and if it hapeneth that hee should Dye without any hayre then . . . my Son tho: Eastwood Should bee posesed with it . . .
. . . wife Elizabeth Eastwood . . . Execq^r^ . . .
. . . my three Sons Richard, thomas and John Eastwood . . .

witnesses: George Horne.
Thomas Ca*to:*
Thomas price.

Richard Eastwood.
Marke.

JOHN ETHERIDGE, Sen[r] of the Southerne Branch of Elizabeth River . . .

Book 5 f. 175.

dated 20 Oct 1691/2

proved 17 May 1692.

. . . unto my Son Edward Etheridge the Lower part of my plantation whereon I Doe now Live . . .
. . . unto my Son Henry Etheridge from the upper part of the Chinkaping towards my Brother thomas . . .
. . . wife my whole Executrix . . .
. . . my two Sons Edward and Henry to Live with my Sons John and thomas . . . untill they Come to Eighteene . . .

witnesses: Jn[o] Etheridge, Jun[r].
thomas Etheridge.
mark.

John Etheridge.
marke.

WILLIAM GOLDSMITH of the County of Norfolk In Virginia . . .

Book 5 f. 175.

dated 4 Mch. 1691/2.

proved 17 May 1692 by Michall fentres and wife and thomas Sally.

. . . unto my Grandson William Whithurst Son to my Son in Law James Whithurst and my Daughter Sarah his wife the one halfe of my Land that is to have it next the Creeke . . . where I now Live . . . but if my Said Grand Son William Die without Lawfull heyres of his Body then to fall to the next male of blod but for want of Such heires to fall to the next female of Blood . . .
. . . unto my Grand Son John Johnson Son of my Son in Law George Johnson and my Daughter Mary his wife the other halfe of my Land . . . if my grandson John Johnson Die without heirs of his body then to fall to my Grandson Samuell Johnson . . . if my grand Son Samuell Johnson Die without heires of his body to fall to my Grandson William Whithurst above mentioned . . .

. . . to my Daughter Mary Johnson a Small Carved box which was her mothers . . .
. . . my Son in Law James Whithurst my Sole Exec[r] . . .
witnesses: Michall ffentris.
Ann ffentris
Thomas Sally.
George Smith.

William Goldsmith & Seale

DAVID MORROW, Jun[r] of the County of Norfolk In Virginia . . .
Book 5 f. 175.
dated 5 Nov. 1691.
proved 17 May 1692.
. . . unto my Eldest Sone John Morrow the plantation formerly Called John Sowses and forty acres joyneing to it . . . alsoe . . . one hundred acres of wood Land Ground where I Doe now Dwell . . .
. . . to my Sone George Morray the plantation I now Dwell on the Cleare Ground to bee made up to one hundred acres . . .
. . . my Sone John Morry Come to the age of one and twenty . . .
. . . my muskett and Cutlas . . .
. . . my Daughter *Eve Mory* one Cow . . .
. . . unto my Daughter Elizabeth Morry one Cow . . .
. . . unto my Daughter Mary Morrow one Cow . . .
. . . unto my Loveing wife Mary Murray all the rest of my Estate . . . my Executrix . . .
. . . all my boyes and Girles to bee free att Sixteene . . .
witnesses: Jeremiah Beck.
John willd bore.
Eliz[a] Willbore.

David Morray & Seale.

ANN CARRAWAY, being aged . . .
Book 5 f. 186.
Dated 13 June 1689.
proved 15 Nov. 1692.
. . . unto my Daughter Mary Lovett, A Great Iron kettle . . .

. . . unto my daughter Elizabeth Nichols a bell mettle morter and pestle . . .

. . . unto my Son Bartholomy Wm Son one Shilling Sterling . . .

. . . unto my Son Jno Carraway one Shilling Sterling . . .

. . . unto my Son Richard Williamson . . . the rest . . . Execo^r^ . . .

witnesses: Lancaster Lovett.
Ben^o^: Burroughs.

Ann Carraway & Seal.
her marke.

JABEZ BIGG . . .

Book 5 f. 188.

dated 18 Sept. 1691.

proved 17 Jan. 1692/3 by Geo. Whidby & Jno. Jennet.
15 Mch 1692/3 by Elizabeth Whidby.

. . . my body to the ground to bee buried at ye disc*resi*on of my ffather . . . my Exec^r^ . . .

. . . my ffather John Bigg Senr both posonall & real . . . my Land . . my whole Estate . . .

witnesses: Thomas Mercer.
the mar of George Whidby.
John Jennet, his mark.
Elizabeth Whidby, her mark.
Dorothy Bigg, her mark.

Jabez Bigg and Seale.
Mark.

AUGUSTINE WHIDDON of the County of Lower Norfolk, Carpenter . . .

Book 5 f. 190.

dated 13 Sept. 1690.

proved 16 May 1693. by Wm Maund & Jno Cherry Senr.

. . . wife Sarah Whiddon . . . my houses and plantation I now live on to her during her naturall life . . .

. . . my Son John Whiddon after the Decease of my Wife the plantation including One hundred acres of Land next adjoyning to it; and the Other hundred to bee Equally devided between my Other Sons Augustine, and William . . .

. . . all three of my Sons, Shall bee free & of Age at Eighteen yeares of Age . . .
. . . my Eldest Son John . . .
. . . if my wife dies, I doe give the Children unto my ffather John Cherry and to his wife . . .
. . . wife Execrix . . .

witnesses: Wm Maund.
John Cherry Senr.
Tho: Bigg,
his mark.

Augustine Whiddon.

DAVID MURRAY, of Elizabeth river in ye County of Norfolk in Virginia . . .

Book 5 f. 196.

dated 5 Nov. 1692.

proved 16 May 1693.

. . . to my Grand Son George Murry & the youngest Son of my Son David Murray Decd (who dyed possesst of what Land I left him formerly) fifty acres of Land wth halfe the Orchard to belong to it . . .
. . . to my Son Alexander Murray two hundred Sixty & two acres of Land, lying to the Westward Side of my Son David Murrays land . . . if . . . Alexander Dyes wthout Issue of his Body . . . to revert to the Next in blood (viz) to my Son Davids two Sons and to my Son Johns Son they three . . .
. . . my Daughter Ann, now the wife of Jeremiah Beck, to her I give Only twelve pence in English money . . .
. . . to my Grandson George Murray the Son of my Son David Murray, Deceast . . . to his Brother John Murray . . .
. . . my Son John Murray Sole Executor . . .

witnesses: John Edwards.
Mary Murray.
her mar
Mary Murray Wido.
her mar

David Murray & Seale.

JOHN IVY . . .
Book 5 f. 201.
dated 24 May 1693.
proved 17 July 1693 by George Horne & Sarah Pucknell

. . . unto my Son John Ivy One Heifer . . .
. . . unto my Daughter Mary Ivy One Heifer . . .
. . . unto my Son Thomas Ivy One Heifer . . .
. . . to my Daughter Elizabeth Ivy . . . One Heifer . . .
. . . these my Children aforesaid . . . when they come to age . . . (viz) my Sons Thomas & John to bee twenty one . . . my daughters Sixteene or att . . . marriage . . .
. . . towards the Schooling of my Children . . . my Gunn to be Sold for a hhd of tobacco . . . if it will yeald Soe much, & if not I leave it to my Son John Ivy . . .
. . . wife Mary Ivy . . . my whole Exec^{r}tx.

witnesses: George Rosseter.
Sarah Pucknell.
her mark.

John Ivy,
mark.

THOMAS WILSON of the Westerne branch of Eliz: River
Book 5 f. 202.
dated 18 Aug. 1692.
proved 17 July 1693 by Capt. Hugh Campbell & Moses Spring.

. . . Secondly It is my will & pleasure & desire, that my wife & my two Sons John & Thomas live in love & the feare of God together upon the plantation I now live upon, injoying my whole Estate (Except Such Legacyes as is after named) but if it shall hapen that they shall not agree & that one or both of my Said Sons, are not willing to live wth there mother then they shall have theire proper *shon*able Share of the Orchard for the full time of five yeares after theire removall, from theire mother . . .
. . . to my daughter Elizabeth the wife of Wm *Deftnell* fower hundred pounds of tobacco . . .
. . . to my grand Child Robert Montgomery One yearling heifer . . .
. . . to W^{m} *At*chison my now Servant a yearling heifer . . . .

. . . The Plantation I now live upon Containing two hundred & forty Six acres by Patent I leave to my wife during her Naturall life . . . after . . . devided, my Eldest Son John to have his first Choice, & my Son Thomas to have the other halfe . . .

. . . That 150 acres of Land w[ch] belongeth unto mee, w[ch] boundeth upon Maj[r] Nickolus line (goeing by the name of the Wilderness) I leve to be Equally devided betwixt my Son John & my Son Thomas . . .

. . . Son John my Sole & Only Exec[r] . . .

. . . I am in Little or Noe debt . . .

. . . It is my Will that there bee Noe apraizm[t] of my Estate . . .

witnesses: Hugh Campbell.
John *Ifie.* his mark.
Moses Spring.

Tho: Wilson & Seal.

MOSES LINTON . . .

Book 5 f. 205.
dated 6 Dec. 1692.
proved 17 July 1693 by Dan[el] Macafasion.
15 Sept. 1693 by Mr. Tho: Brett & Mary Lindon.

. . . unto my Son William all my Land of what Quallity or Condition Soever, and after the Death of my Said Son William, I give and bequeath my Said Land to Moses the Son of my Son William . . . ; but for want of Such Issue, then to the next heires of my Son William forever:——— whereof I did formerly give to my Son Moses Decd, a Certaine tract of Land & possessed —— of it, & Assigned a bill of Sale to him, for the Same, but Never was Recorded I doe for the Confirmation of that Guift, give & bequeath the Same Tract of Land to Moses Linton the Son of my Son Moses Linton Decd . . .

. . . to my Daughter Elizabeth Ball the wife of Richard Ball one Trunk One Cold Still, One third parte of my Pewter, after the decease of Elizabeth, my wife . . .

. . . to my Son William, the whole remamed[r] of my psonall Estate, as is Exprest On the Other Side . . .

. . . my Son William Linton my whole & Sole Ex*ecer* . . .

witnesses: Thomas Brett.
Daniell Macafasion.
Mary Lindon
her mar.

Moses Linton.
his mar.

JOSEPH TOWNSEND . . .

Book 5 f. 205.

dated 28 Aprill 1692.

proved 15 Sept. 1693 by Jn° Jolliff & Th°: W*orsle.*

. . . wife One Cow . . .
. . . my Daughter Mary One Cow . . .
. . . my Daughter Jean One Cowe . . .
. . . my Son Joseph One heifer . . .
. . . my three Children . . . at the age of Sixteen . . . Girles, and at Eighteen . . .
. . . to my Sone Josiah . . .
. . . my Loveing Neighbo^r^ & kinseman Edward E*th*eridge & John Jolly Junr to Overse . . . .

witnesses: Jn° Jolliff.
Tho: *N*orsle.
Edw: E*th*eridge.

Josiah Tou*nsend* &
Seale.

JOSEPH MILLER, Senr of the County of Lower Norfolk Planter . . .

Book 5 f 207.

dated 4 Jan. 1689.

proved 15 Sept. 1693 by John Cherry & Wm Maund.

. . . my body to bee buried in the parrish of Elizabeth River according to the Discression of my wife Elizabeth Miller . . . my Executrix . . .
. . . unto my Son Benj. Miller & my Son Moses Miller, & my Son Edward Miller the Plantation I now live On . . .
. . . my Son Joseph Miller and my Son Wm Miller . . . bee Overseers of my three Sons afore Mentioned . . . that my afore mentioned three Sons, bee at age att Eighteen yeares Old a peece . . .

witnesses: Wm Maund.
Jn° Cherry, his mar
Rebeckah Cherry.

Joseph Miller & Seale.

JAMES THILABALL of Eliz. River prish in the County of Lower Norfolk, Gent.

Book 5 f. 208.

dated 3 Aprill 1692.

proved 15 Sept 1693, by Coll. Lemuell Mason & Mr. Thomas Mason.

. . . well stricken in yeares . . .

. . . buried in Christian manor . . .

. . . unto my loveing Son ffrancis Thelaball One hundred Acres of land, more or less, lying neare the plantation, formerly belonging to Wm Doughan Decd, which Sd. Land I formerly designed to give unto my Son Lemuel Now Decd., and Now the above Said ffrancis and his heires forever . . . one Negro woman . . . one Negro boy . . . a high bed steed & a feather bed . . . with Green Curtains & *Dallians,* wth Silk fring and a Greene Woosted Rugg . . . a Hamaker . . . another feather bed & boulster which Comonly Lyeth on the Trundle bed steed wth a White Rugg and long table wth ff*orne* to itt & a Joyners Cubbard & a Chaire of Joyners Worke . . . a great Copper kettle & two pott Racks . . . One Iron Spitt, and Smale pr. of Andjrons, & a paire of Helſeards and a paire of Brass Skales wth fower pnds of brass weights & a Cross Cutt Sawe, and fower Iron Wedges, & a Silver porringer & two Silver Spoons mark I T E & three pewter Dishes & a pewter bason, the aforesdd goods bequeathed to my Said Son ffrancis are not to bee Delivered him, until after the Decease of my wife Elizabeth without her Consent and likeing.

I give & bequeath unto my loving Son James Thelaball a Negro girle . . . one feather bed and boulster, and a paire of Sheets, wch Comonly Lyeth in the Shedd at the End of the Dwelling house, & a blew Woosted Rugg, & a flock bedd, One Silver Salt cellar, two Silver spoons marked I T E & One brass Morter & Pestle & one pewter flaggon, & one Copper Still & One large Chest wth a double Locke & One toole Chest and all the tooles therein, & One pr. of great Andjrons & One Iron Spitt & One Anvill . . . Not to bee Delivered, untill after the Decease of my Wife Elizabeth, wthout her Consent and likeing . . .

. . . . unto my loving Daughter Margaret Langley three Silver spoons, and One Silver wrought wine Cupp, & One Smale Copper kettle & one Smale pewter Still, and a brass warming pann . . .

. . . unto my Loving Daughter Elizabeth Langeley, one Negro girle . . . three Silver Spoons & One Smooth Silver wine Cupp & one Smale Copper kettle . . .

. . . unto my loving Daughter Mary Chichester, One Silver beere bole, One Silver Dram Cupp, One Smale Silver Spoone, One Couch with feather bed and pillow in it & a Rugg . . .

. . . unto my loving Cosen W^m^ P*orten* all my ffrench books . . .

. . . my Said wife Elizabeth my whole & sole Executo^r^ . . .

witnesses: Lemuel Mason.
Thomas Mason.
Mary Mason.

James Thelaball & Seale.

THOMAS HALLOWELL . . .

Book 5 f. 208.

dated 16 June 1693.

proved 15 Sept. 1693. Eleazer Tart & Bartholome Highsmith.

. . . unto my Daughter Mary Hallowell fower hundred acres of Land. lying & being at the head of the westerne branch of Elizabeth River . . .

. . . unto my Sons Thomas and John Hallowell a prcle of Land, being pte. of the Land wch I live upon, being at the fishing Creeke and Soe running to the white Oak branch & Soe Right Over to Morris Deales, my Son Thomas to have that parte where I live and my Son John to have that part Next the fishing Creek . . . my wife must have her thirds of the plantation . . .

. . . the rest of my land backward . . . unto my Sons William and Luke . . . when they Come to Age . . .

. . . unto my Daughter Mary One feather bed . . . to bee Delivered to her at the day of her Solemnization of her marriage.

. . . my Loving wife Sarah Hallowell . . . Exe^rix^ . . .

. . . my Children (vizt) John, William, Elizabeth, Kathrin and Luke . . .

. . . John & William . . . when they Come to age . . .

witnesses: the mark of
Bartholeme Highsmith
Eleazer Tart
John Nickells.

Tho: Hallowell & Seale.

WM. COOPER Sen[r] . . .

Book 5 f. 210.

dated 3 May 1686.

proved 15 Nov. 1693. by Jn[o] Williamson & Dorkas Williamson.

. . . unto my Son W[m] Cooper all my books, Excepting great Sermon book, that I give unto my Sonn John Cooper . . .

. .. . wife Ann Cooper all my Cattle & Hoggs & Cheepe, and my horse if hee bee alive . . . the Plantation, Soe long as Shee liveth . . .

. . . my two Sons W[m] Cooper & John Cooper . . .

. . . wife Ann Cooper fully & holy Execu[rix] . . .

witnesses: John Williamson.
Dakiss Williamson.
the 8th Day of June 1693.

William Cooper & Seale.

THOMAS WALK . . .

Book 5 f. 212.

dated 5 Jan[ry] 1693/4.

proved 5 Jan[ry] 1693/4, by fower Evidences.

. . . I give and Bequeath the Plantation I now live upon unto my Son Thomas Walke . . . likewise . . . halfe that tract of Land I bought of W[m] Hilliard lying at Curituck Bay . . .

. . . unto my Son Anthony Walke my Plantation lying at the head of the Southern branch Called Possum Neck adjoyning to the Land of Jn[o] Dixons, the Said Plantation or the pduce thereof I Impower my Exec[rs] to Dispose of for his best advantage. and to add thereunto One hundred ponds Sterld Out of my psonall Estate, before any Devesion thereof, all which is to purchase him a good Convent[t] plantation . . .

. . . . unto my Sister Ann Chambers of Barbadoes, and unto Each of her Children Shee Now hath five pnds Sterld a peece . . .

. . . . unto my Daughter Mary Walke, my young Negro Woman Called Peggy . . .

. . . . unto my Brother Robert, my Sister Margarett and my Sister Margery of Barbadoes, unto Each of them twenty Shillings to buy them a Ring a peice . . .

. . . . unto my Loveing ffriends Left. Coll. Anthony Lawson, M[ris] Mary Lawson, Margarett, Elizabeth & Anthony Lawson Jun[r] unto Each of them twenty Shillings to buy them a Ring a peice . . .

. . . . unto my Loveing frends: Edward, W[m] & John Moseley . . . twenty Shillings to buy them a Ring a peice . . .

. . . . unto W[m] Moseley Sen[r] forty Shilings to bee paid him out of my Owne wareing Cloathes . . .

. . . . unto Margarett Moseley the wife of the Said W[m] Moseley forty Shillings to bee paid her out of my wives wareing Cloathes . . .

. . . . unto the Widdow Elder forty Shillings . . .

. . . . Remaining . . . unto my three Children, Thomas, Anthony and Mary Walk . . .

. . . . the Vessells, I am Concerned with . . . bee fitted Out and my goods this yeare to bee Shypt off in them to Barbadoes . . .

. . . . ffriends Left Coll Anthony Lawson, Edward Moseley Sen[r] & W[m] Moseley Jun[r] to bee my Execr[s] in trust . . .

witnesses: George Moseley.
John Smith.
Morgan Bryan.
Anthony Lawson, Jun[r]

Tho. Walke & Seale

WILLIAM DUNDAS . . .

Book 5 f. 213.
dated 11 July 1692 & 3.
proved 15 Jan[ry] 1693/4.

. . . . my Loving Sister Christian Kennan, wife of M[r] Andrew Kennan and to her Children after her Decease, all my whole Estate . . .

. . . Collonell Anthony Lawson and Mr Thomas Walke bee my Sole Execrs . . . and to remitt my Said Estate to my aforesaid Sister in Dublin in Ireland by bills of Exchange for London if possible, or as the Said Christian Kennan or her husband Mr Andrew Kennan Shall Order . . .

witnesses: Edward Moseley, Senr.
John Hodgis.

William Dundas & Seale.

JOHN GAMON . . .

Book 5 f. 215.

dated 4 Oct. 1693.

proved 15 Mch. 1693/4.

. . . unto my Son in Law Daniel Glasco and to my Daughter Mary his wife . . . "Eighty acres of Land, beginning at a Marked Poplar Standing upon Richford Swamp at the head of land & from there down the Said Swamp to the first branch Issueing out of Richford Swamp, and from the said Poplar along the head line of my land, Soe farr upon a Square Small make up the Said Eighty Acres" . . .

. . . unto my Daughter Susanna the whole pte. of land Called the White Pine Woods between the Cypress Swamp & the Gum branch . . . & for want of such Issue, to my Son Robert . . .

. . . unto my Son Robert Gamon the whole remainer of my land . . . the manor Plantation . . . Except that . . . to the two Daughters . . . but Not to posess the manor Plantation, *till* after the death of Susana my wife . . .

. . . wife . . . Executrix . . .

. . . my loving friends Tho: Butt & Richard Brett Overseers . . .

witnesses: Charles Cartwright.
Tho: Miller.
Rachell ffreeman.

John Gamon & Seale.

WILLIAM NICHLIS of the County of Norfolk in Virginia Book 5 f. 215.

dated 9 Aug. 1693.

proved 15 Mch. 1693/4.

. . . unto my Son Andrew Nichlis this my Plantation where I now live . . .

. . . unto my three Sons, William, John, Nathaniell three hundred & twenty acres of Land Joyning to Warren Godree called by the name of Lyons quarter . . . butt if my Son Andrew Should bee dead, or Never come againe, then I give unto my Son William my Plantation where I now live . . . and my . . . Lyons Quarter to my two Sons John & Nathaniell . . .

. . . unto my Daughter Elizabeth M*aclenahan* twelve pence in money . . .

. . . unto my Daughter Mary twelve pence . . .

. . . unto my Daughter Ann twelve pence . . .

. . . unto my Daughter fflorence a Cowe & Calfe which useth at the Southerne branch . . .

. . . wife Elizabeth and my Six Children ffrancis, William, John, Martha, Sarah, Nathaniell, all the rest . . .

. . . wife Executrix . . .

. . . unto Richard ffarmer my Plantation att Lyons Quarter . . . use during his naturall life . . .

witnesses: Mary R*av*ing, her mark.
John Branton.
Thomas Selley.

William Nichlis & Seale.

JAMES WILSON boatright of the Southerne branch in the County of Norfolk . . .

Book 5 f. 218.

dated "July the 24th Day 1693. Elizabeth River."

proved 15 May 1694 by Elizabeth Williams & Tho: Coope.

. . . Estate holy to his wife Elizabeth Wilson . . .

witnesses: James M*ohun*.
Eliza: Williams
Tho: Coope.

James Wilson

JOHN WATTFORD . . .

Book 5 f. 219.

dated 29 Aprill 1694.

proved 15 May 1694.

. . . all my land unto my brother Solomon Manning, the youngest Son of my ffather in law Tho: Maning . . .
. . . unto my Cozen Joseph Walford one Cow Calfe . . .
. . . to my ffather & Mother the Cow . . . Dampell . . .
. . . unto my brother John Maning One heifer . . .
. . . to my Sister Sarah maning . . . One heifer . . .
. . . unto my brother Thomas Maning three Sowes and a young barrow . . .
. . . my Bible . . .
. . . due to mee from Richard Bacon . . .
. . . my father in Lawe Tho: Maning Exec^r . . .

witnesses: George Horne.
Rich. Eastwood.
Xtopher Lee.

John Watford & Seale.
mark.

WALTER COSTEN . . .

Book 5 f. 220.

dated 7 June 1688.

proved 15 May 1694, by Thomas Butt & Mary Lindon.

. . . unto John Sickes the Son of Walter Sickes, all that plantation & tract of land whereon Walter Sickes Now liveth . . . after ye Decease of Walter Sickes and Jane his wife to whom I give the Plantation that they Now live On and all Other priviledges of the whole tract of Land Equally with the Said Jno Sickes during theire Naturall lives, they not baring the Said John Sickes from making a plantation upon the Said Tract of land when hee comes to the Age of One & twenty yeares . . .
. . . unto John Gamon Senr Eight hundred foot of Land upon Costins Island . . . to build a house upon . . .
. . . unto Thomas Sickes & Walter Sickes Junr & Costen Sickes . . . the remainer. of Costen Island . . .
. . . unto Walter Sickes Junr Son of Walter Sickes . . . One hundred Sixty & Seaven Acres of land bounding upon the land of Joseph Curling. together wth the plantation whereon I now live . . .

. . . unto Thomas Sickes Son of Walter Sickes & his heires forever One hundred & Sixty Seaven acres of that tract of land I now live On Next Ajoyning . . . from the Richford Swamp Eastward to the head line . . .
. . . unto Costen Sickes One hundred & Sixty acres of that land I now live On Next ajoyning upon the land of Jn° Edmonds from Richford Swamp to the head line . . .
. . . Apoynt my Loving Cozen Walter Sickes Senr my Sole Executo^{r} . . .

witnesses: Tho: B*utt*.
John Weston.
Mary Linton.

Walter Costen & Seale.

WILLIAM HAYLY of the Southerne branch of Elizabeth River in the County of Lower Norfolk . . .

Book 5 f. 224.

dated 31 May 1694.

proved 12 July 1694 by Henry Cornelius & Jn° Batcheor.

. . . to be buryed at the Discrecon of my ffriend Thomas Mercer . . .
. . . unto Thomas Mercer all my Estate . . .

witnesses: the mark of
Giles Randall.
John Batchelor.

the mark.
William Hayley & Seale.

HESTER BRIDGE, Widdow the wife of .Thomas Bridge lately Decd . . .

Book 5 f. 230.

dated 27 Jan. 1686/7.

proved 15 Mch. 1693/4. by Symon Handcock and Edward Moseley.

. . . my Negro Servt maide Elizath . . .
. . . bought of Mr. Peter Smith . . .
. . . unto my God Son David Dun*c*on all the rest of my Estate . . . my Executo^{r} . . .

witnesses: James Peeters.
Simon Hankock.
Edward Moseley.

Hester Bridge & Seale.

ROBERT GRIMES of the County of Lower Norfolk . . .
Book 5 f. 230
dated 31 July 1692.
proved 15 Mch. 1693/4, by Jno Whimfell & Henry Pope.

. . . to my Son John Grimes all my land lying On the North Side of a Creeke, between me and Robert Hatton . . .

. . . to my Son James Grimes all the rest of my land together with my Housein . . . my hole Executo[r] . . .

witnesses: Jn[o] whimfell.
Henry Pope.
Ann Wright.

Robert Grimes
his mark & Seale

JOHN ffROST . . .
Book 5 f. 231.
dated 28 Mch. 1687.
proved 15 Mch. 1693/4. by W[m] Wennam & John Aell*e*t.

. . . my Plantation to my wife for her life & after her Decease to my Daughter Mary . . .

. . . my Wife Exec[r]x . . . (wife Julia See top of Book 5 f. 231) . . .

witneses: W[m] Wenham
John Aell*o*tt, his mar.
W[m] Clements, mar.

John ffrost & Seale.

AARON SPRING . . .
Book 5 f. 231.
dated 22 Nov. 1693.
proved 15 Mch. 1693/4. by Robert Drisedayle & Edward Outlaw.

. . . unto my Son John, the plantation that now I live On being a hundred Akers, and my half of the Mill . . . to Inheritt at the Age of Eighteen & in Case hee dye w[th]out Eares then to be Equally devided to his three Sisters . . .

. . . unto my daughter Elizabeth One hundred akers of Land, Lying in the Woods, at the head of Jn[o] ffreemans line Called by the name of the I*nehamed* Ridge . . . to Inheritt at the Age of Eighteen . . .

. . . unto my Daufter S*arie* my Negro Gemey by name . . . at . . . Eighteen . . .

. . . unto my Dafter Elizabeth two thousand pnds. of tobacco which is in my Brother Robert Springs hands . . . at . . . Eighteen . . .

. . . unto my wife Elizabeth . . . Executrics . . .

witnesses: Robert Driesdayell.
Sam[l] Porter.
his marke.
Edward Outlaw.

Aaron Spring & Seale.

HENRY NICKLIS being bound for the Sea . . .
Book 5 ff 229 & 232.
dated 20 Aprill 1694.
proved 16 Nov. 1694.

. . . to my Wife ffrancis, her being on the land, wth the use of all my Housen, during her life . . .

. . . my Son Richard Nicklis Shall bee at age . . . at . . . Eighteen . . .

. . . to my Son Richard all my lands lying and being, in the Easterne Branch of Elizabeth River . . . my two Gunns, wth my Pistoles & halsters, and my New Bible . . .

. . . my Wife ffrances Nichlis . . . Sole Exec[r] . . .

witnesses: W[m] Nicholson.
John Smith.
Henry Whitehurst.

Henry Nicklis & Seale.

JEANE GREEN . . .
Book 5 f. 241
dated 27 March 1694.
proved 15 Jany 1694/5. by Samuell Walker.
15 March 1694/5. by Eleazer Tart.

. . . unto my Grandson Jn[o] Winfeld One Mare . . .

. . . unto my grandaughter Eliz[a] Walker One bed . . . my pestle . . .

. . . unto my Grand Son Rich[d] Bunting, One gunn . . .

. . . unto my Grand daughter Eliz[a] Bunting, One pewter dish . . .

. . . unto my Grand Children my Son Thomas his Children (vizt) Jane Green 1 Cow . . . to Ann Green One Cow . . . & to Tomisen One Cow . . .

. . . unto my Grand daughter Eliz[th] Walker, One great Chest . . .

. . . unto Henry Culpeper, One little Chest . . . my piggeons . . .

. . . my Grand Daughter Tomasen Green . . .

. . . my Grand daughter Alice Norcott, my Smoothing Iron One fflesh forke . . .

. . . my Son in lawe Rich[d] Bunting . . . Exec[r] . . .

witnesses: Henry Culpeper,
his marke.
Sam: Walker,
his marke.
Eleazer Tart.

Jeane Green
her marke.

Since the wrighting of the above Will . . .

. . . unto my Daughter in Law Bridgett Bunting One p[r] of little Sheers . . .

dated 13 Aprill 1694.

witnesses: Eleazer Tart.
Samuell Walker.

The marke of
Jeane Greene.

RICHARD WILLIAMS of the Little Creek in the County of Lower Norfolk Planter . . .

Book 5 f. 244.

dated 27 Jan. 1688/9.

proved 15 Mch. 1694/5. & 15 May 1694/5.

. . . to my Loveing wife Edy[o] the plantation whereon I now live with that tract of land, I bought of Nicholas Huggins . . .

. . . to John Griffin Sen[r] . . . what land belongeth to John *Oseb*evine Plantation . . .

. . . wife Edy my . . . Exec[r]ix . . .

. . . to James Smith one Cow . . . after he Cometh to perfect Age . . . but he the Said Smith to Continue with my wife during her time . . . likewise my plantation after my Wifes Decease . . . but in Case the

Said Smith Dieth with out Issue . . . to John Griffin Junr . . .
. . . to Thomas Griffin wch I desere his father John Griffin to See after . . .

witnesses: John Thrower,
the marke of.
Thomas Mason, Junr

Rich. Will*e* & Seale.

GEORGE BRADLEY of Newport On Road Island M^{r}cht.
Book 5 f. 247.
dated 24 Aug. 1694 In the Sixth yeare of theire Maj^{ties} Reigne Over England & C.
. . . being now bound Out upon a Voyage to Sea, . . .
. . . comend my Soul into the hands of Almighty God, . . .
. . . & my body Comitt to the Earth, to bee Decently buryed, . . .
. . . all my debts and funerall Charges Shall bee first paid . . .
. . . unto my Grandfather John Ward five pound to buy him a Ring . . .
. . . unto my trusty well beloved friends Mr Weston Clarke & Mr Robert *Kittle* both of New Port in Road Island Each five pounds to buy them a Ring . . . appointing them ffeoffeefe in trust of this my last Will & Testam^{t} . . .
. . . If it should happen that my wife Margarett, Should Now bee wth Child, and it Should be borne into ye world Alive and Should happen to bee a Son, I desire his Name may bee called George, & I will & bequeath to him three hundred pounds; and if a Daughter; then I will & bequeath her two hundred, & the Same to bee Mannaged for them by my wife Margarett during her widohood, & upon her Intermarrying againe; the Same to bee Mannaged for his or her use, till come of fitt age to look after it her Selfe, or Marry) by my ffeeffes, or Exec^{r} in trust, who I desire to bee his or her Guadians. All the rest and residue of my psonall Estate Good & Chatteles whatsoever; Land, or Tenemt^{s} whatsoever to me Imediately belonging, be they heare or Elcewhere I doe give & bequeath unto my Deare & loving Wife Margarett; full & Sole Exec^{r}ix . . .

witnesses: Jeames Clarke.
Sam^{ll} Cranston.
Willes Wilson.

George Bradley & Seale.

James Clarke & Sam[ll] Cranston two of the Witnesses to the above sd. Will apeared before mee the 11[th] Day of the Second Month Called Aprill 1695, and upon theire Engag—[t] According to law. ° testifieth that the above Said George Bradley, did in theire p[r]sence Owne the within written Will to bee his last Will & Testam[t] taken before mee

John E*a*ston Gov[r]

The above written is a true Coppey of the last Will & Testam[t] of George Bradly late of New Port M[r]cht. as is Attested by mee with Ord[r] for the truth there of to bee Sealed with the Seale of the Collony of Road Island & Pvidence plantations. John E*u*sti*n* *C[e]ll.*

Signed wth the Seale of the Collony as
Attest. *West* Clarke Recd[r]
Recorded according to an Ord[r] of Norfolk County Court held 15th July 1695. Test. Mala Thruston, C[l] Cur.

JOHN MURDEN of Norfolk County Planter . . .
Book 5 f. 249.
dated 8 Jan. 1693/4.
proved 15 June 1695.

. . . Shortly intending a voyadge for England . . .
. . . unto my Son John the one Moyty or halfen Deal of my Plantation & land whereon I Now Dwell . . . to have the North part, . . .
. . . unto my Son William the other Moytey & Halpen Deale . . . to have the South parte . . .
. . . John or William . . . Dye, before he accomplish his age . . .
. . . if both my Said Sons . . . Dye, before they accomplish therre age . . . unto my three Sons Jeremiah, Robert & Edward . . .
. . . unto my three Sons, Jeremiah, Robert, & Edward . . . all the land that I bought of Coll. Thomas Milner . . . when the Eldest accomplish the Age of One & Twenty . . .
. . . Elizabeth my wife . . . Execr[x] . . .
. . . unto Son John after the Decease of his Mother Elizabeth my wife . . .
. . . to my Daughter Mary . . .
. . . unto my Daughter Elizabeth . . .

witnesses: Jere B*e*ck.
Edward Tranter.
Tho: Abington.

John Murden & Seale.

N. B.—Book 6 which I will now abstract is about one half illegible. This is due in part to old age and in part to the failure to care for the preservation of the Volume. Many wills formerly therein contained are missing, and the Originals lost.

JOHN WILSON of the Western branch of Eliz. River . . .

Book 6 p. 15.

dated 29 July 1695.

proved 15 Jan. 1695/6, by Jean Hall & Robert Dayeslayed.

. . . unto my Cozen Robert Mountgomery, One Cowe . . .
. . . unto my Cozen Mary Davenell, One Cowe . . .
. . . unto my Cozen Wm Davenell, One Cowe . . .
. . . unto my Sister Eliz^a^ Davenell, my bed . . .
. . . unto Robert Dresedasle, One heifer . . .
. . . unto my Brother Wm Davenell, my Cast*o*r Hatt . . .
. . . unto my Brother Thomas Wilson, all the rest . . . Exec^r^ . . .

witnesses: William Huchinson.
Jeane Hall.
Robert Dryesdayell.

John Wilson & Seale.
hismar.

CHARLES CARTHRITE . . .

Book 6 p. 33.

dated 14 Sept. 1695.

proved 15 May 1696. by Theodor & Ann Taylor.

. . . unto my Son in lawe Robert Gamon One Cow & Calf . . .
. . . unto my Daughter Susan Gamon, One Cow . . .
. . . unto my Deare Wife Susan Carthrite, One Cow . . . rest . . .
. . . wife . . . my whole Executrix . . .

witnesses: Theoeer Taylor.
Joseph Hodges.
Ann Taylor.

Charles Cartright & Seale.

WILLIAM KNOTT Marriner now Resident in the Towne of Norfolk County in Virginia . . .

Book 6 p. 76.
dated 6 aprill 1694.
proved 15 Mch. 1696/7, by Simons, Suggs & Wilkins.

. . . unto my Godson Wm Porten Son of Mr Wm Porten Deceased my two lotts of land, where I now live in the Towne of Norfolk County . . . Joyning to Peter Smiths & Next to ye River Side . . . when hee shall ataine to the age of twenty-one . . .

. . . unto John Thruston the Son of Malachy Thruston, my other Lotts of land, in the Said Towne lying opposite to that I Now live On, and On the Northwards Side of the Street, & Joyning to the back Creek . . . when hee Shall Ataine the Age of twenty one . . .

. . . unto John Adams, the Son in Law of Thomas Brent of Norfolk County aforesaid . . . when hee Shall ataine to the age of twenty One . . .

. . . unto Elizabeth Branton Wid^o . . .

. . . unto David Dunson . . .

. . . unto the poore of the Towne of Norfolke County the Sum of five thousand pounds of tobacco, to bee disposed of to Such poore pSons of the Said Towne, as the Vestry Shall at time or times Convent^t to them the Said Vestry of Elizabeth River parrish adjudge Most Charitable, Needfull Expedient for Reliefe.

. . . friend Malachy Thruston Now Clerk of the Court of Norfolk County . . . Sole Exec^r . . .

witnesses: Wm Wilkins.
Geo. Newton.
James Simons.
Joseph Sugg.

Wm Knott & Seale.

JOHN BIGG of Elizabeth River in the County of Norfolk in Virginia . . .

Book 6 p. 77.
dated 4 Sept. 1694.
proved 15 Mch. 1696/7 by Joseph Hodges, Jno. Portlock, Tho: Nash & Thomas Etheridge.

. . . to my Son John Bigg . . . (my Sole Only and Absolute & lawfull heire) . . . all my Estate both reall

& psonall Except Such leagecyes hearafter mentioned, (that is to say) I Give him my Said Son John Bigg all my land I am Now possessed off (viz[t]) my Mannon plantation, and all the land belonging to the Same . . . Including a Small pcell of Land that George Whidby lives upon by my pmission dureing my life; allsoe the Land w[ch] my Son Jabez held in his life time by Pattent bareing Date the 23[d] Day of Aprill 1688, w[ch] Said Land is allsoe my pper Rights, all which with the land I hold Now by my Owne Pateent bearing date the 21th Day of Aprill An[o] Dom[i] 1690; I Give to my Said Son Jn[o] Bigg . . . , but if my Said Son John Shall Dye without Issue as aforesaid; then . . . to my Grand Son John Whidby, and the heires of his body . . . and for lack of Such Issue, to my Grand Son George Whidley and his heires . . ., & for lack of Such Issue, then to Descend to the rest of my Daughters Elizabeths Children . . . , and for want of Such Issue, then to my Daughter Katherine Mercers Children, . . . and for want thereof . . . to the Next right heires of mee the Said John Bigg, the ffather . . .

. . . to my Son Thomas Bigg, my Daughters Ann *Faux,* Kathern Mercer, Elizabeth Whitby, Jeane S*ik*es, Phebe Bigg, Dorothy Bigg to Each of them . . . twelve pence or One Shilling . . .

. . . unto my Son in law Mathew Caswell & my Grand Child Joh*n Hafsald* & Martha ffrancis, William Jabez, Jeane & Mathew Caswell . . . One Shilling Sterld . . .

. . . my Son John Bigg . . . Onley Executor . . .

witnesses: John Portlock.
Tho: Nash.
Tho: Etheridge
Joseph Hodgis
W[m] Maund
W[m] Etheridg
his mark.
Robecka Hodgis
her mark.
"and many Others."

John Bigg & Seale.

DANIELL MACKAFARSON . . .

Book 6 p. 78.

dated 31 Dec. 1695.

proved 15 Mch. 1696/7.

. . . to my two Sons Daniell & Andrew, my plantation with all the land to be Equally Devided between them . . . Sole Exec[rs] . . .

witnesses: Roger Hodgis.
John Creekmore.
Thos. Butt.

Daniel Mackaferson & Seale.

HESTER HITCHCOCK . . . (Nuncupative) . . .

Book 6 p. 78.

The Deposition of Elizabeth Bayley Aged about 59 yeares . . . Sworne Sayeth: That being with her Sister Hester Hitchcock when shee lay upon her Death bed Sick whereof Shee Dyed . . . shee did give all Shee had, unto her Cozen this Depon[ts] Daughter Elizabeth, and made her whole Executrix . . . to her I comitt the Care & Charge of my Sister Mary Knott during her naturall life . . .

Sworne in Court 15th March 1696/7

Elizabeth Bayley.

The Deposition of Joseph Bayley Aged 20 yeares . . . Sayeth That his Aunt Hitchcocke . . . did give all . . . to her Cozen Elizabeth Bayley and made her Sole Executrix . . .

Sworne in Court 15th March 1696/7

Joseph Bayley.

JOHN NICHOLS of the Westerne branch of Elizabeth River in Norfolk County in Virginia, being Aged . . .

Book 6 f. 96.

dated 11 Nov. 1696.

provey 17 May 1697, by Mathew Spivy, Malachy Thruston, W[m] Tart & Eleazer Tart.

. . . unto my loving Vertueuse & tender Wife Judeth Nichols . . . the plantation I now live On . . . and allsoe all the profits, and advantages Shee my Said Loveing Wife can Make to her Self of in & to One hundred Acres of land Called an Island, at the Northwest River in this Count of Norfolk . . . during her naturall life which

Shee is to Enjoye as a full Compensation of her Dower of my Lands.

. . . . unto my Son in law Mathew Spivie, the Son of my p^r^sent Wife Judeth Nichols the Said plantation I Now live On, being five hundred Acres of Land after the Decease of his Mother my Said wife . . . Swamp land, upon the head of the Said five hundred acres, which Eleazer Tart hath Entered, together with some that is on the head of his land, and it being Agreed that Each of us, Shall have & Enjoye that pte. of the Said Entry Joyning upon Each of o^r^ lands; I . . . give . . . unto him the Said Mathew Spivye . . .

. . . . unto my Daughter in Lawe Ann Spivye, the Daughter of my Said Wife Judith . . . One hundred Acres of land at the North West River . . . called an Island, after the Decease of my Said Wife her Mother . . . purchased from Dan^ll^ Br*owne* . . .

. . . . Sett free my two Molattos (Viz^t^) a Boy Named John Lovina, and a Girl Named Sarah Lovina, both being Children of my Negro Woman Named Jean Lovina . . . boy is now aprentice to one Nathan Newby a Smith living in Nansimond County . . .

. . . . unto the above Said Molato Girl Sarah Lovina two hundred Acres of Land lying & being in the Southerne branch of Elizabeth River Now in the posession & Occupation of Daniell B*urne* being pte. of a Tract of land, Containing three hundred & fifty Acres . . . Shee to have the said two hundred Acres upon the Northern Runn Mentioned in the Plott . . .

. . . . to Molattoe boy Named John Lovina One hundred & fiftie acres of Land joyning upon the Said two hundred & fifty acres . . . unto the above Said Molattoe boy John Lovina One & Six acres . . . in Westerne branch of Eliz^th^ River and Joyning upon the land late of William Davenell Decd. which I formerly bought of John fflower^s^ . . . a Water Mill . . . the head of Southerne branch of Elizabeth River which I bought of John Ives, being formerly Capt Carvers . . .

. . . . wife Judeth Nichols . . . the remainer . . . my whole & Sole Executrix . . .

witnesses: Tho: Russell
Eleazer Tart.
Mathew Spivy.
Wm Tart.
Mala Thruston.

John Nicholls & Seale

WILLIAM HESLETT of Norfolk County . . .
Book 6 f. 105.
dated 22 Aug. 1697.
proved 16 Sept. 1697.

. . . Appoynt . . . my . . . Wife Ann Heslett . . . Sole Executrix . . .

. . . unto my Said Loving Wife . . . all my Negroes . . . my Houses & Lotts in the Towne of this County, which I now live On, together with my plantation, in ye Westerne branch of Elizabeth River, and all my lands thereto Adjoyning being about three. One of which (vizt) Either the Howses, and Lotts in the Towne aforesaid, or the Said Plantation in the Westerne branch . . . Shall bee by my . . . Executrix aforesaid Sold; if Shee Shall Soe Occasion for & Towards the payment of the Estaees of the Orphants of Joseph Copeland Decd remaining in my hands, and what thereof *to* shall Not be Sold . . . . to her my . . . wife Ann . . .

. . . unto my Son Cary Heslett, my Plantation I lately bought of Dan^{ll} Macoy and John Ross in the Southern branch of Elizabeth River, and all my land joyning thereto being about two hundred and fifty Acres . . .

. . . unto my Daughter Ann Heslett, my due Share & part of a Patent of land, Granted to my Self, Edmond Creekmore, & Henry Dale, at the North West River, Con^{t} about two thousand two hundred Acres, my part thereof being about Seaven hundred Acres more or less, as by an Instrum^{t} of Devision, Now in the Custody of Malachy Thruston may appeare . . .

. . . all the rest and remainder of my lands at and towards the North West River, and Elsewhere, being Severall pcells, as may apeare by my Wrightings & Deeds for ye Same unto my Said Son Cary Heslett, and the Child my Loving Wife Now goes wth Child withall if . . . borne & live, to Each of them the One halfe . . . butt in Case . . . be not borne and liveth the half of the Said land as aforesaid . . . unto my Daughter Ann Heslett . . .

. . . unto John Thruston the Son of Malachy Thruston my greate Surveying Instrument, and appurtenances to the Same in my Leather Case with hasps to itt, that it lyes in . . .

witnesses: Sam^{ll} Boush.
Alice Boush.
Mala Thruston

Wiliam
Heslett & Seale.

PETER HOBSON, of Elizabeth River, in ye Towne of Norfolk County . . .

Book 6 f. 107.

dated 14 Sept.—(torn)—

proved 25 Sept. 1697. by—(torn)—Power, Malachy Thruston and —(torn)—tt,—

. . . . my Lott of Land and howsing thereon in this Towne where Now I live upon my Son John Hobson, and free liberty of timber & fire Wood for ye use of the house of and from any part of my land Purchased of Ann Stoneham and John Adams . . .

. . . . all my Land Purchased of the Said Ann Stoneham & John Adams being Six hundred acres Except the liberty of timber & fire wood above reserved to my Son John, the Said Six hundred Acres I Give unto my Daughter Phillis and my Daughter Mary Hobson . . .

. . . . unto my Daughter Elizabeth for and towards her Education in learning thirty pounds Sterling . . .

. . . . my woman Servt Margarett Scott . . . freedom . . .

. . . . remainer of my psonall Estate . . . bee Converted into Money & kept in bank . . .

. . . . Son John Hobson, my Daughter Phillis Hobson, and my Daughter Mary Hobson . . . , son John Hobson . . . when he Shall ataine to the Age of twenty yeares . . . Daughters Phillis & Mary . . . at sixteen . . .

. . Elizabeth my wife, who by her *Evil* Action I Esteeme unworthy the of Wife having in a Most unaturall manner gon away from mee, and her Children & having Conveyed away a Viry Considerable pte. of my Estate . . .

. . . . freinds Mr. Samuele Boush, and Malachy Thruston to Each of them thirty Shillings to buy Each of them a Ring . . .

. . . . friends and Neighbo^rs, Mr. Samuell Boush and Malachy Thruston . . . Sole Executors . . .

witnesses: Samp^son Power.
Edmond Shea.
Ann Heslett.
Mala Thruston.

Peter Hobson & Seale.

LEWIS CONNER—(torn)—

Book 6 f. 111.

dated—(torn)— August—(torn)—

proved—(torn)—

. . . to my loving Wife—(torn)—
. . . my fower Sons Lewis Conner, Ceader—(torn)—
. . . wife Elizabeth during her na—(torn)—
. . . above Said Shipp . . .
. . . Briginteen that is Now—(torn)—Soe Soon as Shee Shall—(torn)—
. . . my Said Eldest Son Lewis C—(torn)—

witnesses: Willi Daines.
William Barrow.
James Downing.
his mark.
John M*aux*.

(Taken from a loose piece):

. . . Plantation . . .
. . . Estate, both in Virginia & England . . .
. . . my Seaven Children . . .
. . . wife Elizabeth Conner . . . Sole Executrix . . .
. . . Seale the 31th Day—(torn)— . . .

Probated: 20 Jan. 1697/8. (See Book 6 f. 114).

ROBERT SCOTT of Nanci*monn* County Carpenter and now in the Towne of Norfolk County . . .

Book 6 f. 123.

dated 27 Jany 1697/8.

proved 18 May 1698.

. . . unto the poore of the lower Parrish of Isle Wright County . . . the debts due unto me . . . Discrecon of the Vestry . . .
. . . unto Malachy Thruston of Norfolk County Towne & James ffowler of Isle Wright County Towne all the Rest . . . Sole Executors . . .
—————— Seale.

Deposition of Malachy Thruston Aged 62 yeares or thereabouts.
Deposition of Patrick Cordon Aged 24 years.

JOHN WINFELL . . .

Book 6 f. —(torn)— (Indexed p. 125)—

dated———Mch. 1697/8.

proved 17 May 1698. by Mathew & Sarah Spivee and Katherin Whimfield.

. . . Rich[d] Buntin to him the Said Thomas Whimfield and . . .

. . . wife Sarah Whinfield . . . whole Executrix . . .

. . . Son John Whinfield . . .

. . . Henry Whinfield . . .

. . . Son George Whinfield . . .

. . . my Children hereafter Named—(torn)—gter Eliz[a] holmes, Tho: Whinfield, & Rich[d] Whinfield & Susan Whinfield and Ann—(torn)—Henry Whinfield & George Whinfield & Abigall Whinfield . . .

witnesses:—(torn)—

Jno Whinfell.

JOHN JOHNSTON—(torn)—branch in the County of Norfolk . . .

Book 6 f.—(torn)—(Indexed p. 126)—

dated 1 Mch. 1696.

proved 16 Mch. 1697/8, by *Ana* Wyatt

17 May 1698, by *Tho:* Wilson.

. . . Westerne Branch . . . I say I doe give my land above Specified—(torn)—liam Johnston, I say I give it to them . . . —(torn)—Owne body forever, and if it should happen or please God—(torn)—without heires his Brother Shall have his parte—(torn)—the houses partaining to itt I doe Give to my Son W[m]—(torn)—

. . . between them . . .

. . . wife—(torn)—Executo[rx] . . .

. . . Son William, wth a gunn . . .

. . . Sons John & William to pay to my Daughter Agnes—(torn)—

witnesses:—(torn)—

John Johnston & Seale.
his mar.

WM. CHICHESTER of—(torn)—

Book 6 f.—(torn)—(Indexed p. 126)—

dated 23 Mch. 1697/8.

proved 17 May 1698 by Lemuel Mason & ffrancis Thelaball.

. . . unto my Loving Wife Mary—(torn)—during her naturall life—(torn)—and after her Decease to Son Wm Chichester, and—(torn)— . . .

. . . my Son James Chichester all that tract of land lying—(torn)—now liveth On . . .

. . . all that tract of land that Wm Morley Now lives On bein—(torn)— . . . unto my Son John Chichester —(torn)—

. . . I doe apoint my two Cozens Thomas Mason & Lemu Mason Junr Overseers . . .

. . . wife Mary Chechester my whole & Sole Exec—(torn)—

witnesses:

Limuel Mason, Junr.
ffrancis Thelaball.

Wm Chichester & Seale.

ROBERT BECKFORD of Virginia Marriner . . .

Book 6 f.—(torn)—(not indexed)—

dated 6 July 1698.

proved 20 July 1698 by James P—(torn)— and —

. . . Intended Voyage . . .

. . . to pay Wm Beverly, son of Mr Robert Beverly—(torn)—

—(torn)— mitt home to my loving Sister Martha Beckford, living in Cocking Towne—(torn)—Darthmouth in the Kingdome of England; . . .

. . . this my last will . . . the Power of Atonney Annexed . . .

Yr affectionate ffriend,
Robert Beckfor.d

JOHN CHERRY . . .

Book ——— (Indexed Book 6 p. 130).

—(missing)—

JOHN ETHERIDGE . . .

Book 6 f.—(torn)— (Indexed p. 136).

dated 20 July 1693.

proved 15 Sept. 1698 by Thomas Nash & Thomas Etheredge—(torn)—

. . . to my Son John Etheredge my Plantation which I now live upon—(torn)—

. . . my Next Son James . . . my gunn & my Sword . . .

. . . wife—(torn)—Executrix . . .

. . . my Daughter Elizabeth; . . .

witnesses:—(torn)—

John Etheredge
Mark

LA*WRENCE* or LA*WCER*—(torn)—

Book 6 f.—(torn)—(Indexed p. 143).

dated—(torn)—

proved—(torn)—

. . . In the Name God A—(torn)—

. . . Clark See my—(torn)—

. . . Barthome Clark—(torn)—

. . . Cambell & B—(torn)— . . .

witnesses: Jun̄o Whimfell.
Cathern Whinfell.

—(Signature torn out)—

JOHN ELLITT—(torn)—

Book 6 f.—(torn)—(Indexed p. 153).

dated—(torn)—

proved 18 July—(torn)—by Capt. William Hatton & Wiliam Wenam.

. . . to my *Dear* Sonns all my land Equally to be—(torn)—heires for Ever lawfully begotted of their boddyes.

. . . please to goe from theire Mother.

. . . —(torn)—She Come to Age of twenty yeare.

. . . one poringer a peace . . .

—(torn)—my Wife and my Daughter Rebeckah to them and —(torn)— . . .

witnesses:—(torn)—

the marke of
John Ellitt.

HENRY CULPEPER of the (torn)—Branch of Elizabe. River in the County of Norfolke, . . .

Book 6 f—(torn)—(Indexed p. 155).

dated 25 July 1698.

proved 17 July 1699. by Geo. Vallentine and Roger Hodgis.

. . . to my Sonn Thomas my hundred acres of Land I bought of Jno Crekmore . . . my Gunn . . . a Cutting knife . . .
. . . to the Child my Wife Goes with one Great Chest
. . . I Give my Sonn Thomas to his Uncle Thomas Richireson and if his Decease—(torn)—father or Grand Mother Richinson . . . untill he is Eighteen yeares . . .
. . . to my brother Robert Cullpeper . . . and to his Daughter Elizabeth . . .
. . . I Give my Gr*ind*—(torn)—Thomas Richinson . . .
. . . wife—(torn)—Whole Executrix . . .

witnesses: Roger Hodgis.
Geo. Vallentine
his marke
William Maund.
Thomas Richison.
his marke.

Henry Cullepeper
his marke.

THOMAS CORDING, of the County of Lower Norfolk . . .

Book 6 f. 162.

dated *4* Oct. 1698.

proved 15 Sept. 1699, by Henry Skyner & Wm Southerland.

. . . unto Elizabeth my beloved wife the Plantation whereon I now live during her Naturall Life . . .
. . . unto my Son Thomas Cordin the One halfe of my land when . . . twenty and one yeares . . . known by the name of Buckes plantation . . . affter his Mothers Decease and if my Son Thomas Shall Chose Buckes Land . . . unto my Son William Cordin . . . the other halfe . . . (vizt) the land I now live On affter his Mothers Decease . . . when . . . twenty and One . . . and in Case they boath dye with-

out Issue . . . the Land bee Equally Devided amongst my Daughters after my Wife Decease . . .
. . . wife . . . Sole Executrix . . . .
. . . Mr John Hodges . . . Gordenship of my Children . . .

witnesses: Henry Skynner.
Tho. Hoffler.
William Southerland.

Tho: Cording & Seale.

MALACHY THRUSTON now Resident in the Towne of Norfolk County . . .

Book 6 f. 170.

dated 14 Mch. 1698/9.

proved 15 Nov. 1699, by Capt. Sam^ll Boush & Maj. ffrancis Sayer.

. . . unto my Son John Thruston all my land beginning *from* the pales that *run* in the Garden from the Street down towards the Creeke, and from thence as aforesaid along the Street as farr the S*uwld* pales upwards, wth Dwelling house Shopp house and other houses, on the said land, which is about three Lotts and wharfe, provided my Sonn John Thruston Doe signe and seale a deed when he shall attaine to the age of twenty one yeares, and acknowledge in Open Court unto his Brother my Sonn James. —(torn)—All the Land, that was given to him my Son John Thruston—(torn)—Capt. William Knott deceased, otherways my Son James Thruston—(torn)—three lots and a halfe, out of the forementioned land—(torn)—given to my Son John Thruston.

I do O—(torn)—that my Land, which was Given unto me by Richard J—(torn)—, called by the name of Brushy-Neck bee Ever kept for the use of my Wife and all my Sons, and that, it shall not be sold by any of them.

. . . unto my Sonn Malachy Thruston all the Land from the forementioned pales that Runn Downe the Garden, to the b*ac*—(torn)—of Doctor Thomas Tabors Lott, with the houses thereon, being by Estimation about three lotts of Land . . . likewise . . . my Plantation I lately lived on at Linhav—(torn)—in Princess Ann County, with about fforty Acres more Joyn—(torn)—to it, which I formerly Exchanged for Other with Randolph Lovet —(torn)— . . . also my Seale Cornealian Ring with Negro boy on it—

. . . unto my Daughter Sarah Thruston my Plantation and Marshes att the back called in Currituck in Princess Ann County, . . . which land I formerly bought of John Booth, . . . likewise . . . thirty pounds Sterling, when She Shall attaine the Age of Sixteene . . .

. . . unto my Daughter Jeane Thruston thirty pounds Ster[l] to be given unto her, when . . . Sixteene . . .

. . . my Loving wife Martha . . . full one third part of all my Lotts and Lands before disposed off During her naturall life

. . . unto my kind loving & vert—(torn)—Jeane Porter thirty pounds Sterling . . .

. . . unto my Sister in Law—(torn)—thousand pounds of tobacco . . .

. . . unto my Brother in law ff*l*—(torn)—three thousand pounds of tobacco: & to b*enif*e*itt*—(torn)—ff*ather beckes* Given him, . . .

. . . unto my Sonn John Thruston my—(torn)— named Luke my S*ervce* Pistolls, Holsters and *Crupper*—(torn)—belt Gunns as his Choice, my S*initer* & best, my Ivory hilted—(torn)—and belt . . . when he shall attaine to the Age of twenty One yeares, as alsoe my Signett Ring with my Coat of Arms—

. . . unto my Sonn James Thruston my Negro boy Mathew als B*u*tt, two of my next best Gunns at his Choice and a *Carabine* my Small Rapier & belt . . . at the age of twenty one . . .

. . . unto my Daughter Sarah Thruston. . . one good ffeather bed & bolster two pillowes one of my best Green Ruggs & a payer of good blank*esudes* & a payer of—(torn)—fine Sheets; my sett of green Serge Curtaines Vallaines . . . Sixe pewter dishes, Sixe pewter plates my Sixe thin flatt handled Silver Spoons . . . and my pett bookes my Oaken Chest of Drawers.

. . . unto my Daughter Jeane Thruston . . . at the Age of Eighteen . . .

. . . unto my Daughter Martha Thruston thirty pounds Sterling . . . & my Redd & white new Stuffe Strippe Curtains & Vall*ances,* Sixe pewter Dishes & sixe pewter plates and my great new Silver Spoone Mark[t] G M: . . . at Eighteene . . .

. . . unto my loving and Vertuous Wife Martha Thruston all and Singular the Rest . . .

. . . I appoynt . . . wife Martha Thruston and my loving Sister in law Jeane Porter . . . Sole Execut[rx] . . .

witnesses: ffrancis Sayer.
Roger H*owesen.*
Sam[ll] Boush.

Malachy Thruston.
and Seale.

MOSES SPRING . . .

Book 6 f. 176.

dated 4 July 1699.

proved 15 Jan. 1699/1700, by Thomas Worsley, Mary Worsia & Edward Pull*en*.

. . . . unto my Son Robert my part of the Mill and all the Land which my ffather left to mee . . . to my Wife while Shee lives . . .

. . . . unto my Sons Moses and Aaron two hundred and twenty foure Acres of Land Called by the Name of the bottle ridge to be Equally Divided . . .

. . . . unto my Son John one hundred Acres of Land Called ff*ancies* Ridge . . .

. . . . unto my three Daughters Ann, Sarah and Martha Each of them a thousand pounds of tobacco . . . .

. . unto my Brother Robert a new Serrg Wescote . . .

. . . . unto my well—(torn)—Ann and to her Desposseing.

. . . . —(torn)— Given to my Children it is to be Delivered to them—(torn)—of Eighteene yeares or the day of mariage.

—(torn)—loved Wife Ann Springe whole and Sole—(torn)— . . .

witnesses: Thoma—(torn)—
Mary—(torn)—
her—(torn)—
Edw: O—(torn)—

Moses Spring.

WILLIAM CRAWFORD of Norfolk County in Virginia, Gent.

Book 6 f. 181.

dated 26 Sept. 1699.

proved "16th of March 1699/1700." Mr Walter Cocke—(torn)—omas Cocke.

. . . I give & beq—(torn)—
Crawford all my Est—(torn)—
Quarter part of the—(torn)—
this prsent Voyage out—(torn)—
Comes from London—(torn)—
all the money Lieing in—(torn)—
appeares by an accoump—(torn)—
in the Said Mr Cock's hands—(torn)—
my Said Grandchild untill he Sh—(torn)—

. . . my One Quarter par—(torn)—
. . . unto my well—(torn)—my personall Estate in Virginia (Except in—(torn)—
Ship Hope . . .
Abigaill Crawford on account of their ffather—(torn)—
make and Ordaine my said Wife to be my—(torn)—
my Last Will & Testament . . .
America Likewise what money I ha—(torn)—
Mathews hands in London.
be remaining after the Death of my—(torn)—
betweene my two Grandchildren William & Abig—(torn)—
. . . my Will is that my Servant Anthon—(torn)—
Sent back to Plymouth & his passage payd for—(torn)—
By this my Will I make Constitute & Ordaine m—(torn) — James Cocke of Plymouth my whole & Sole Exec—(torn) —Relating to me in Europe (onely Excepting w—(torn) —Mr Mathews hands in London which I have—(torn)—
. . . Appoint my Trusty—(torn)—Mr Thomas Hodges Mr Samuell Baush Mr H—(torn)—Scot Overseers . . .
Wife Margaret Crawford Should Chance to m—(torn)—William & Abigaill Crawford till the day—(torn)—being of the Age of Eighteene yeares, & in Cas—(torn)— . . .

William Craford & Seale.

. . . ——— GWINN . . .

Book 6 f. 193. (folio taken from Index).

dated 5 Feb. 1696.

proved 15—(torn)—May 1700 (taken from conveyances on same folio).

. . . the plantation whereon I l—(torn)—
. . . halfe the Orchard and—(torn)—
Sd wife the one halfe of my Cattle—(torn)—
house hold Goods During her Natura—(torn)—
I Give unto my Sonn William G—(torn)—Pattent . . .
. . . unto my Grand Sonn Alexander Gwin—(torn)—
I doe appoynt my Sonn William Gwinn my—(torn)— . . .

witnesses: Edward Weston
The marke of
Ann Weston.

—(Signature torn out)—

JOHN CORPEREW of Norfolk County . . .

Book 6 f. 197.

dated 13 gbr 1700.

proved 27 Nov. 1700.

. . . unto my Son John Corperew my Mannor Plan—(torn)—and Lands belonging to it as for as black wallnutt branch: . . . and if he Should Depart this Life without Issue . . . to his brother James Corprew: and Soe to Intale to ye next Survivor.

. . . unto my Son Thomas Corprew all my Lands—(torn)—on the Other Side of black wallnutt branch And Soe to run a So: East Corse j—(torn)—e fork of the Sd. Branch and Soe to the head line . . . and if he should Depart this Life without Issue then to return to the next Survivor.

. . . unto my two Sons: John and Thomas Coprew all my Other Lands to be Equally Devided betweene them and It is my will that my Son Thomas Should have free regrees of the Ceder Swamp: and to have part of the Orchard till he raises one.

. . . unto my Daughter Mary Dickson one Negro . . .

. . . unto my Daughter Grace Holloway one Mollato boy . . .

. . . unto my Daughter Elinor Brough one Cowe . . .

. . . unto my Grand Child Mary Courtney one young Maire . . .

. . . unto my Grand Child Mary Dickson one young maire . . .

. . . unto my Daughter Elinor Broughs fower Children fower young heifers . . .

. . . all the rest of my personall Estate unto my *true* beloved Wife & my two Sons John and Thomas Corperew . . .

. . . Wife and my Son John . . . Sole Execr . . .

witnesses: James Wilson.
Danll Leigh.
Joseph Curling
his marke.

John Corperew & Seale

JOHN ANDEREWS . . .

Book 6 f. 198.

dated 2 Aug. 1700.

proved 15 Nov. 1700; by Eliz[a] Gray & Johana *P*aton.

. . . unto Doctor Richard Bolton of Norfolk County my mare bridle and Sadle and that the said Doctor Richard Boulton Doth owe mee . . .

. . . to Capt. Plumer Bray of Princess Ann County five pounds . . .

. . . unto Alexander Murfry five hundred pounds of toba[c] . . .

. . . unto Sampson Powers three hundred pounds of tobacco . . .

. . . Ordaine Doctor Richard Boulton my Sole Oenly Execu[r] . . .
making voide all wills . . . by me formerly made in Virginia . . .

witnesses: Eliz[a] Gray.
Johana — Paton.
Gett Clanagin.

John Andrews.

THOMAS TABOR of Norfolk . . . of Norfolk County towne Gent . . .

Book 6 f. 201.

dated 8 Jan. 1700.

proved 15 Jan. 1700/1.

. . . unto my Son John Tabor one ——— land Situate . . . in Norfolk Towne which Said Lott I ——— hased of Lemuell Lizmore ajoyning to M[r] Thrustons (Deced) . . . my medicons plate Instruments Steal Instruments with my Great Chest Morters and P*eptells* of all sorts Stills and Seales and waights or any the Else that may be Called or Doeth belonge to Surgery . . .

. . . Mary my wife . . .

. . . bookes Called as followeth (viz[t]) a book Named Hill-*eiacoeus* one a N*otmie* Called Killeia a booke of the Gen[ll] practice of Phisick one booke of a Pothercary Dispensatory One booke more Called *Male* One book being *Rekins Gearbell* One booke more Called Woodells Mate . . . One Gunn . . .

. . . unto my Second Son Thomas Tabor my lott of land Seituate . . . in Norfolk Towne . . . ajoyning to the lott of Lizemores which sd. lott I tooke up the place where I Now live . . . five pounds . . . at the age of Sixteen . . .

. . . unto my Daughter Rosamond Taba one parcell of Land . . . in Norfolk Towne . . . ajoyning unto Cornealius *T*ulys lott Containing About two lotts of Land . . .

. . . unto Mary Tabor my Loving wife first of all her dwelling In the afforesd bequeathed Plantation or in my Dwelling house in towne . . . for the term of her naturall life . . .

. . . my Brick kill Oyster Shells . . .

. . . Plate buttons . . .

. . . my Servt boy Patervis Welch his full time of service . . .

. . . Mary . . . wife . . . Sole Executrix . . .

witnesses: Sam[ll] Boush
Richard Bolton.
Samp[n] Powers.

Thomas Tabor & Seale.

THOMAS CRANKSHAW of Norfolk County Virginia, Putterer . . .

Book 6 f. 205.

dated 20 Aprill 1701.

proved 16 May 1701.

. . . all my moules Tooles and all other instruments belonging to my Trade of a Putterer, and all Tooles belonging to a Glaser, to Cary Heslett . . .

. . . unto the Said Cary Heslett . . . Two hundred and fifty Pound of Putter, made, up in milke basons . . . Dishes and Plaites.

. . . unto Bartholomew Cle*r*ke, my best coate . . .

. . . Cary Heslett . . . Soule Executor . . .

. . . George Newton Gent and Patrick Cordon to over See . . .

witnesses: Barth[o] Clerke.
his marke
Ann Clerke
Sampson Powers.

Thomas Crankshaw and Seale.

GEORGE BALLINTINE *sr* of the Southern Branch of Elizabeth River in the County of Norfolk . . .

Book 6 f. 206.

dated 2 Sept. 1700.

proved 15 May 1702. by John Portlocke & Thomas Nash.

. . . I first make my Two Sonns, Thomas and William Ballintine Joynt Executors . . .

. . . unto my Sonn George, one Putter Dish and the other Putter Dish unto my Sonn John Ballintine . . .

. . . unto my Sonn Alexander Balintine a great table . . .

. . . unto my Sonn Richard Balantine the little table . . .

. . . unto my well beloved Daughter Mary the wife of Roger Hodges a Gold Ring and . . .

. . . unto my Loving Daughter Dorothy wife of John Creekmore a loocking Glass and Candle Coup . . .

. . . unto my Loving Daughter Frances wife of Henry Deale a Silver Dram Coup . . .

. . . unto my Sonn Daniell the best feather bed . . . my great bible . . .

. . . my Grandaughter Mary Hodgis . . . one trunk . . .

. . . unto my Wives grand Daughter Margarett *Macklanan* one Ewe . . .

. . . wife ffrances . . .

. . . Son David bee at age at Sixteen . . .

witnesses: Thomas Nash.
John P—(torn)—ke.

Goerge Balantine and his marke.

JOHN WALLIS . . .

Book 6 f. 206.

dated 20 July 168—(torn)—

proved 16 July 1701.

. . . buried at the Disposing of my Wife Martha Wallis . . .

. . . unto my Sonn John Wallis, all the houseing—(torn)—around, and al the wood Land ground adjoining it to a branch below the f*fisheing*—(torn)—and Soe to a branch runninge off the Creeke, adjoyning to Edward Davis and right—(torn)—the Said Davises house. . . .

. . . unto my Sonn William one *Necke* of Land—(torn)—being Point boundeing on the branch adjoyning to the Little house, Point, and my Sonn—(torn)—*n* the other Side . . .

. . . unto my Sonn Thomas, one Necke of Land Called—(torn)—Necke and So adjoyning to my Sonn Willie So bounding on a branch, where Anthony L*apus*—(torn)—the barr, kill . . .

. . . my Sonn Richard all my Land on the Westerne Side ———ame branch with one hundred and fifty acres of Land, which I bought of Anthony Lopas . . . these Parcels of Land to my foure Sonns . . . Neither of them, shall make any Conveyance or Sale, of Either of there parts unles it be—(torn)—Each other . . .

witnesses: Roger Hodgis.
Mary Hodgis.
her marke.

John Wallis and Seale
his marke.

JOHN DUNN . . .

Book 6 f. 209.

dated 19 Mch. 1700/1.

proved 15 July 2.

. . . unto my loving wife *Amie* Dunn one feather bed . . .
. . . unto my Sonn John Dunn, a small bed . . .
. . . wife . . . Executrix . . .

witnesses: Elizabeth Gray.
Sampson Powers.

John Dunn and Seale.

WILLIAM WHITTHERST of Elizabeth River . . .

Book 6 f. 210.

dated 8 Dec. 1699.

proved 15 July 1702, by John Blandwell & Rich. Whitherst.

. . . all my Land to the Child which my wife is now bigg wth, but my wife to have to the, Soul Prop*ridey* thereof During her life, but if the Child Dies then my land to fall to my two Cosens, (Vitz) Rich[d] and William Whitthorst, my Brother Richards Sonns; . . .

. . . my Brothers and Sisters and for T*orakey* Ridge, where John Blandle Lives, I Doe give to the Said Blandle, During his life Payeing one hundred Pounds Tobacco yearly . . .

. . . wife Jane Whitthurst my Soull Executrix . . .

. . . my two Brothers Rich[d] and James Whittherst Overseers . . .

witnesses: John Edwards.
Rich[d] Whittherst.
William Whitthurst.
John Blandwell.
marke.
William Smith
Humphry Smith
his marke.

W—(torn)—Whitthorst and Seale.

JAMES JACKSON . . .

Book 6 f. 211.

dated ————

proved 16 July 1702 by James Lowrey & Hugh Daniell.

. . . unto my Sonn Simon Jackson a peace of land by the head of Tanners Creeke Called T*ames* quearter, to him and the heires of his body lawfully begotten for Ever this land never to bee Morgaged *or* laid out by any *loveing lac*f by the Space of three yeares . . .

. . . the plantation . . .

. . . I give him againe, the Land now *that* I live upon . . .

. . . to my wife Margra Jackson for as long as Shee Continues a Widow, after that to my Son James Jackson . . .

. . . unto my two Eldest Girles A*fifa* and Mary Jackson a Cow Calfe a peace . . .

. . . to my Daughter *Alise* Jackson a Peutter Bason . . .

. . . to my Daughter Mary Jackson a Peutter Dish . . .

. . . to my Daughter Margarett Jackson, a heffer . . .

. . . to my Wife that peace of Land that is by John *Jordins* that if Shee Should have any Ocasion to Sell it that it may bee Solde, by my wife Margarett Jackson, for the bringeing up of the Children . . .

. . . unto my Daughter Elizabeth Joanes twelve pence . . .

witnesses: James L—(torn)—
Hugh Da—(torn)—
his marke.

James Jackson,
his marke.

THOMAS WILLSON . . .

Book 6 f. 243.
dated 18 Feb. 1701/2.
proved 15 May 1702.

. . . unto my Sonn Thomas Willson one ffeather bed . . . att the Age of twenty one; And the Plantation where I live after the Decease of my Loveing Wife Sarah Willson; . . .

. . . unto my Sonn John one Good new ffeather Bed, . . . at the Age of twenty one years And my Plantation by the Deepe Runn—(torn)—I lived before, where my Sonn Thomas may live when he comes to Age, if he like not to live with his Mother, till my Son—(torn)—Comes to Age to take it himselfe . . .

. . . bequeath my Land towards the Southerne Branch known by the Name of the Wildernesse to be Equally Diveded between my two Sonns, and my Daughter Sarah being one hundred & fifty Acres That is fifty Acres a piece . . .

. . . wife . . . Sole Executrix . . .

. . . if my wife marry, my two sonns Thomas and John shall bee free and for themselves at the Age of Sixteene . . .

. . . my Brother in Law Thomas Cherry . . .

. . . John Johnstone . . .

witnesses: William Johnston.
John Johnston.
Eleazer Tart.

Thomas Willson,
his marke & Seale.

ELNATHAN TART . . .

Book 6 f. 245.
dated 17 Sept. 1701
proved 15 May 1702.

. . . unto my Sonne Thomas Tarte one hundred and fifty Acres of Land joyning upon the Land of Lemuell Powell . . . , and in Case he decease without heires as afores[d] then the said . . . land . . . unto my Sonne Elnathan Tarte . . .

. . . unto my Son The: Tart . . .

. . . unto my Sonne Joseph Tarte . . . when he shall come to the Age of Sixteene . . . if he think good to

Clear and Plant, upon my part of my Land which is not yet Cleared, he may, and live upon it During his Naturall Life, And at the Age of twenty one . . .

. . . Unto my Daughter Mary Tarte . . . Cattle . . . In Nansemond County at the Plantation of William Hay . . .

. . . unto my Daughter Elizabeth Tarte . . .

. . . unto my Grand Daughter Mary Queene . . . said Mary's ffather John Queene . . .

. . Unto my Sonne Enoch Tarte the Plantation where I live, being one hundred & fifty Acres . . . and in Case of Defeat of Such—(torn)—Then to my Sonne Joseph Tarte . . .

. . . my Brother Eleazer Tarte . . .

. . . my Loving Wife Alice Tarte . . .

. . . Wife and Sonn Enock Tarte my whole and Sole Executrix and Executo^r . . .

witnesses: Joseph Hodges.
Henery *Givvins.*
marke.
Eleazer Tarte.

Elnathan Tarte & Seale.

—(torn)—**HATTON,** of Eliz: County . . .

Book 6 f. 257.
dated—(torn)—
proved—(torn)—by Richd Webb—(torn)—
I Doe Give and bequeathe unto—(torn)—
Hannah Hatton the Plantation—(torn)—
& Orchards & Still for her Life but—(torn)—
or ff*ee*male then the s^d Child To ha—(torn)— . . .
the s^d Child Dye of my Wife Hannah—(torn)—
Decease to goe to francis Wright—(torn)— . . .
I Doe alsoe give unto my Grand Son—(torn)— . . .
I Doe Give unto my Wife—(torn)— . . .
Daughter Ann Gregory A—,torn)— . . .
Hatton & my Daughter Ann g—(torn)—
Wife Hannah Hatton & my d—(torn)—Gregory—(torn)—
Execut^rx es To see this my las—(torn)— . .

witnesses: Henery Bowes.
John L—(torn)—
Richard—(torn)—
Ann—(torn)—

John Hatton & s—(torn)—

LEMUELL MASON of Elizabeth River pish in the County of Norfolk, Gent. . . .

Book 6 f. 258.

dated—(torn)—

proved 15 Sept. 1702.

. . . unto my Loveing Wife Ann the Plantation
—(torn)—on I now live for and during her naturall
—(torn)—that is to say, that one hundred Acres of
—(torn)—sd by my ffather ffrancis mason Deceased
—(torn)—art of the produce of the Orchard on the
—(torn)—where I now live which said third part
—(torn)—and Bequeath to my Sonn Thomas Mason. . . .
—(torn)—my three Sonns Thomas—(torn)— . . .
—(torn)—& George Mason or to Either of—(torn)— . . .
—(torn)—to my Said Sonn Thomas Mason all the
—(torn)—*terrest* that I have to the timber upon a prcell
—(torn)—By Mr James Thelaball, and my Selfe, lying at
—(torn)—alsoe twenty Cutts of good boards & timber from
—(torn)—ich I purchased of George Kemp Deceased . . .
I Give and bequeath Unto—(torn)—
Daughter Alice the Widdow of—(torn)— . . .
I Give and Bequeath to Mr—(torn)—
Elizabeth on Shill—(torn)—
I Give and Beq—(torn)—
Margaret—(torn)—
I Give and B—(torn)—
Ann *lenn*—(torn)— . . .
Brother Thelaball Lan—(torn)— . . .
Ordaine my two Sonns Th—(torn)— . . .
whole and Sole Executrix of—(torn)—
—(torn)—my Sister Elizabeth Thelaball . . .
witnesses: —(torn)—

Lemuell Mason & Seale.

ARTHUR MOSELEY—(torn)—

Book 6 f. 270.

dated—(torn)— *1* Febry. 1700.

proved—(torn)—1702/3.

. . . my Executrix . . .
I Give and Bequeath Unto my Wife Ann—(torn)—
whereon I now Live during the time &—(torn)—

Life and after her Decd: I Give the s[d] La—(torn)—Joseph Moseley to him & to his heires for Ever . . .

. . . my Sonn Benj—(torn)—

. . . my Sone William—(torn)—

. . . my Sonn Arth*ur*—(torn)—

. . . my Sonn Edward—(torn)—

. . . Sonn George—(torn)—

. . . to my Daughter Mary Wife—(torn)— . . .

. . . to my Daughter Susan—(torn)—Pierce—(torn)—

. . . Sonns Joseph; Benjamine, Amos, Anthony—(torn)—

witnesses: John—(torn)— llis.
John—(torn)—ddon.
Joseph Bayly.

—(torn)—Moseley & Seale.

THEODORE TAYLOR . . .

Book 6 f. 271.

dated 7 Feb—(torn)—

proved 15—(torn)—

. . . my Executrix . . .

. . . unto my Son William Taylor that

—(torn)—I now live on . . .

—(torn)—my Said Son William Taylor ffifty acres

—(torn)—y bounding on James—(torn)—ens Land

—(torn)—of Murdens line . . .

—(torn)—John Nicholson ffifty acres of

—(torn)—, the s[d] Nich[o]lson to Enjoy

—(torn)—y Deed to him & to his heires for . . .

—(torn)—all my Land over the

—(torn)—Murdens & John Nicholson Land & ffifty acres of Land by—(torn)—

bounding on the Green—(torn)— . . .

. . . unto my—(torn)—Ann Taylor During her Naturall Life And after her d—(torn)—Divided among my Children . . .

. . . wife Ann Taylor my Sole Executrix . . .

witnesses: James Wilson.
The mark of
James Wardein,
The mark of
Walter Curlin.

Theodor—(torn)—

(Taken from a Loose Scrap of the Will torn off).

. . . unto my Son Thomas Taylor—(torn)—

Swampp lying between James—(torn)—

—(torn)—**GILLIGAN** . . .

Book 6 f. 285.

dated 25 Feb. 1700.

proved—(torn)—March 1703/4, by—(torn)—

proved 16 Aug. 1703, by Thomas Nash—(torn)—

. . . to my Br—(torn)—
. . . to Thomas Matheys—(torn)—
. . . by my Sd. Brother . . .
. . . John Portlock shall Execute my Will . . .

witnesses: Thos Nash.
Patrick Holloway.
his marke
Catherine Holloway.
her marke.

ff—(torn)—do Gilligan & Seale.

WILLIAM JOHNSON . . .

Book 7 f. 26.

date 7 July 1703.

proved 15 Mch. 1703/4.

. . . unto my two Sons (viz) James and William Johnson all my Land to be Equally Divided betweene them, when they shall Come to the Age of Eighteene yeares old. But if It please God that, that Child which my Wife is now burthened with Should be a Sonn, . . . he shall have the one third part of my Land . . .

. . . that my Son James have my Mannor Plan*tation* after the Dec*ed*. of my present Loving Wife Mary. . . . my present Loving Wife my whole and Sole Executrix . . .

witnesses: Nathall Ludgall
his marke.
Willm Dafnall
his marke.
Mathew Spevy.

William Johnson & Seale.

MATTHEW CASEWELL of Norfolk County . . .
Book 7 f. 29.
dated 19 May 1703.
proved 16 Mch. 1703/4.

. . . Unto my Youngest Son Mathew Casewell . . . the Land or Plantation whereon I now Dwell; With *an* hundred Acres of Land belonging thereto, and my Mill stones betwixt him & his Brother Jabezes Casewell: Butt if my Son Matthew Casewell Die without heires or Issue that then this Plantation wth the hundred acres of Land appertaining thereunto to fall unto my son Jabezes the next heire.

. . . unto my Son Jabezes Casewell . . . an hundred Acres of Land Joyning unto the Gum Swamp: But if he Dies wth heires or haveing any Issue that then the hundred acres of Land to fall to his Brother William Casewell.

. . . unto my Son William Casewell one hundred acres of Land Lying on the Eastern side of my Plantation Lying betweene the hundred acres of Land I Gave unto my Son Matthew Casewell But if my Son W^{m} die wthout heires or having Issue that then the hundred acres of Land to fall unto my Daughter Jane, (or *is* any way is undutifull unto his Parents till such time comes at yeares then I Matthew Casewell Cutts the s^{d} Willm Casewell off with twelve pence,) and her heires Lawfully begotten:

. . . unto my Daughter Jancel Casewell . . . An hundred & ffifty acres *of* of Land Lying betwixt St*anhop* Butts & Benjamine Hollowells; but if she die wthout heires or having Issue that then the hundred & ffifty acres of Land to fall unto her sister Constant Casewell.

. . . unto my Daughter Constant Casewell and her heires Lawfuly begotten of her body the hundred acres of Land wth I bought of William Lewis; but if she dies wthout heires or Issue to fall unto the next heire.

. . . unto my Daughter Martha . . . twelve pence . . .

. . . unto my Oldest Son ffrancis Casewell . . . twelve pence . . .

. . . Coul*t* w^{cb} I bought of Walter Curling . . .

. . . unto James Wilson one young mare . . . when he comes at yeares . . .

. . . my wife . . .

. . . Exec^{rs} . . . Willaby M*areland* and Thomas Corphew . . .

witnesses: John Edmonds.
Henry Parkinson.

Mathew Casewell.
his marke and Seale.

JAMES JORDAN &c . . .

Book 7 f. 34½.

dated 10 Feb. 1703/4.

proved 15 May 1704.

. . . unto Mary Porter the Daughter of Sam[ll] Porter . . . one Ewe . . . .

. . . my Wife Jane Jordan all my Personall Estate Dureing her Naturall Life, And after her Dece[d] to be Equally Divided betweene William Bottons Children and Ann Taylors Children . . .

witnesses: Robert Drisdrall.
Tho: Hobgood.
marke
John Lovina.

James Jordan & Seale.

JUDITH RISE of Norfolk County . . .

Book 7 f. 52.

dated 8 June ——.

proved 15 Sept. 1704.

. . . my Sonn John Joyce my whole & Sole Executor & Trustee . . .

. . . to my Daughter Eliz. Maning all my Wearing Clothes Except Some y[t] I shall give to my Daught[r] Taylor & one Gold Ring . . .

. . . to my Grand Daught[r] Eliz. Maning one young Ewe . . . to Nicholeis Manning for y[e] use of his Daught[r] . . .

. . . unto my Daughter Judeth Taylor Nine yards of black Crape . . .

. . . to Joseph Pearl the boy w[ch] I brought up, one young Cow . . . to y[e] Age of twenty one . . . to his Sister Elizabeth Jones one Sow . . .

witnesses: Jno. Gibson, mark.
Eliz. *Gwinn*, mark
Jno. Willis

Judith Rise & Seale.

ffRANCIS THELABALL of the County of Norfolk . . .

Book 7 f. 73.

dated 12 Dec. 1702.

proved 15 Mch. 1704/5

. . . unto my Son James Thelaball . . . the plantation where I doe Live with two hundred acres of Land *there* Containing.

. . . to my Son Dyer thelaball the plantation where I did live with two hundred Acres of Land their containing.

. . . to my Son ffrancis Thelaball . . . One hundred Acres of Land in broad Neck & Soe up to the Swamp.

. . . to my Son Lemuel Thelaball . . . the Neck of Land on the other Side of the Greate branch bounding on Hugh Purdys Line here be itt one hundred acres more or Less.

. . . to my Daughter Sarah Thelaball Eight yards of good Serge . . .

. . . to my Loving wife Margery Thelaball the best bed . . . also the old Negro Wooman Call bess after my Mothers Decease . . .

. . . to my youngest Son one Cow . . . when hee Comes to . . . twenty one . . .

. . . to my Son James Thelaball the Negro . . . affter My Mothers Decease, my Son . . . paying to his Mother in Law the Sum of twenty Shillings yearly her widohood.

. . . Son James Thelaball my Execur and my Lovein wife Margery Thelaball Joyntly Executrix . . .

witnesses: Arthur Blake.

ffrancis Thelaball & Seale.

EDWARD DAVIS Senr of ye County of Norfolke . . .

Book 7 f. 76.

dated 8 Oct. 1703.

proved 15 May 1705.

. . . buried at ye discretion of my wife . . .

. . . my wife bee the full Sole Executrix . . .

. . . my Son Edward Davis have after his Mother decease my best bed . . . & my Grandson Edward Davis my Gun . . .

. . . the rest of my Estate after my wifes Decease be equally divided amongst my five children . . .

witnesses: Henry Perkinson
Edwd Davis, Junr.

Edwd Davis Senr & Seale.
his marke.

JOSEPH HOLLOWELL . . .

Book 7 p. 88.

dated 5 May 1705.

proved 15 gb^r^ 1705.

. . . unto Joseph Small ye Son of John Small all my Land Northerly from ye little bridges to ye red oake branch *quite* acrosse my Land . . . , & he come to age . . .

. . . unto my well beloved wife Grace halfe the remaining part of my Land & halfe my plantation & other conveniences thereunto during her life . . .
ing part of my Land & plantation . . . and after her . . .
Mothers decease to have the part that was given her Mother . . . & for want of such heires to John Hollowell ye Son of Thomas Hollowell . . . if noe Such heires to Thomas Hollowell the Son of Henry Hollowell . . .

. . . a Cow unto Mary Dixon ye daughter of Jno. Dixon . . .

. . . unto John Dixon Junr my pistoles & holsters . . . & Edward Dixon my Sword . . .

witnesses: James Willson Junr.
George Burgesse.
Adam Macoy.

Joseph Hollowell (S).

. . . unto my Brother John Hollowell two Steers . . .
. . . wife Grace my whole & Sole Executrix . . .
. . . 5th of May 1705.
. . . "The additionall part proved . . . 15th of g^br^ 1705"
. . . unto my daughter in Law Mary Courtney the remaine-

JOHN BOWERS of the western Branch of Elizabeth River . . .

Book 7 p. 98.

dated 26 Jan. 1705/6.

proved 15 Feb. 1705/6.

. . . unto my Son John Bowers a plantation of fifty Acres of Land more or Less known by the name of Nitting *Saryes* with a Nursery of Aple Trees now Standing on the plantation I now live on . . . the Said Land being already bounded with a Surveyers Mark.

. . . unto my Son Robert Bowers at tract of Land *Ly* Containing fifty Acres of Land be it more or Less known and Called by the Name of Deep nick being already marked and bounded as aforesaid . . .

. . . unto my Son James Bowers the plantation I now live on being Sixty Six Acres more or Less after the decease of my present Loveing wife Susanna Bowers not that She Shall hinder or molest my Son James from Liveing on the sd. Land when he Shall Come to age, the Said plantation being Marked and bound as aforesaid . . .

. . . if please God that every one of my Sons Viz John Robert or James Should dye without heires of theire body as aforesaid that then the Deep Nick being the Midle part of my Land Shall be equally devided between the two Survivors . . .

. . . my Children Viz John Elizabeth Robert Judah Susana and James Bowers . . . as they Shall Come to age . . .

. . . wife Susana Bowers to be my whole and Sole Executrix . . .

witnesses: Tho. price, by his marke.
Henry Whinfield.
John Bowers Jun[r]
Mathew Spivey.

John Bowers and Seale.

MORRICE VEALE of the County of Low[r] Norfolk planter . . .

Book 7 p. 100.

dated 28 June 1705.

proved 15 Feb. 1705/6.

. . . Wife Elizabeth and my Son William Executors . . .

. . . my Son Morrice and my Son John . . . when the Shall attaine to the age of nineteen . . .
. . . my Six Children my Son William and my daughter Mary and my daughter Elizabeth Mayson Morris and my Son John and my daughter T*enny* . . .

witnesses: John Tully.
The marke of
Mary Tully
John Willis.

Morris Veall & Seal.

THOMAS WALLICE of Norfolk Town in Norfolk . . .
Book 7 p. 102.
dated 29 Octo. 1705.
proved 15 Feb. 1705/6.

. . . my house in this Towne be repaired and mended . . .
. . . unto my Son William . . . my house in this Town and my Plantation Joyning uppon the Town and if my Son William Should die before he Comes to Age then the house and Plantation to fall to my Son Thomas . . .
. . . my Land in the Norwest Woods be Sould for my Son Thomas . . . when he Comes to Age.
. . . my Three Rings be given unto my Son William one to my Son Thomas and one to my brother William Wallis.
. . . my five Children . . .
. . . brother William Wallis hole and Sole executor . . .

witnesses: Thomas Sayer.
Henry Perkinson
John Joyce

Thomas Wallis & Seal.

JOHN GRIFEN of the County of Norfolk . . .
Book 7 p. 104.
dated 19 May 1705.
proved 15 Feb. 1705/6.

. . . wife Isabell Griffin . . . Sole Executrix . . .
. . . to my Son Thomas Griffen a parcell of Land Lying on the eastward Side of the Reedy branch belonging to this Land where now I live on In Alexander Menf*re*ys pattent . . .

. . . all my estate holy to my Loveing wife Isabell Griffen dureing her Life and afterwards to be equally devided amongst my Children.

witnesses: Arthur lake.
Cuthen Jones
her mark
Mary Smith
her mark

John Griffen & Seal.

RICHARD CHURCH . . .

Book 7 p. 106.

dated 5 Jan. 1705.

proved 15 Feb. 1705/6.

. . . to my daughter Sarah Nichols one feather bedd . . .
. . . to my daughter Abigall Church a feather bedd . . .
. . . my wife Naturall Life . . .
. . . to my daughter Patience Church a feather bedd . . .
. . . Nott to transport the Said Negroe out of this County . . .

witnesses: Mathew Godfrey.
William Nicholson.
John H*ebdo*n.

(Codocil):
. . . to my Son Joseph Church my Negroe . . . .
. . . to my Grandson Richard Nichols . . . Negroe . . . and alsoe I doe further give to my Said Son all my Lands that I have in this County or elsewhere . . . not debaring my wife to have her thirds of all my Lands during her . . .
. . . to my daughter Corbin a Negroe . . .
. . . my Grand daughter Ann Sally and after her death to Leaddy Sally . . .
. . . 5 Feb. 1705.

(Codicil):
. . . to my Daughter Ann Trevathan two pewter dishes . . .
. . . unto my daughter Mary Murrow a third part of my Sloope . . .
. . . to my Grand Daughter Led*dae* Butt a young horse . . .

. . . to my Grand Daughter Ledda Sally Six good new Napkins . . .

. . . to my Loveing wife Elizabeth Church all my other estate . . . my Executrix . . . and my Son Joseph my Executor . . .

. . . 5 Feb. 1705 . . .

(Codicil):

. . . 6 Feb. 1705 . . .

ANN MASON of Elizabeth river parish in ye County of Norfolke Gentlewoman . . .

Book 7 p. 117.

dated 30 Octo. 1705.

proved 15 M^r^ch 1706/5. by Coll. Thomas Willoughby & Mrs Ann Porter.

Recorded 22 M^rch^ 1706/5.

. . ye death of my decd. husband Coll. Lemuel Mason . . .

. . . Christian buriall at ye discretion of my executors hereafter Named or at ye descretion of my three Sonnes Thomas Lemuell & George Mason.

. . unto my Loveing Daughter ffrancis Sayer ye Sume of Seven pounds ten Shillings . . . without being accountable to her husband . . .

. . . unto my Loveing Daughter Alice Boush . . . w^th^out being accountable to her husband . . .

. . . unto my Loveing daughter Mary Cock . . . without being accountable to her husband . . .

. . . unto my Loveing daughter Dinah Thorowgood . . .

. . . unto my Sonne Thomas Mason . . . the paire of andjrons that are in ye Chimney where I commonly are my Selfe, my decd. husband promising ye Same to my Said Son Thomas above twenty years past.

. . . my Seale Skinnd trunke . . .

. . . said three Sonns . . . Sole Executo^rs^ . . .

witnesses: Tho: Willoughby.
Elizabeth Newton.
Ann Porter.

Ann Mason & Seale.

DENNIS MACOY Senr of ye Southern branch of Elizabeth river . . .

Book 7 p. 118.
dated 4 Feb. 1705.
proved 15 Mch. 1706/5.
Recorded 22 Mch. 1706/5.

. . . all my estate both reall & personall to my Sonn Dennis Macoy Jun[r] . . . my whole And Sole Executo[r] . . .

witnesses: Jn[o] Edwards.
Edw: Etheridge, m[r]k.
Rich[d] Chapman. m[r]k.

Dennis Maccoy. Seale.

ROGER BRYAN Sen[r] of County of Norf[o], Virg[a] . . .

Book 8 f. 14.
dated 1 May 1708.
proved 15 June 1708.

. . . my loving Son Roger Bryan Jun[r] to be my whole & Sole Exec[r] & trustee of my said Estate . . .

. . to my daughter Dorothy Wakefield one Shilling . . .

. . . to my Loving Son Roger Bryan . . . all & Singular my Lands & tenem[ts] goods & Chattles with all & every part & parcell of my Estate both reall & personall, Except the fifty acres of Land bought of Tho: Parker to him my s[d] Son Roger Bryan & his heirs forever.

witnesses: W[m] Powell Sen[r]
John Collins.
Joseph Powell.

Rog[r] Bryan Sen[r]. Seale.

WILLIAM SUGGS of Norfolk County yeoman . . .

Book 8 f. 23.
dated 10 Feb. 1704.
proved 16 Aug. 1708.

. . . unto my Eldest Son William Sugg my planta*con* . . . w[ch] I now Dwell on w[th] halfe my Land including my planta*con* . . .

. . . unto my Son Thomas Sugg y[e] other halfe of my Land . . . in Case my Son William Trouble or Mollest my Son Thomas in his part of my Land given as afor[e]sd. y[t] Then and in that Case I give . . . my Manner plan ta*con* w[th] y[e] one halfe of my Land y[e] planta[t]ion to be In Cluded . . . to my Son Thomas . . .

. . . personable Estate . . . Equally devided Betwixt my Loving wife Mary and my Six Children (viz) William Thomas Joseph Mos[es] my Sons and my Two daughters Margett and Sarry . . my Three sons Thomas Joseph and Moses receive there part of my Estate at y[e] age of Eighteene . . . my two daughters . . . there parts . . . att . . . Sixteene or day of Marriage . . .

. . . my Son William Suggs and my brother George Suggs my full and whole Exec[rs] . . .

witnesses: Lem. Wilson.
Joseph Suggs.
George Suggs.
marke
Dan[ll] Davis,
marke

William Suggs and Seale.

Post Script.

. . . I give This old plantation to my Son W[m] and y[e] next ajoyning over y[e] branch to my son Thomas and y[t] I bought of my brother Joseph I give to my Son Joseph . . .

. . . my wife & her two Children . . .

27 Octo. 1706.

Teste: William Maund.
Thomas willowby.
marke.

William Sugg.
(By Tho. Willoughby).

ROGER KELLSALL Minister of Elizabeth River parrish . . .

Book 8 f. 51.
dated *14* Sept. 1708.
proved 15 Feb. 1708/9.

. . . to my Loveing wife Katherine Kellsall all the Land I am now possest with in Virginia . . .

. . . my Negro boy Samson which I give to my Son John Kellsall when he attaine to the age of Sixteen

. . . upon this condition faithfully and Truly gett or Cause to begott a True and perfect Cop*ia* off the Last will and Testament of ye Reverand M[r] Roger Kellsall formerly Minister of Royden deceast in which the S[d] Roger Killsall Decd gave & bequeathed to me a Certaine Estate knowne by y[e] name of B*a*ers S[t] Marys Lying and adjoyning Nigh unto Colchester as alsoe an other Estate Lying in *N*ayland Cornall which was left to me and my heirs for Ever whereof my Son John Kelsall is True and Lawfull heir intaile upon him and his heirs male Lawfully begotten for Ever: . . .

. . . wife holely and Solely Executrix . . .

. . . Coll James Wilson and W[m] Wilkins. . . . overseers . . .

witnesses: Lem[ll] Wilson.
Willis Wilson.
W[m] Wilkins.
James Cumming.

Roger Kelsall. Seal.

ROBERT GO*DIN* of Norfolk County . . .

Book 8 f. 64.

dated 7 March 1708/9.

proved 16 May 1709.

. . . unto my Son in Law Tho[s] Collings one heifer . . .

. . . to my wife Eliz[a] Gooden all and Singular y[e] rest of my whole Estate . . . Leaving my wife whole and Sole Executrix . . . Dureing her naturall Life . . . that after . . . my Sonne in Law Tho: Collings shall be y[e] Sole heire . . . .

witnesses: Andrew Colling.
Phillip E*ddens*.
Thomas Powell.

Robert Gooden & Seale.

JOHN THRUSTON now resident in the Towne of Norfolk County . . .

Book 8 f. 92.

dated 1 July 1709.

proved 15 Nov. 1709 by Mr. Robert Tucker.

" 15 Dec. 1709 by Mrs. Elizabeth Thruston.

. . . unto my Dear and Loving Mother Mrs. Matha: Thruston Six pounds Sterl: To buy her a Suite of Morning Cloathes . . .

. . . unto my Loveing and Virtuous wife Margaret Thruston all the rest of my personall Estate . . .

. . . unto my Loveing brother Malachy Thruston my Negroe man called Luke to be possessed with him when he shall attaine to ye age of Twenty one . . .

. . . Mother Mrs. Matha Thruston . . . Sole Executrix . . .

witnesses: Robert Tucker.
Eliz^th^ Thruston. Jno Thruston and Seale.

THOMAS WAKEFIELD Senr . . .

Book 8 f. 130.

dated 2 Dec. 1709/10.

proved 15 Feb. 1709 by Jno Warde & Elizabeth Tart.

" *15* Mch 1909/10.

. . . my plantation unto my Loveing wife Sarah Wakefield During her Naturall Life and after . . . my Sone Edward Wakefield shall have itt . . . he paying unto his brothers Jno and Joseph Wakefield Six hundred pounds of Tobacco, with Cask a piece . . .

. . . unto my Sone Jno Wakefield my Gun . . .

. . . unto my Son Edward Wakefield one Little Gun . . .

. . . unto my Son Joseph a Sword . . . an Iron pestle . . . to be D D to him at the age of Eighteen . . .

. . . unto my Daughter Elizabeth Wakefield one Cow . . . after her Mother Decease . . . and one Lineng wheele . . . at ye age of Sixteen . . .

. . . unto my Daughter Sarrah Wakefield one Cow . . . after her Moothers Decease . . .

. . . unto my Sone Thomas Wakefield one Cow . . . after his Mothers Decd . . .

. . . wife . . . Sole Executrix . . .

witnesses: Jno Warde.
Liz^a^ Tarte. The Marke of
Eleazar Tarte. Thos Wakefield & Seale.

EDWARD HEWS Senr of ye Southerne branch of Elizabeth River Parrish in ye County of Lower Norfolk . . .

Book 8 f. 131.
dated 16 Aug. 1709.
proved 19 *Feby* 1709.

. . . unto my Loveing Son Edward Hews three hundred Acres of Land being part of a pattent of four hundred & forty Acres of Land bearing Date ye 20th Day of November 1683 ye Said Land I now Live upon & Lying on ye North Side of paradice Creek Soe Called . . . butt if he my Sone Edward Should Die withoutt heire Male or ffemale . . . fall to my Loveing Sonn Elijah Hews . . . the Said three hundred Acres of Land Running up ye Maine Runn & Soe up to my Greatt Tarkile & Soe along to Whinfields Line . . . this my Intaillmentt of ye Land aforesd I Doe hereby Declare itt is my Intent and will that my Sone Edward make Noe Lease Sale nor Morgae . . . for above ye Space or time of Seven years at one time . . .

. . . to my Loveing Son Elijah Hews four hundred Acres of Land Situate Being Lying (vizt) beginning upon y^{t} South Side of a Creek Called Paradice being part of a pattent bearing Date ye 20th of November 1683 & Soe Runing a Long Richard Lewelline his Line & Runing Likewise A Long ye Line of ye Land Given before to my Sonn Edward till he will have Enoufe to make Good his four hundred . . . butt & if he my Sonn Elijah Should Die without any Such heirs that then itt Shall fall & Returne to my Son Sollomon . . .

. . . to my Loveing Sone Sollomon Hews Eighty five Acres of Land being ye one halfe part of a pattent of one hundred & Seventy Acres & bareing Date Twenty first Day of Aprill 1690 ye Said Land being on the North Side of paradice Creek & Commonly known by ye name of ye Landingfield . . . for want of Such heirs, to fall & returne to my Son Elijah Hews. . . .

. . . to my Daughter Hester Hews Eighty five Acres of Land itt being part of a patt. of 170 Acres bareing Date ye 21th of Aprill 1690 Runing up towards a branch Commonly Called Hickory Branch . . . want of such . . . to my Sone Elijah Hews . . .

. . . to my three Sons Edward Sollomon & Elijah Hews a Certaine percell of Swamp Land bineing binding on Lows & Munns & Scott & veall & winfield Containing aboutt three hundred Acres . . .

. . . all ye Rest of my Lands that is Left & not given away before . . . Shall be Sould by my Executor . . .

. . bequeath Daughter Hester one bible . . .

. . . to my Two sons Sollomon & Elijah Hews all ye Rest of my bookes . . .

. . . to my Daughter Vasthie Hews one feather bed . . .

. . . my three Guns . . .

. . . gratte Pewter Tankard . . .

. . . my five Children Edward Sollomon Elijah Vasthie & Hester all my pewter . . .

. . . to bind . . . to a good . . . trades man my Son Elijah . . .

. . . my Loveing Son Edward Hews . . . Sole Executor . . .

witnesses: Richd Lewelling.
Edward Lewelling.
John Vallentine.

Edward Hews & Seale.

ROBERT ROSE . . .

Book 8 f. 133.

dated 3 Sept. 1698.

proved 15 Feb. 1709 by Joseph Hodges & Jno Rose.
" 15 *June* 1710 by Abraham Bruce

. . . unto my Sonn William Rose . . . Lying on ye North Side of ye plantation whereon I Now Live being one hundred & Twenty Eight Acres . . .

. . . unto my Sone Jno Rose one hundred and twenty Eight Acres of Land Lying on ye Southwest of ye plantation whereon I now Live . . .

. . . unto Son George Rose . . . one hundred & twenty nine Acres of Land ye manor plantation whereon now I Liveth after my beloved wife Martha Rose Decease . . . And as for ye Rest . . . unto my beloved wife . . . During her Naturall Life and afterwards to be Equally Devided between my three Sons William Jno George & my Daughter Mary Carny ye wife of John Carney . . .

witnesses: Joseph Hodges.
William Wright.
Jno Rose.
Abraham Bruce.

Robert Rose & Seale.

WALTER SIKES of Norfolk County . . .

Book 8 f. 142.

dated 9 Nov. 1709.

proved 15 March 1709. by Henry Shaller & Jn° White.
15 May 1710 by Henry Butt Sen[r]

. . . unto three of my Sons that is to Say James Sikes, W[m] Sikes & Joseph Sikes one hundred & twenty Acres of Land beginning at y[e] Siprous Swamp & Soe Runing to y[e] head to be Equally Devided Amongst my aforesd three Sons & not to be Exposed to Saile Excepting from one to y[e] other . . .

. . . unto my Son Costin Sikes . . .

. . . unto my Daughter Eliz[a] Sikes one Cow . . .

. . . wife Jane Sikes & my Son James Sikes my full & whole Executrix & Executor . . .

witnesses: Henry Shaller.
Jn° White.
marke
Henry Butt.

Walter Sikes. Seale.

WILLIAM TUCKER of Norfolk County . . .

Book 8 f. 152.

dated 4 Feb. 1709/10.

proved *15 May 1710.*

. . . to my beloved wife Ellinor Tuck all my Lands & Giveings & Worldly Goods to y[e] Said Ellener Tuck*er* my wife . . .

witnesses: Tho. fanshaw, marke
Rich[d] Etheridge
Marmerduck Etheridg.
Daniell Savill.

William Tucker. Seale.
marke

JOHN JOYCE, of Norfolk County Virginia . . .
Weaver . . .

Book 8 f. 158.

dated 18 June 1707.

proved 15 May 1710.

. . . to my Daughter Mary Ivee my bed and furniture & one Deale box . . .

. . . to my Son David one Cow & Calfe & one Muskett well fixed and one pair of pistolls and Holsters . . .

. . . to my Son Jn° Joyce one Cow . . .

. . . to my Son Edward Joyce one Cow . . .

. . . to my Loveing wife Rachell . . . Sole Executrix . . .

witnesses: Nicholas Maning.
Richd Lewelling.
Jn° Willis.

John Joyce and Seale.

JOHN GODFREY of Norfolk County . . .

Book 8 f. 160.

dated 5 Aug. 1708.

proved 15 May 1710 by Richard Ball, Richard Butt Junr and Samp. Powers.

. . . the Plantation whereon I Now Live on to my well beloved wife Mary Godfrey During her Naturall Life; provided Shee please to Dwell on ye Same and after her Decease . . . unto my Loveing Son Matthew Godfrey . . . and for want of Such heirs to ye next of kinn & Soe from Generation to Generation for Ever . . .

. . . unto my Said Son Matthew Godfrey that parcell of Land that I have joyning upon this plantation (before bequeathed) that I Now Live on which Land was bought of Mr William Portten by me and my brother Mathew Godfrey . . . and for want of such . . .

. . . to my Said Son Matthew Godfrey five hundred acres of Land belonging To Mossy Neck Pattent During my said wife Mary Godfrey's Life And after ye Decease of my wife Mary . . . to my Son William Godfrey . . . and for want of Such heirs To ye Next of kinn . . . Excepting a percell of Land Called Long point . . . bequeath unto my Said Mathew Godfrey . . .

. . . And what Land I have belonging to ye branches of the Northwest River To be Equally Devided between my Said two Sons Mathew Godfrey and William Godfrey . . . Matthew . . . Shall have that part adjoyning To Henry Halstead . . .

. . . To my Daughter Annie Godfrey . . . negro . . .
. . . unto my Daughter *Anne* Godfrey one feather bed . . .
. . . unto my Daughter Anne & To my Daughter Amie one Acre of Land in Norfolke Towne being Two Lotts to be Devided between them my Daughter Ann To have ye fore Street Lott and my Daughter Amie To have ye Back Street Lott . . .
. . . unto my Son Matthew ye Mill in my one Dwelling Hous after my wife Marry her Decease . . .
. . . unto my Daughter Mary the wife of James Whithurst Two Ewes . . .
. . . wife Mary my Sons Matthew & William . . . Sole Executors . . .

witnesses: Daniell Godfrey
Moses Ball
Samp^n^ Power

John Godfrey & Seale.

NOTE.—It is the intention of the abstractor of the foregoing wills to follow the above work by a second Volume, covering the years 1710 to 1800.

LIST OF WILLS

1637-1710

Adams, John, p. 86.
Aldridge, Francis, p. 58.
Andrews, John, p. 175.
Andrews, Wm. p. 47.
Ashall, George, p. 37.
Axstell, John, p. 99.
Axwell, Thomas, p. 59.

Bachelor, Richard, p. 84.
Ballentine, George Sen[r], p. 177.
Banks, John, p. 46.
Barley, Robert, p. 84.
Barrnes, Peter, p. 9.
Barton, Walter, p. 135.
Bass, Samuel, p. 130.
Bass*n*et, Wm., Sen[r], p. 112.
Beckford, Robert, p. 167.
Bell, Alexander, p. 124.
Bigg, Jabiz, p. 140.
Bigg, John, p. 159.
Blake, Robt., p. 37.
Blanch, Elizabeth, p. 77.
Blanch, Thomas, p. 43.
Bouling, Richard, p. 31.
Boulton, John, p. 6.
Bouring, John, p. 54.
Bowers, John, p. 189.
Bradley, George, p. 156.
Branker, Nar[th], p. 97.
Bray, Robert, p. 77.
Bridge, Hester, p. 152.
Bridge, Thomas, p. 101.
Brinson, Mathew, p. 78.
Brinson, Thomas, p. 47.
Brock, William, Sen[r], p. 111.
Browne, Christopher, p. 50.
Browne, Henry, p. 33.
Browne, John, p. 32.
Browne, Thomas, p. 24.
Browne, Thomas, p. 31.
Bruks, John, p. 109.
Bryan, Roger, p. 193.
Buckmaster, Elizabeth, p. 27.
Burdas, William, p. 26.
Bustian, John, p. 121.
Bustian, Margaret, p. 122.
Butt, Rob[t], Sen[r], p. 48.

Camarell, Wm. p. 66.
Cameron, Osborne, p. 35.
Canareth, Lucas, p. 42.
Cannon, Elizabeth, p. 92.
Cannon, Thomas, p. 92.
Carney, Wm., Sen[r], p. 85.
Carraway, Ann, p. 139.
Cartright, Charles, p. 158.
Casewell, Matthew, p. 185.
Chambers, Richard, p. 115.
*Ch*armice, Samuell, p. 10.
Cherry, John, p. 167.
Chesey, Thomas, p. 14.
Chichester, Wm., p. 167.
Church, Richard, p. 191.
Clarke, Michaell, p. 22.
Clemens, William, p. 121.
Cockruft, William, p. 103.
Cokee, Eliz[th], p. 55.
Collins, Giles, p. 43.
Connor, Lewis, p. 165.
Cooke, John, p. 8.
Cooke, Richard, p. 106.
Cooper, William, p. 147.
Cording, Thomas, p. 169.
Cornwell, Joshua, p. 107.
Corperew, John, p. 174.
Costen, Walter, p. 151.
Craford, William, p. 172.
Craig, James, p. 35.
Crankshaw, Thomas, p. 176.
Creekmon, Edmund, p. 75.
Cremor, George, p. 72.
Cubbidge, John, p. 12.
Culpeper, Henry, p. 169.
Cuningham, Jno., p. 31.

Daffnell, William, p. 99.
Davis, Edward, Sen[r], p. 187.
Davis ,Elizabeth, p. 29.
Davis, Robte, p. 21.

NOTE—When the name of the testator, in the caption of the will, differs in spelling from the signature, the index follows the signature.

Deanes, William, Senr, p. 116.
Digby, Robert, p. 25.
Dolley, Dennis, p. 112.
Duglas, Daniell, p. 118.
Dundas, William, p. 118.
Dunn, John, p. 178.
Dyer, Wm., p. 41.

Eastwood, Richard, Senr, p. 137.
Edgerton, Charles, p. 29.
Elliott, Abraham, p. 52.
Ellitt, John, p. 168.
Emperour, Mary, p. 48.
Etheridge, John Senr, p. 138.
Etheridge, John, p. 168.
Etheridge, Thomas, p. 36.

Falk, John, p. 132.
Fanshaw, Thomas, p. 30.
Felwood, Roger, p. 79.
Fenford, Thomas, p. 72.
Fenwick, Mary, pp. 69 and 73.
Finch, Francis, p. 37.
Fitsgarrall, Katherin, p. 60.
Fitsgarrall, Morris, p. 59.
Fleetwood, Francis, p. 134.
Foreman, Alexander, p. 123.
Forinhaugh, John, p. 4.
Foster, Richard, p. 7.
Fowler, Francis, p. 69.
Fowler, Robert, p. 10.
Fowler, Sidney, p. 129.
Frederickson, Christian, p. 24.
Frisell, Jno., p. 127.
Frost, John, p. 153.

Gamon, John, p. 149.
Gee, Thomas, p. 40.
Gie, Patrick, p. 122.
Gilcrist, John, p. 107.
Gilham, John, p. 7.
Gilligan, F——do——, p. 184.
Godby, Thomas, p. 102.
Godbye, Thomas, p. 11.
Godfrey, John, p. 200.
Goldsmith, William, p. 138.
Gooch, John, p. 3.
Goodaker, Thomas, p. 119.
Goodaker, William, p. 89.
Gooden, Robert, p. 195.
Gooscott, John, p. 133.
Gouldinge, John, p. 19.
Gradwell, Edward, p. 8.
Grandy, Charles, p. 115.
Green, William, p. 43.
Greene, Jeane, p. 154.
Greene, John, p. 41.
Griffien, John, p. 190.
Grimes, Robert, p. 153.
Gwinn, ——, p. 173.

Hall, Edward, p. 44.
Hall, Richard, p. 4.
Hall*a*well, Thomas ,p. 146.
Hancocke, William, p. 113.
Hargrove, Richard, Senr, p. 100.
Hatch, Anthony, p. 125.
Hatton, Francis, p. 120.
Hatton, John, p. 6.
Hatton, John, p. 181.
Hatton, Robert, p. 82.
Hav*ast*, Mary, p. 34.
Hayes, Ann, p. 5.
Hayes, Owen, p. 40.
Hayes, Thomas, p. 95.
Hayley, William, p. 151.
Herbert, John, p. 44.
Herbert, John, p. 65.
Heslit, William, p. 163.
Hews, Edward, Senr, p. 197.
Hill, Richard, p. 99.
Hitchcock, Hester, p. 161.
Hobson, Peter, p. 164.
Hodge, Edward, p. 4.
Hodge, Robert, p. 79.
Hollewell, Thomas, p. 113.
Hollowell, Joseph, p. 188.
Hollstead, Henry, p. 94.
Hookey, William, p. 136.
Horner, George, p. 6.
How, Thomas, p. 62.
Howell, Cob, p. 20.
Hughby, Thomas, p. 117.
Hugins, Nicholas, p. 135.
Hurle (y), Joseph, p. 49.

Ivy, George, p. 123.
Ivy, John, p. 142.
Ivy, Thomas Vis, p. 91.

Jackson, James, p. 179.
Jacobs, John, p. 77.
Jarmice, Samuell, p. 10.
Jermy, William, p. 22.
Johnson, Benjamin, p. 51.
Johnson, James, p. 38.
Johnson, John, p. 71.
Johnson, William, p. 184.
Johnston, John, p. 166.
Jones, Rice, p. 25.
Jones, Richard, Senr, p. 85.
Jones, Richard, p. 134.
Jordan, James, p. 186.
Joyce, John, p. 199.
Joyce, Martin, p. 71.
Julian, Sarah, p. 5.

Keeling, Adam, p. 86.
Keeling, Elizabeth, p. 33.
Keeling, Thorowgood, p. 67.
Kelsall, Roger, p. 194.
Kemp, Ann, p. 58.
Kemp, George, p. 47.
Kendall, James, p. 63.
King, Richard, p. 98.
Knott, William, p. 159.

Lake, Joseph, p. 115.
Lambert, Thomas, p. 52.
Land, Renat*res*, p. 76.
Laurrance, John, p. 90.
Laurence, John, Michaell, p. 68.
Lawrence, Richard, p. 110.
Lawrence, ———, p. 168.
Lawson, George, Junr, p. 56.
Linton, Moses, Jr., p. 53.
Linton, Moses, p. 143.
Lo*u*rry, William, p. 106.
Loveday, Robt, p. 60.
Levinsgton, Wim., p. 81.
Lov*i*tt, Lancaster, p. 38.

Maccoy, Dennis, Senr, p. 193.
Maczkaferson, Daniell, p. 161.
Mack*eel,* Dorman, p. 93.
Macoy, Michaell, p. 83.
Mamakes, William, p. 116.
Marks, Peter, p. 20.
Marks, Stephen, p. 32.
Martin, Johnathan, p. 129.
Mason, Ann, p. 192.
Mason, Lemuell, p. 182.
Mason, Trustran, p. 56.
Mathews, James, p. 70.
Mtahias, Mathew, p. 30.
Maune, John, p. 3.
Mc——lallen, John, p. 61.
Miller, Joseph, Senr, p. 144.
Mills, William, p. 26.
Moore, John, p. 81.
Moore, Morgan, p. 128.
Moore, William, p. 87.
More, Cason, p. 108.
Morgan, Thomas, p. 44.
Morray, David, Junr, p. 139.
Morris, Thomas, p. 94.
Morton, Anne, p. 83.
Moseley, Arthur, p. 182.
Moseley, Will, Senr, p. 16.
Moyser, Thomas, p. 68.
Mullakin, James, p. 28.
Mull*i*gan, James, p. 28.
Murden, John, p. 157.
Murfee, John, p. 46.
Murray, David, p. 141.

Nash, Francis, p. 118.
Nedham, Thomas, p. 19.
Newell, Henry, p. 75.
Newman, Alice, p. 127.
Nichlis, William, p. 150.
Nicholas, Andrew, p. 15.
Nicholas, Henry, Senr, p. 52.
Nich*olls*, John, p. 161.
Nichols, Richard, p. 51.
Nichlis, Henry, p. 154.
Norman, John, p. 93.

Odeon, William, p. 22.
Offley, Henry, p. 58.
Olivant, Wm., p. 39.
Oliver, Emanuel, p. 73.

Pead, John, p. 55.
Peeters, Simon, p. 74.
Fere, Henry, p. 40.
Pette, Thomas, p. 42.
Piggott, Sarah, p. 126.
Pinner, Richard, p. 26.
Pitts, Thomas, p. 94.
Plumer, Lawrence, p. 12.
Poole, Richard, p. 42.
Poore, John, p. 70.
Pope, William, p. 131.
Porten, Sarah, p. 57.
Porten, Wm., p. 56.
Porten, James, p. 88.
Porter, John, Senr, p. 45.
Porter, Robert, p. 25.
Foslett, Edward, p. 30.
Powell, John, p. 120.
Powell, William, p. 132.
Powes, Robt., p. 7.

Rallings, Edward, p. 110.
Rayner, John, p. 133.
Reaven, William, p. 131.
Riglesworth, Peter, p. 10.
Rise, Judith, p. 186.
Robinson, Nicholas, p. 54.
Rogers, Wm., p. 96.
Rose, Allexander, p. 102.
Rose, Robert, p. 198.
Ro*w*se, Robert, p. 109.
Russell, Richard, p. 27.

S*alm*on, John, p. 71.
Savell, Richard, p. 100.
Scott, Robert, p. 165.
S*hrilles,* William, p. 110.
Sibsey, John, p. 9.
Sidney, John, p. 22.
Sikes, Walter, p. 199.
Skevengton, Thomas, p. 130.
Smith, Robert, p. 68.

Smith ,Robert, p. 104.
Smithers, Thomas, p. 111.
Snaill, Henry, p. 19.
Spratt, Henry, p. 105.
Spring, Aaron, p. 153.
Spring, Moses, p. 172.
Spring, Robert, p. 61.
Sternell, Richard, p. 16.
Stow, Thomas, p. 62.
Straton, Henry, p. 63.
Suggs, William, p. 193.

Tabor, Thomas, p. 175.
Tanner, Daniell, p. 11.
Tarte, Elnathan, p. 180.
Taylor, Margarett, p. 68.
Taylor, Mary, p. 23.
Taylor, Richard, p. 65.
Taylor, Theodore, p. 183.
Thelaball, Francis, p. 187.
Thelaball, James, p. 145.
Thorowgool, Adam, p. 96.
Thruston, John, p. 196.
Thruston, Malachy, p. 170.
Toppin, Arthur, p. 35.
T*ownsend*, Joseph, p. 144.
Trigs, Paul, p. 64.
Tucker, Thomas, p. 53.
Tucker, William, p. 199.
Tuttie, John, p. 30.

Vaughan, William, p. 125.
Veall, Morris, p. 189.
Vincent, William, p. 14.

Wakefield, Thomas, p. 196.
Walke, Thomas, p. 147.
Wallis, John, p. 177.
Walli*s*, Thomas, p. 190.
Walston, Samuell, p. 103.
Ward, Edward, p. 29.
Ward, Thomas, p. 13.
Watford, John, p. 151.
Watking, John, p. 5.
Weblin, John, p. 106.
Wisgate, Henery, p. 18.
Whiddon Augustine, p. 140.
Whinfell, John, p. 166.
White, John, p. 76.
White, William, p. 91.
Whiteh*er*st, Robt., p. 62.
Whitehurst, Ellen, p. 13.
Whitehurst, John, p. 136.
Whitford, David, p. 104.
Whith*o*rst, William, p. 178.
Willer, Edward, p. 117.
Wilkerson, Arnald, p. 12.
Williams, Evans, p. 34.
Williams, Nicholas, p. 61.
Will*iams* (or Will*e*), Rich, p. 155.
Williamson, John, p. 49.
Willou*ghby*, Sarah, p. 41.
Willson, Hugh, p. 129.
Willson, Thomas, p. 180.
Wilson, James, p. 150.
Wilson, John, p. 158.
Wilson, Thomas, p. 142.
Wishart, James, p. 73.
Woodhouse, Henry, p. 17.
Woodhouse, Henry, p. 101.
Woodard, Francis, p. 67.
Workman, John, p. 45.
Workman, Thomas, p. 13.
Wright, Thomas, p. 15.

Yates, Joane, p. 23.
Yates, Richard, p. 64.

INDEX OF NAMES

Though it is proper that, in the text, the variations in spelling in the recorded wills should be followed, it is felt that in an index this is not necessary except when required for identification.

It should be borne in mind that though a name may appear several times on a page, only one reference is given in the index.

In the "Miscellaneous Index" all place-names are given except "Elizabeth River" and "Lynnhaven," one or the other of which appears in practically every will.

Abott, John, 28.
Abington, Thomas, 157.
Adams, Alice, 53, 86; Barbery, 19; Henry, 26; John, 61, 86, 159, 164; John, Jr., 86; Richard, 86; Thomas, 19; William, 127.
Aellott, John, 153.
Aldridge, Francis, 58; Jane, 58; Thomas, 109, 121.
Alexander als Sharp, Majere, 48; Margone, 27.
Allen, Thomas, 10, 18, 20.
Aubray, ———, 103.
Anderson, Andrew, 72; Jenit, 106.
Andre, Francis, 73; John, 73; Oliver, 73.
Andrews, John, 175; William, 47; Winifred, 47.
Angus, Patrick, 81, 105, 115.
Anis, William, 62.
Anthony, ———, 21.
Arden, Robert, 86.
Ashall, Anne, 20; Elizabeth, 20; George, 20, 37; George (Jr.), 37; Mary, 37, 38; Richard, 20, 37, 38; Susan, 38.
Ashby, Denis, 53.
Ashworth, John, 42.
Atchison, William, 142.
Axtel, John, 78.
Axstell, John, 99, 100; Deborah, 100; Ruth, 100.
Samuel, 100; Thomas, 100.
Axwell, Margaret, 59; Thomas, 59.
Auere, Oliver, 73.
Ayres, Joseph, 34.
Bacon, Richard, 62, 118, 119, 151.
Bachelor, Alice, 84; Ann, 84; Edy, 84; John, 84; Joseph, 84; Richard, 84; Richard, Jr, 84.
Bain, George, 102.
Baker, Francis, 57, 61.
Ball, Elizabeth, 143; Moses, 201; Richard, 143, 200; Samuel, 130.
Ballentine, Alexander, 177; Daniel, 177; George (Sr.), 177; George (Jr.), 177; John, 177; Richard, 177; Thomas, 177; William, 177.
Banks, Elizabeth, 46; Henry, 46; James, 19, 74; John, 13, 46; Margaret, 46; William, 46.
Banneshers (Bannester?), Will, 12.
Barley, Robert, 84, 85.
Barlow, William, 29.
Ba:nes, Anthony, 115; Elizabeth, 111; Peter, 9.
Barrett, George, 12; Thomas, 12.
Barrington, Isaac, 51; William, 98.
Barrow, William, 165.
Barry, John, 40.
Barsley, William, 105.
Barttee, Robert, 89.
Barton, John, 135; Thomas, 135; Walter, 135.
Basnett, William, Sr., 101, 112, 113; William, (Jr.), 112, 113.
Bashaw, Andrew, 75, 75.
Batchelor, John, 152.
Bateman, William, 131.
Bathurst, William, 85.
Bayley, Elizabeth, 161; Joseph, 161, 183.

Baxter, Edward, 66.
Beane, Elizabeth, 11.
Becher, Hester, 130.
Beacher, ———, 131.
Beck, Jeremiah, 139, 157.
Beckford, Martha, 167; Robert, 167.
Bell, Alexander, 124.
Bellamy, Adam, 8.
Belt, Alexander, 26.
Bence, Mary, 63.
Bennett, Anne, 19, 29, 98; Edward, 29; Elizabeth. 29; Mary, 29, 90; Philip, 5; Thomas, 19, 20, William, 68.
Benson, John, 45, 99, 100; Thomas, 45.
Beody, Edward, 29.
Bery, Edmond, 131.
Beverley, Robert, 167; William, 167.
Bigg, Dorothy, 140, 160; Phebe, 160; Jabez, 140, 160; John, 45, 140, 159; John (Jr.), 159, 160; John (3rd), 160; Thomas, 84, 141, 160.
Black, Jeremia, 99.
Blake, Arthur, 37, 136, 187; Mrs. ———, 37.
Blanch, Elizabeth, 43, 77; Mary, 43; Thomas, 43; Thomas (Jr.), 43; William, 43.
Blandie, John, 179.
Blandwell, John, 178, 179.
Bock, Jeremiah, 128.
Bolton, John, 6; Richard, 175, 176.
Bonney, Richard, 39, 95, 101, 108.
Boney, Robert, 109.
Boodington, John, 78.
Booles, Henry, 117.
Bordas, Thomas, 26; William, 26.
Bouling, Dorothy, 31; Elizabeth. 31; Elizabeth (Jr.), 31; Mary, 31; Richard, 31; Richard (Jr.), 31.
Bouring, Edward, 54, 87; John, 32, 54, 61; John (Jr.), 54.
Bouroughs, Burroughs, Burrows, Benjamin, 119; Benony, 39, 79, 80, 81, 89, 91, 93, 95, 140; Mary, 93; William, 66, 93.
Bottom, William, 186.
Boush, Alice, 163, 192; Lemuel, 163, 164, 170, 171, 173.
Bouskine, John, 68; Moses, 69.
Bowers, Elizabeth, 189; Henry, 181; James, 189; John, 119; John (Jr.), 189; Judah, 189; Robert, 10, 113, 118, 119, 189; Susanna, 189; Susanna (Jr.), 189.
Bowles, Henry, 113.
Bowman, Edward, 17.
Boymus, Boymens, John, 10; John (Jr.), 10.
Bradley, George, 156, 157; Margaret, 156.
Bradford, William, 125.
Bragger, Edward, 38.
Brakes, Henry, 6, 8, 12.
Branch, Giles, 74.
Bransgrove, Benjamin, 118.
Branker, Edward, 98; Nathaniel Jr.), 98; Robert, 97.
Branton, Elizabeth, 134, 159; John, 118, 150; Thomas, 21, 24, 83, 134.
Bray, Edward, 77, 78; John, 20, 78; Mary, 21; Plummer, 21, 78, 91, 112, 175; Robert, 34, 42, 52, 58, 77; ———, 67.
Breach, Thomas, 51, 56.
Brent, Thomas, 159.
Brett, Richard, 149; Thomas, 143.
Bridge, Hester, 101, 106, 152; John, 18; Thomas, 10, 18, 19, 28, 39, 77, 101, 152.
Bright, John, 27, 36.
Brighthouse, Edward, 110, 111, 112.
Brittnoey, Richard, 37.
Brinson, John, 47, 130; Mathew, 47, 78, 79, 128; Robert, 58, 63, 70; Susanna, 70; Thomas, 47, 58.
Brocke, John, 111; Mary, 112; Thomas, 111; William (Sr.), 111; William (Jr.), 111; William (3rd), 111.
Brooke, Sarah, 94.
Brough, Elinor, 174.
Brown, Browne, Ann, 31, Christopher, 24, 32, 33, 50; Daniel, 162; Edward, 30; Elizabeth, 25; Henry, 24, 32, 33; James, 50; John, 24, 32, 50, 118; Mary, 25, 33; Thomas, 6, 24, 31, 32, 50; Thomas (Jr.), 24; William, 24, 32, 33, 50, 70, 73, 124.
Browning, Mrs. ———, 17.
Brownley, John, 97, 98.
Bruce, Abraham, 120, 198.

Bruks, Grace, 109; Job, 109; Jane, 109; John, 109; John (Jr.), 109; Sarah, 109.
Brunt, Alice, 127; Thomas, 127.
Bryan, Morgan, 148; Roger (Sr.), 193; Roger (Jr.), 193.
Buckmaster, Elizabeth, 27.
Bullock, Thomas, 3.
Bunting, Bridget, 155; Elizabeth, 31, 154; Richard (Sr.), 155; Richard, 17, 154.
Burdas, Henry, 27.
Burges, Robert, 75.
Burton, Richard, 79.
Bustian, Christopher, 59, 121; John, 121, 134; Margaret, 121, 122.
Butler, Robert, 11.
Butt, Henry (Sr.), 199; Henry, 48, 70; Jane, 48; Leddae, 191; Mary, 25; Richard, 48; Richard (Jr.), 200; Robert (Sr.), 48; Robert, 94, 102; Robert (Jr.), 48; Thomas, 48, 149, 151, 152, 161.
Butts, Stanhope, 185.

Cabeito, Sarah, 93.
Caisen, Abigail, 107.
Camaron, Elizabeth, 36; Katherine, 36; Mary, 35; Osborne, 35; William, 36.
Campbell, Hugh, 107, 142, 143.
Camerell, Elizabeth, 66; Katherine, 66; William, 66.
Canarads, Lucus, 42.
Canney, Dany (? Daniel), 110.
Cannon, Edward, 42, 91, 92, 93, 112; Edward (Jr.), 92; Elizabeth, 92; John, 92; Sarah, 92, 112; Thomas, 42, 91; Thomas (Jr.), 92.
Capps, Denis, 112; Robert, 10; William, 22, 128.
Carmady, Susanna, 68.
Carney, Abigail, 85; David, 85; James, 85; John, 85, 198; Mary, 85, 198; Richard, 85, 110; William, 85.
Carraway, Ann, 22, 139; John, 7, 16, 114, 127, 140.
Carrey, Richard, 60.
Carter, Edward, 75; James, 136.
Catherite, Charles, 158; Susan, 158.
Cartwrite, Alice, 51.
Cartwright, Charles, 149; Peter, 102.
Carver, John, 26; Richard, 78; William, 25, 27, 47, 85; "Capt.," 162.
Casewell, **Caswell**, Constant, 185; Francis, 160, 185; Jabez, 160, 185; Jane, 185; Jancel, 185; Jean, 160; Martha, 160, 185; Mathew, 84, 160, 185; Matthew (Jr.), 185; William, 160, 185.
Catterell, William, 103.
Cato, Thomas, 137.
Cattlin, Henry, 41.
Ceader, ———, 165.
Ceay, Will, 6.
Chambers, Ann, 148, Richard, 115.
Chamberlin, Mary, 134; Thomas, 94, 95.
Chamioe, **Charmice**, Rose, 10; Samuel, 10.
Chapman, Henry, 105; Richard, 193.
Cherry, John, 140, 141, 144, 167; Rebecca, 144; Thomas, 180.
Chesey, Jeane, 14; Robert, 14; Thomas, 14.
Chichester, Mary, 68, 98, 146; William (Sr.), 49; William, 43, 68, 72, 98, 133, 167.
Church, Abigail, 191; Elizabeth, 192; Joseph, 191, 192; Patience, 191; Richard, 22, 99, 191.
Clark, Bartholomew, 168; Elizabeth, 22; James, 156, 157; John, 10; Michaell, 22; Weston, 156, 157.
Clanagin, Gett, 175.
Clemens, Mary, 121; William, 121.
Clements, Wm., 32, 153.
Clerke, Ann, 176; Bartholomew, 176.
Cocke, James, 173; Mary, 192; Thomas, 98, 99, 105, 118, 172; Walter, 172.
Cockroft, **Cockruft**, Jehu, 103, 104; John, 104; Sarah, 104; Sarah (Jr.), 104; Thomas, 103, 104; William, 16, 103, 114; William (Jr.), 103, 104.
Codd, Thomas, 3.
Cokee, John, 55; Elizabeth, 55.
Collins, Andrew, 195; Crane, Crany, 31, 62; Elizabeth, 18; Giles, 18, 43; Giles (Jr.), 43; Henry, 43; John, 43, 193; Joannah, 135; 136; Judith, 43; Thomas, 195.
Conell, William, 79.

Coniers, Walter, 134.
Conner, Elizabeth, 165; Lewis, 87, 165; Lewis (Jr.), 165.
Conor, Walter, 135.
Conquest, Richard, 9, 11, 15.
Cooke, John, 8; Richard (Sr.), 106; Richard, 107.
Cooper, Ann, 147; Edward, 10, 19, 20, 21, 70, 110; Edward (Jr.), 21; John, 110, 127, 147; Thomas, 150; William (Sr.), 127, 147; William, 49, 50; William (Jr.), 147.
Copeland, Joseph, 163.
Corbett, John, 39; Mary, 42; Richard, 42; Sarah, 42.
Corbin, ———, 191.
Cording, Ann, 25; Elizabeth, 169; Richard, 25; Roger, 26; Thomas, 33, 50, 169, 170; William, 169.
Cordon, Patrick, 165, 176.
Corker, ———, 16.
Cornelius, Henry, 152.
Cornewell, Joshua, 107; Rebecca, 107.
Cornick, Ann, 93; Barbara, 92; Martin, 125; Simon, 92, 93; William, 41, 52, 67, 70, 79, 92, 93, 102, 125; William (Jr.), 92, 93.
Corprew, James, 174; John, 76, 78, 110, 115, 174; John, (Jr.), 174; Thomas, 174, 185.
Coseland, Martha, 36.
Costen, Walter, 151.
Cotton, Thomas, 33.
Courtney, Mary, 174.
Cox, Richard, 104.
Craig, James, 35.
Cranberry, Elinor, 109.
Cranston, Samuel, 156, 157.
Crankshaw, Thomas, 176.
Crawford, Crafford, Abigail, 173; George, 108; Margaret, 173; Mary, 34; William, 107, 172, 173.
Creck, Thomas, 128.
Creed, Thomas, 63.
Creekmore, Creewmon, Dorothy, 177; Edmund, 75, 163; Edmund (Jr.), 75; Edward, 75; Elizabeth, 75; Jane, 75; John, 75, 161, 177.
Cremor, George, 72; James, 72; John, 72.
Crockett, Francis, 49.
Cruch, Henry, 46.
Crutchett, Mary, 133.
Cubbidge, John, 12.
Cubbick, John, 8.
Culpeper, Henry, 43, 155, 169; Robert, 169; Thomas, 169.
Cumming, James, 195.
Cunningham, John, 31.
Curling, Joseph, 151, 174; Walter, 183, 185.
Cuthrill, William, 103.
Cyech, Richard, 121.

Daffnell, Deftnell, Elizabeth, 142; William, 99, 142, 184; William (Jr.), 99.
Dale, Henry, 163.
Daller, Adam, 51.
Dallowe, John, 32.
Dally, Dolly, Dennis, 41, 112; Elizabeth, 42, 112; John, 112, 118; Margaret, 112; Sarah, 112.
Daniel, Hugh, 179.
Dang, James, 113.
Davenell, Elizabeth, 158; Mary, 158; William, 158, 162; William (Jr.), 158.
Davis, Daniel, 194; Edward (Sr.), 187; Edward, 177; Edward (Jr.), 187; Edward (3rd), 187; Elizabeth, 29; Elizabeth (Jr.), 29; Elizabeth (Taylor), 65; John, 12, 42, 46, 69; Margaret, 29; Robert, 21; Thomas, 124; Winford, 124; Mrs. ———, 187.
Dayeslayed, Robert, 158.
Daynes, Daines, Thomas, 14; William, 14, 32, 60, 165.
Deall, Frances, 177; Henry, 177.
Deales, Morris, 146.
Dean, John, 120.
Deanes, Mary, 116; William (Sr.), 116; William (Jr.), 116.
Debbs, Richard, 101.
Deseme, Joseph, 109.
De Potter, John, 14.
Deuester, John, 44.
Dickson, Mary, 174.
Digby, Ann, 25; John, 25, 26; Robert, 25.
Dixon, John, 147.
Donnell, Myles, 40.
Doughan, William, 145.
Douglas, Bridget, 118; Daniel, 89, 118.
Downing, James, 165.
Doyley, Denis (see Dalley), 29.
Draper, Robert, 97.

Drisdrall (etc.), Robert, 153, 158, 186.
Drout, Richard, 69, 107.
Dubar, John, 15.
Duncan, David, 152.
Dundas, William, 105, 148.
Dunn, Amie, 178; John, 178; John (Jr.), 178.
Dunson, David, 159.
Dunstan, Peleg, 56.
Dyer, Mary, 41; Sarah, 28; William, 41, 52; William (Jr.), 41.

Easton, John, 157.
Eastwood, Elizabeth, 137; John, 137; Richard, 9, 137, 151; Richard (Sr.), 137; Richard (Jr.), 137; Thomas, 137.
Eddens, Philip, 195.
Egerton, Ann, 57; Charles, 29, 57.
Edmonds, Bridgett, 14; Elizabeth, 14; John, 52; Katherine, 14; Thomas, 14.
Edwards, John, 27, 34, 36, 48, 54, 64, 72, 85, 96, 107, 108, 141, 179, 185, 193; William, 105.
Efreag, John, 24.
Elder, Miss ———, 148.
Elliott, Abraham, 22, 52; Alice, 53; Jane, 53; Sarah, 53.
Ellis, William, 31.
Ellitt, John, 168; Rebeckah, 168.
Elliz, Philip, 26; William (Jr.), 26; William, 26.
Emperour, Francis, 48; Mary, 48; Tully, 48, 51; William, 48, 66; ———, 16;.
English, Thomas, 104.
Etheridge, Andrew, 36; Christian, 36; Edward, 36, 64, 138, 144, 193; Elizabeth, 64, 89; Henry, 138; John (Sr.), 36, 138, 168; Marmaduke, 36, 64, 199; Mary, 64; Richard, 64, 199; Susan, 36, Thomas, 36, 138, 159, 160, 168; Thomas (Jr.), 36; William, 36, 54; 160.
Ewell, Sarah, 111; Thomas, 111.
Evans, John, 59.
Eyre, Robert, 7.

Falke, Ann, 132; John, 132.
Fanshaw, Mary, 24, 30; Thomas, 30, 199; Thomas (Jr.), 30.
Farmer, Richard, 150.
Faux, Ann, 160.
Felwood, Roger, 79.
Fenford, Sarah, 72; Thomas, 36, 72; Thomas (Jr.), 72.
Fentris, Ann, 139; Michael, 138, 139.
Fentres, Mrs. ———, 138.
Fenwick, Mary, 69, 73; Thomas, 69, 70.
Ferebee, Elizabeth, 71; John, 41, 43, 71, 84, 87, 109, 132.
Ferguson, Adam, 115; Bridget, 115; Thomas, 115, 120.
Fernall, George, 40.
Finch, Francis, 37; John, 3, 10.
Finckley, F., 102, 109.
Fitsgarrall, James, 107; Henry, 60, 129; Katherine, 44, 59, 60; Morris, 44, 59, 65; ———, 59.
Fleetwood, Francis, 134; Henry, 122, 134.
Flewellen, Edward, 65; Richard, 65.
Forbes, John, 28.
Foreman, Alexander, 85, 123; Dorothy, 123; Elizabeth, 123; John, 123; Richard, 123.
Fornihaugh, Deborah, 4; John, 4.
Foster, Richard, 7.
Founder, Richard, 8, 60; Elizabeth, 60.
Fountayne,. Roger, 7, 12, 21; Roger (Jr.), 21.
Fowler, Frances, 45, 69; George, 10, 29, 38, 45, 69, 129; James, 165; Mary, 10; Pembrook, 69; Robert, 10, 69; Robert (Jr.), 10; Sidney, 69, 129.
Franklin, Simon, 101, 104, 106.
Frederickson, Christian, 24; Frederick, 24; Mrs. ———, 24.
Freeman, Isaac, 134; Rachel, 149.
Fresell, Daniel, 63.
Frisell, Daniel, 88, 127, 128; John, 127, 128; Francis, 127, 128.
Frost, John, 153; Julia, 153; Mary, 153; William, 87. 116.
Fundermull, Lewis, 11.
Fulcher, Thomas, 23, 25; "Mr.,"

Gage, Mathew, 62.
Galley, Thomas, 34.
Gammon, Gamon, John (Sr.), 151; John, 62, 149; Robert, 149, 158; Susan, 158; Susanna, 149.
Gariot, Jane, 40.
Gascatt, John, 99.

Gaskin, Gaskins, Job, 104; Samuel, 3.
Gee, Thomas, 40.
Genings, Henry, 121.
Genilian, ———, 97.
Gesborne, John, 63.
Gewalsene, Josias, 24.
Gibson, Henry, 40; John, 40, 186.
Gilbert, Thomas, 31, 33.
Gilchrist, Agnes, 107; John, 107.
Giles, Mary, 134.
Gilham, John, 7, 8; John (Jr.), 7.
Gilligan, ———, 184.
Givvins, Henry, 181.
Gisborne, John, 110.
Glasco, Daniel, 149; Mary, 149.
Godand, John, 119.
Godby, Ann, 11, 27, 28, 77, 103; Thomas, 11, 27, 85, 102.
Godfrey, Anne, 201; Daniel, 201; John, 35, 57, 200; Mary, 51, 200; Matthew (Sr.), 200; Matthew, 35, 57, 191, 200; Warren, 35, 57, 72, 96, 150, 200.
Gorring, Daniel, 108, 124.
Goldsmith, William, 13, 27, 138.
Gooch, John, 3.
Goodacre, **Goodaker**, Elizabeth, 28; John, 89; Joseph, 89, 119; Robert, 89, 105, 119; Thomas, 89, 119; William, 89, 119; William (Jr.), 89.
Gooden, Elizabeth, 195; Robert, 195.
Goodrich, Thomas, 14, 19; ———, 17.
Goole, George, 42.
Gooscott, Bridget, 133; John, 133.
Gordon, Thomas, 87.
Gorvis, Robert, 3.
Gouldinge, John, 19.
Gradwell, Edward, 6, 8.
Grady, Mary, 60; Owen, 66 .
Graham, John, 116.
Grandy, Charles, 115; John, 116; Mary, 113; Thomas, 113; William, 116.
Granger, Benjamin, 67.
Grant, Ann, 81.
Gregory, Ann, 181; Thomas.
Gray, Elizabeth, 175, 178.
Griffith, Herbert, 83; John, 110.
Grigman, John, 55, 62.
Grimes, James, 153; John, 153; Robert, 153.
Grinto, William, 108.
Green, **Greene**, Ann, 62, 155; Elizabeth, 62; Henry, 62; Jane, 155; Jeane, 154; John, 28, 38, 41; Katherine, 28, 41, 110; Sarah, 43; Thomas, 41, 62, 155; Thomisen, 155; William, 28, 31, 41 43.
Griffin, Isabel, 190, 191; John (Sr.), 155; John, 29, 37, 55, 190; John (Jr.), 156; Thomas, 156, 190.
Guardian, William, 135.
Guy, James, 68; Hester, 68.
Gwinn, Alexander, 173; Elizabeth, 186; William, 173; ———, 173.
Gye, Elizabeth, 122; James, 122; John, 122; Margery, 122; Patrick, 122; Patrick (Jr.), 122.

Hadesly, Johanna, 46; Margaret, 46; Sarah, 46.
Hafder, Mary, 116.
Hafeald, John, 160.
Hagging, Nicholas, 90.
Hall, Edward, 4, 21, 44; Humphrey, 44, 45; Jean, 158; Katherine, 45; Richard, 4; Thomas, 12.
Halstead (see also Holstead), Briget, 99; Henry, 200.
Hambelton, John, 124.
Hammon, Martin, 27.
Hancock, Edward, 114, 126; Frances, 114, 126; George, 114, 126; John, 114; Mary, 114, 126; Robert, 126; Samuel, 114, 126; Sarah, 114; Simon, 7, 74, 114, 126, 127, 130, 152; Susan, 126; William, 51, 59, 69, 89, 100, 104, 113, 118, 126; William, Jr., 114;
Hannay, Hannah, Robert, 94, 104, 106, 107, 128, 131.
Harding, Thomas, 31.
Hargrove, Benjamin, 100, 135; Richard (Sr.), 100; Richard (Jr.), 100.
Harread, Thomas, 45.
Harris, Richard, 68.
Harrison, Joseph, 26.
Hartle, Hartley, Charles, 110, 112.
Hartwell, Richard, 45.
Hasatt, Mary, 34.
Hatch, Anthony, 125; Anthony (Jr.), 125; Elizabeth, 125.
Hatfield, William, 54.
Hattersley, Mary, 116; Pall, 116; William, 29; Sarah, 45.

Hatton, Dorothy, 6; Elizabeth, 82; Elizabeth (Jr.), 82; Francis, 50, 68, 82, 120; Hannah, 181; John, 6, 25, 82, 116, 120, 181. John (Jr.), 6; Martha, 24; Robert, 82, 153; Robert (Jr.), 82; Sarah, 120; William, 168; Mrs. ——, 181; "Capt.," 87.
Haveild, Luke, 116.
Havast, William, 35.
Hawood, Sarah, 113.
Hay, William, 181.
Hays, Hayes, Adam, 5, 13, 109, 112; Ann, 5, 40; Hoge, 26; Isabella, 95; Nathaniel, 5, 13; Owen, 14, 40; Richard, 51, 56; Robert, 5; Thomas, 95.
Hayly, William, 152.
Hayword, Roger, 20.
Hebdon, John, 30, 191.
Heigham, George, 4.
Henley, Charles, 63; Jeane, 18.
Henry, George, 38.
Herbert, John, 44, 65; John (Jr.), 44, 65; Mary, 44.
Heslett, Ann, 163, 164; Ann (Jr.), 163; Cary, 163, 176; William, 163.
Hetherington, Etterington, Jane, 109; Thomas, 36.
Hewlin, Joseph, 50.
Hews, Edward (Sr.), 197; Edward, 72; Edward (Jr.), 198, 199; Elijah, 197, 198; Hester, 197, 198; Solomon, 197, 198; Vasthie, 198.
Highsmith, Bartholomew, 146, 147.
Hill, John, 6, 17; Richard (Sr.), 93; Richard, 83, 99.
Hilliard, William, 147.
Hitchcock, Hester, 116, 161; ——, 161.
Hobgood, Thomas, 186.
Hobson, Elizabeth, 164; John, 164; Mary, 164; Peter, 164; Phyllis, 164.
Hocker, Isaac, 47; Mary, 58.
Hodge, Alexander, 80; Alice, 80; Edward, 4; John, 80, 81; John (Jr.), 81; Robert, 40, 66, 79, 80; Robert (Jr.), 81; Samuel, 4; Thomas, 80; John, 109, 149, 170; Joseph, 158, 159, 160, 181, 198; Mary, 177; Rebecca, 160; Richard, 65; Robert, 177, 178; Roger, 66, 68, 132, 161, 169; Thomas, 86, 87, 109, 113, 120, 173.
Hodgkins, Bartholomew, 16.
Hoffler, Thomas, 170.
Holloway, Catherin, 184; Grace, 174; Patrick, 184; Sarah, 132; Thomas, 43.
Hollowell, Alice, 113.
Hollewell, Benjamin, 113, 185; Edmund, 113; Elizabeth, 113; Henry, 113; John, 113, 146, 147; Joseph, 113; Katherine, 146; Luke, 146; Mary, 109, 146; Sarah, 146; Thomas, 113, 146; Thomas (Jr.), 113, 146; William, 146, 147.
Hollstead, Ann, 94; Henry, 94; Henry (Jr.), 94; John, 94; Symond, 94.
Holmes, Edward, 39; Elizabeth, 68, 166; Henry, 13, 39, 66, 68; Hester, 26; Jane, 39; John, 5, 6, 12; Lemuel, 39; Robert, 39; William, 39.
Hone, Katherine, 49; Theophilus (Jr.), 49; Thomas, 49.
Hookey, James, 136; Sarah, 136; William, 136;.
Horne, Elizabeth, 23; George, 82, 110, 137, 142, 151; Hanna, 23; Thomas, 23.
Hornes, George, 6.
Horton, Robert, 44.
Hoskings, Hugh, 54.
Host, Godwin, 115, 116.
How (or Stow), Thomas, 62.
Howard, Ann (Sr.), 4; Cornelius (Sr.), 4; Elizabeth (Sr.), 4; Samuel (Jr.), 4; Matthew (Sr.), 4; Matthew (Jr.), 4 .
Howell, Cobb, 20.
Howesen, Roger, 171.
Huchinson, William, 158.
Hudgins, Alice, 135.
Huggens, Nicholas, 39, 43, 66, 122, 135, 155; Philip, 136.
Hughley (or Hughby), Thomas, 117.
Hunter, William, 74, 78, 82.
Hurle, Joseph, 49.

Itson, Ann, 70; Mary, 70.
Ives, Elizabeth, 50; John, 121, 134, 162; Mary, 99; Timothy, 85; Timothy (Jr.), 50; William, 121.

Ivy, Agnes, 91; Alexander, 123; Alice, 91; Alexander, 77, 80, 91; Elizabeth, 77, 91, 124, 142; Frances, 91; George, 54, 77, 123; George (Jr.), 77, 123; Hannah, 77, 123, 124; John, 123, 142, 143; John (Jr.), 142; Joseph, 124; Lemuel, 91; Ludford, 91; Mary, (Sr.), 142; Mary, 142, 200; Samuel, 77, 123; Thomas, 9, 72, 77, 91, 123, 142; Thomas Vizt, 91; ———, 27.

Jackson, Alice, 174; Anthony, 135; Aphia, 179; James, 86, 179; James (Jr.), 179; Joseph, 50; Mary, 179; Margaret, 179; Margaret (Jr.), 179; Simon, 179.

Jacob, John, 77; William, 10.

James, John, 108, 109.

Jameson, Alexander, 136; John, 135; Mary, 136.

Jarmice (or Charmice), Samuel, 10.

Jenings, Henry, 46, 121; Richard, 46.

Jenkins, Jane, 50; Lazarus, 52, 53.

Jennet, John, 131, 140.

Jermy, Ann, 23; William, 5, 9, 22.

Jolly, John (Jr.), 144.

Jolliff, John, 55, 144.

Jones, Ann, 25; Charles, 49; Cuthen, 191; Edward, 95; Elizabeth, 98, 179, 186; Francis, 108; Herbert, 72; Hester, 134; John, 95; Mary, 85; Ralfe, 19; Rice, 25; Richard, 85, 134; Richard (Jr.), 30, 85; Thomas, 70, 99.

Johnson, Ann, 24, 71; George, 138; Benjamin, 51; Catherine, 38; Elizabeth, 38; Elizabeth (Jr.), 38; Jacob, 60, 61, 65, 74, 90, 124, 130; James, 28, 38, 184; James (Jr.), 38; Jane, 38, 41; John, 20, 71, 138; John (Jr.), 52, 117; Job, 129; Mary, 38, 52, 139, 184; William, 12, 117, 184; Samuel, 138.

Johnston, Agnes, 166; John, 166, 180; John (Jr.), 166; William, 166, 180; William (Jr.), 184.

Jordan, James, 186; Robert, 85; Jane, 186.

Joy, Kate, 22; Viressinus, 22.

Joyce, David, 200; Edward, 200; Elizabeth, 71; John, 71, 186, 190, 199; John (Jr.), 200; Judith, 71; Martin, 71; Rachel, 200.

Juggins, Francis, 33.

Julian, Sarah, 5.

Keeling, Adam, 39, 42, 45, 54, 82, 86, 87; Alexander, 33, 47, 63, 78, 86, 93, 103; Ann, 67, 86, 93; Elizabeth, 33, 34, 86; John, 86, 103; Luce, 45; Lucy, 67; Lucy (Jr.), 67; Thomas, 23, 86; Thorowgood, 33, 34, 44, 58, 67.

Kelsall, Katherine, 195; John, 195; Roger, 194; Roger (Sr.), 195.

Kemp, Ann, 41, 47, 58; Elizabeth, 58; George, 5, 16, 47, 59; James, 47, 59, 91; Job, 47, 58, 105; John, 47, 105; Maudling, 8; Mary, 8; Sarah, 5.

Kendall, James, 63.

Kennan, Andrew, 148, 149; Christian, 148.

Key, Stephen, 8, 12.

King, Elizabeth, 98; Jeane, 27; Richard, 98.

Kittle, Robert, 156.

Knott, Mary, 161; William, 159, 170.

Ladd, Bethsheba, 39; John, 39.

Lake, Annie, 115; Arthur, 191; Elizabeth, 115; Francis, 65; Henry, 65; Isabel, 40; Joseph, 40, 67, 115.

Lambert, Jane, 52; Thomas, 9, 14, 39, 52.

Lamont, James, 94, 104.

Land, Elizabeth, 34, 76; Edward, 76; Francis, 119, 105; Jasper, 67; Philip, 3; Renatus, 67, 76; Robert, 76.

Landingfield, 197.

Lane, Robert, 91, 93; Elizabeth, 91, 5.

Langley, Elizabeth, 146; Joyce, 35; Margaret, 145; Robert, 50; Thomas, 123, 124; William, 22, 69, 124.

Latny, Henry, 63.

Lawrence, Andrew, 90; Cary, 90; Dorothy, 90; John, 45, 90; John (Sr.), 90; Margery, 68; Michael, 68, 69; Richard, 28, 41, 49, 110, 120, 121; (or Lawcer), ———. 168.

Lawson, Anthony, 42, 56, 58, 60, 61, 66, 78, 79, 80, 81, 87, 91, 93, 96, 97, 105, 114, 130, 148, 149;

Anthony (Jr.), 80, 148; Elizabeth, 148; George, 118; George (Jr.), 56; Margaret, 56, 148; Mary, 56, 148; Mary (Jr.), 56; Thomas, 56.

Leake, Elizabeth, 64; Francis, 64; Mary, 64.

Lee Christopher, 151; Mary, 28; Richard, 11, 28.

Leigh, Daniel, 174.

Lemon, Edward, 45; Katherine, 45; James, 45, 104, 135.

Lenier, Daniel, 56.

Lenton, Ann, 98.

Leonard, Daniel, 75.

Letherington, Thomas (Jr.), 66.

Lewelling, Edward, 198; Richard, 197, 198, 200.

Lewis, Alice, 35; James, 37, 65; Jophall, 25; William, 185.

Levingston, Katheren, 82; William, 81; William (Jr.), 82.

Lindon, Mary, 151.

Linton, Mary, 143, 152; Moses, 53, 141; Moses (Jr.), 54, 141; Moses (3rd), 143; William, 136, 143.

Littleton, Edward, 97, 98.

Lizmore, Lemuel, 175.

Lloyd, Cornelius, 4; Edward, 5.

Londes, Lowndes, Dorothy, 19; Thomas, 53, 55.

Lopas, Anthony, 178.

Loveday, Dorothy, 60; Mary, 60; Robert, 32, 60; Sarah, 60.

Lovett, Ann, 38, 39; Elizabeth, 39; John, 38, 39; Lancaster, 13, 38, 140; Lancaster (Jr.), 38, 39; Mary, 39, 139; Randolph, 39, 170; Thomas, 39.

Lovina, Jean, 162; John, 162, 186; Sarah, 162.

Loving, John, 26; William, 26.

Low, ———, 197.

Lownes, John, 19.

Lowrey, James, 106, 179; William, 106; Yorley, 106.

Ludgall, Nathaniel, 184.

Lues, Richard, 110.

Lully, Rauland, 63.

Lurton, Thomas, 119.

Macafasion, David, 143.

Mackaferson, Andrew, 161; Daniel, 161; Daniel, (Jr.), 161.

Macklanan, Margaret, 177.

Mackeel, Ann, 93; Anthony, 93; Daniel, 93; Darman, 93; John, 93, 136; Margaret, 93; Thomas, 93.

Maclanahan, Elizabeth, 150.

Macoy, Anne, 83; Daniel, 30, 36, 163; Dennis, 193; Dennis (Jr.), 193; Hannah, 83; James, 83; Mary, 83; Michael, 83; Michael (Jr.), 83.

Mahony, Carnellis, 46.

Malbone, Peter, 21; Sarah, 57.

Mamaken (Mamakes), William, 116.

Manning, Elizabeth, 22, 186; Elizabeth (Jr.), 186; John 132, 151; Nicholas, 186, 200; Sarah, 151; Solomon, 151; Thomas, 68, 119, 151; Thomas (Jr.), 151.

Moreland, William, 185.

Markham, John, 24.

Marks, Ann, 32; Elinor, 32; John, 32; Mary, 32; Peter, 20; Richard, 72; Stephen, 32; Stephen (Jr.), 32.

Martin, John, 18, 20, 38, 39, 86; Jonathan, 129; Juell, 78; ———, 5.

Mariatre, Edward, 27; Honnor, 27.

Mason, Alice, 11, 182; Ann, 11, 182, 192; Barbery, 56; Elizabeth, 56; Frances, 35, 41; Francis, 182; George, 41, 133, 182, 192; Henry, 87; Lemuel, 6, 11, 15, 18, 41, 69, 70, 80, 96, 97, 98, 99, 122, 123, 133, 146, 167, 182, 192; Lemuel (Jr.), 23, 192; Margaret, 41; Mary, 146; Nicholas, 8; Thomas, 56, 69, 133, 145, 146, 182, 192; Thomas (Jr.), 156; Tristram, 9, 56.

Masters, John, 35.

Mathews, Elinor, 70; Elinor, (Jr.), 70; James, 70; "Mr.," 173; Thomas, 59; Tobias, 10; John, 30, 118, 128.

Mathias, Mathew, 30.

Matheys, Thomas, 184.

Maund, Elizabeth, 3; Isabel, 3; John, 3; John (Jr.), 3; William, 85, 132, 140, 144, 160, 169, 194.

Maux, John, 165.

Mayo, Trustram, 71.

Memmox, William, 62.

Menfrey, Alexander, 190.

Mercer, Katherine, 160; Thomas, 132, 140, 152; William, 40.
Michael, Darbey, 22.
Middleton, Andrew, 31; Elizabeth, 106; Estell, 106; Henry, 106.
Miles, Gulies, 23; John, 44; William, 23.
Milicent, Samuel, 72.
Miller, Benjamin, 144; Edward, 144; Elizabeth, 144; Joseph (Sr.), 144; Moses, 144; Thomas, 149.
Mills, William, 26.
Milner, Thomas, 108, 157.
Minchen, George, 39, 79.
Minignand, Dominick, 107.
Mograk, Charles, 10.
Mohun, James, 150.
Monyerd, Dominick, 106.
Moone, Sarah, 89.
Moore, More, Alice, 128; Cason, 108; Cason (Jr.), 108, 109; Caton, 101; Edward, 109; Henry, 108, 109; Jacob, 128; John, 81; Mary, 101; Morgan, 128; Morgan (Jr.), 128; Thomas, 98, 109, 128; Sarah, 101, 108, 109; William, 87, 101, 103, 109, 128.
Morgan, David, 44; Thomas, 44; Treharne, 44.
Morris, Elizabeth Mason, 190; Josiah, 94, 95; Thomas, 94.
Morrow, Morry, Murray, Ann, 30, 83; David, 30, 83, 128, 139; Dorothy, 98; Elizabeth, 139; Eve, 139; George, 139; John, 139; Mary, 139, 191.
Morse, Francis, 125.
Mortene, Johana, 24; William, 24.
Morton, Anne, 83; William, 83.
Moseley, Amos, 183; Ann, 182; Arthur, 16, 100, 114, 182, 183; Anthony, 183.
Moreley, Benjamin, 183; Edward, 56, 58, 89, 91, 100, 114, 126, 148, 149, 152, 186; George, 83, 148; John, 127, 148; Joseph, 183; Margaret, 148; Mary, 126; Susan, 16, 126, 183; Susannah, 126; William, 16, 28, 103, 114, 126, 148, 183; William (Jr.), 16.
Mosier, Thomas, 68.
Motlen, John, 129.
Mountgomery, Robert, 142, 158.
Moy, John, 21; Richard, 21.
Mullakin, James, 28, 105; Jane, 28; Rosamond, 22, 28.
Mumford, Thomas, 101.
Munn, ———, 197.
Muncrest, John, 130.
Murden, Edward, 157; Elizabeth, 157; Elizabeth (Jr.), 157; Jeremiah, 157; John, 157; John (Jr.), 157; Mary, 157; Robert, 157; William, 157; ———, 183.
Murfee, Edward, 46; John, 46.
Murfrey, Alexander, 175.
Murray, Alexander, 141; David, 141; David (Jr.), 141; George, 141; John, 141; Mary, 139, 141; Mary (Sr.), 141.
Murten, Alexander, 97.
McEllalen, Jane, 61; John, 61; John (Jr.), 61; Mary, 61.

Narne, Nearne, William, 49, 59, 69, 74.
Nash, Elizabeth, 119; Francis, 118; Frances, 118; John, 118; Martha, 118; Thomas, 159, 160, 168, 177, 184.
Naskun, William, 15.
Nayland, Connall (Conswall?), 195.
Neblin, John, 26.
Nedham, Elizabeth, 26; Jane, 5; Nathaniel, 19; Thomas, 19.
Newby, Nathan, 162.
Newell, Henry, 75; Henry (Jr.), 75.
Newman, Alice, 127; William, 134.
Newport, William, 67, 115.
Newton, Elizabeth, 192; Frances, 57; George, 57, 74, 84, 85, 108, 132, 159, 176.
Nickells, John, 147.
Nichlis (Nicholas?), Andrew, 150; Ann, 150; Elizabeth, 150; Florence, 150; Frances, 154; Francis, 150; Henry, 154; John, 150; Martha, 150; Mary, 150; Nathaniel, 150; Richard, 154; Sarah, 150; William, 150; William (Jr.), 150.
Nicholls, Nichols, Dorothy, 116; Elizabeth, 51; Eleanor, 16; Elizabeth, 140; Henry, 51; John, 109, 161, 162; Judith, 161, 162; Mary, 34; Richard, 51, 191; Richard (Jr.), 51; Sarah, 191.

Nicholas, Andrew, 15, 89; Elinor, 52, 89; Elizabeth, 15, 89; Elizabeth (Jr.), 16; Henry (Sr.), 52; Henry, 13, 16, 136; Henry (Jr.), 52; Mary, 50, 52; Mary (Jr.), 52; William, 15, 89; ———, 143.
Nicholson, John, 183; William, 128, 154, 191.
Noland, ———, 27.
Nolcott, Norcott, Ann, 36; Alice, 155; Giles, 36.
Norman, John, 93.
Norwood, Edward, 131.

Oakes, John, 32.
Odeon, Odien, Ellen, 22; Richard, 22, 48; Elizabeth, 135; William, 22; William (Jr.), 22.
Offley, Henry, 42, 46, 58.
Okeham, Ann, 35; John, 35, 78; Mary, 33, 78; ———, 34.
Old, Edward (Sr.), 131; Edward, 63; Edward (Jr.), 63.
Olephant, Olivant, William, 13.
Oliver, Imannuel, 73.
Osebev'ne, John, 155.
Outlaw, Edward, 62, 99, 153.
Overington, Richard, 85.
Owens, Elinor, 66; John, 106; Richard, 5; Rose, 42; William, 68.

Paine, John, 9.
Parker, Thomas, 193.
Parkinson, Henry, 185.
Parsons, Thomas, 136.
Paterson, Hick Sander (? Alexander), 100.
Patten, Samuel, 108.
Pattman, John, 57.
Payne, Florentine, 11.
Payton, Paton, Johana, 175; William, 134.
Pead, John, 37, 55; John (Jr.), 55; William, 55.
Pearl, Joseph, 186.
Peale, Malachi, 80.
Pearse, John, 54, 127.
Peatre, Robert, 118.
Penewell, John, 37.
Pere, Ann, 40; Henry, 40.
Perkinson, Henry, 190.
Peter, Elizabeth, 135.
Peters, Alice, 74; Ann, 74; Elizabeth, 135; Jacob, 75; James, 40, 55, 74, 122, 152; Rebecca, 75; Margery, 75; Sarah, 74, 108; Simon, 74, 75; Simon (Jr.), 74.
Petie, Robert, 105.
Pette, Thomas, 42.
Petty, Elizabeth, 42; Joseph, 58.
Pew, Stephen, 96.
Phillips, Elizabeth, 48, 129; James, 8; Katherine, 8; Lemuel, 88, 101, 104; Mary, 48.
Philpott, Richard, 43, 62.
Phipp, ———, 3.
Piggott, Sarah, 126, 127.
Pill, Thomas, 4; Thomas (Jr.), 4.
Pinner, Richard, 9, 26; Richard (Jr.), 26; William, 26.
Piper, William, 44.
Pitts, Elizabeth, 94; Jeane, 94; Joseph, 61, 94; Joseph, 111; Thomas, 94.
Platt, Henry, 52.
Plumer, Anne, 12; Francis, 63; Lawrence, 12.
Poole, Ann, 39; Blandina, 42; John, 112, 113; Richard, 25, 38, 39, 42.
Poore, Elizabeth, 70; John, 70.
Pope, Henry, 153; William, 131.
Poslett, Edward, 27, 30; Mary, 30.
Porten, Sarah, 35, 56, 57; William, 35, 56, 96, 97, 146, 159, 200.; William (Jr.), 159.
Porter, Ann, 192; Edward, 25; Florentius, 88; Francis, 88; James, 70, 73, 88; John (Sr.), 41, 45, 91; John, 27, 28, 69, 70, 118; John (Jr.), 45, 91, 130; Mary, 45, 88, 186; Robert, 25; Robert (Jr.), 25; Samuel, 186; William, 41; ———, 66.
Portlock, John, 77, 159, 160, 177, 184.
Porvis, Robert, 18.
Powell, Ann, 132; Dorcas, 120; Elizabeth, 120, 121, 132; John, 120, 121; John (Jr.), 120; Joseph, 193; Katherine, 120; Keziah, 132; Lemuel, 120, 180; Mary, 120, 132; Richard, 120, 121; Sarah, 120, 132; Susan, 120, 121; Thomas, 195; William (Sr.), 193; William, 120, 121, 132.
Powers, Sampson, 164, 175, 176, 178, 200, 201; ———, 164.
Powes, Powys, Mary, 7; Robert, 7, 14, 20; Robert (Jr.), 7, 8.
Poyner, Peter, 122.
Prescott, John, 75.
Preist, John, 20.

Preston, Doctor, 100.
Price, Thomas, 137, 189.
Prince, Sarah, 111.
Pucknell, Sarah, 99, 142.
Pullen, Edward, 172; Robert, 172.
Purdy, William, 46, 124, 125.
Purvine, Lewis, 63; Mary, 63.

Queene, John, 181; Mary, 181.

Rallings, Edward, 110; Jane, 110.
Randall, Giles, 152.
Rasby, Sarah, 81.
Raving, Mary, 150.
Rawlings, Edward, 63, 67, 71.
Ray, Jane, 106.
Raymond, Lemuel, 29.
Rayner, Ann, 134; John, 133; John (Jr.), 133; Richard, 134.
Raynolds, Christopher, 10.
Read, Matthew, 5.
Reaven, Elizabeth, 131; Eleanor, 131; Jeane, 131; William, 131; William (Jr.), 131.
Remmington, Edward, 21.
Rene, Robert, 88.
Reene, John, 101.
Reinolds, Sarah, 17.
Retch, Willie, 24.
Retchford, William, 24.
Reynolds, Elizabeth, 38; Thomas, 38.
Rich, John, 7.
Richards, Dorothy, 14.
Richeson, John, 87; Thomas, 169; William, 74.
Richinson, Thomas, 169.
Ridley, George, 4.
Rigglesworth, Dorothy, 10; Jane, 10; Mary, 10; Peter, 10; George, 26.
Rise, Judith, 186.
Roberts, Margaret, 100, 117; Samuel, 74, 108, 117.
Robinson, Ann, 54; Elizabeth, 48; Henry, 14; John, 21; Mary, 48; Nicholas, 54; Tully, 48, 95; Wm., 4, 48, 95, 105, 118; ——, 27.
Roe, Ann, 26; Richard, 26.
Rogers, Ann, 96; William, 116, 137.
Rothe, John, 36.
Rouse, Robert, 109.
Rose, Alexander, 102; Alexander (Jr.), 102; Ann, 102; George, 198; Isabel, 102; Jane, 102; John, 102, 198; John (Jr.), 198; Martha, 102, 198; Robert, 198; William, 198.
Rosseter, George, 142; John, 99.
Ross, John, 163.
Rowe, Anne, 31.
Rowell, Dorothy, 80.
Russell, Mary, 79; Richard, 27; Robert, 12; Thomas, 78, 79, 162; Thomas (Jr.), 79; William, 28.
Rutland, Edward, 10.
Rye, John, 34.

Sallmon, Elizabeth, 71, 72; John, 71, 72; Mary, 71; Susanna, 71; William, 72.
Sally, Ann, 191; Leaddy, 181, 192; Thomas, 138, 139.
Sanford, John, 38, 59, 60, 86, 87, 103, 115, 130; ——, 131.
Savill, Daniel, 199; Mary, 8, 100; Richard, 100.
Sawyer, Lawrence.
Sayer, Arthur, 48; Frances, 192; Francis, 22, 25, 26, 27, 44, 59, 84, 86, 87, 103, 106, 134, 135, 136, 170, 171, 190; Richard, 85; Thomas, 87, 120, 135.
Scott, David, 105, 133; Francis, 122; Margaret, 164; Robert, 165; ——, 197; Thomas, 105, 106, 108, 130.
Seeley, John, 48; Thomas, 150.
Sewell, John, 76; Mary, 76.
Shaller, Hussey, 199.
Shanks, Thomas, 53.
Shanky, Thomas, 49.
Sharood, James, 113.
Shaw, Charles, 84.
Shea, Edmund, 164.
Sheane, Daniel, 95 .
Sheen, Jermyen, 94, 95.
Shepherd, Mary, 80, 81; Peter, 80, 81.
Sherpoles, Margery, 30.
Sherwood, James, 76; James (Jr.), 76.
Sherley, Daniel, 11; Thomas, 11.
Sholand, Elinor, 83.
Shreefes, Shrilles, William, 110.
Sibsey, John, 9; Mary, 9.
Sidney, John, 22, 69.

Sikes, Costen, 151, 152, 199; Elizabeth, 199; James, 199; Jane, 199; Jean, 160; John, 151; Joseph, 199; Thomas, 151, 152; Walter, 151, 152, 199; Walter (Jr.), 151; William, 199.
Simonds, Henry, 75; James, 11, 50; Thomas, 50.
Simons, James, 159; Thomas, 61.
Skevington, Elizabeth, 130; Thomas, 130.
Skynner, Henry, 169, 170.
Slavin, James, 61.
Smart, George, 90, 124.
Smith, Elizabeth, 44, 82, 104; George, 95, 139; Henry, 88; Humphrey, 179; James, 155; John, 9, 148, 154; Margaret, 105; Mary, 191; Peter, 107, 108, 130, 152, 159; Richard, 60, 82, 104; Sarah, 89, 105; Robert, 66, 89, 97, 104; Thomas, 31; William, 95, 179.
Smithers, Ann, 111; Thomas, 73, 111.
Smythe, Roger, 12.
Snayle, Ann, 29; Jane, 60; Henry, 18, 19, 73; Henry (Jr.), 19.
Southerland, Ann, 32, 33; William, 169, 170.
Southerly, David, 9.
Sothren, Charles, 17.
Sowse, John, 139.
Speks (Speke?), Thomas, 25.
Spencer, John, 6, 8.
Spivie, Ann, 162; Sarah, 166; Matthew, 161, 162, 166, 189.
Spevy, Mathew, 184.
Spratt, Henry, 37, 105, 108; Henry (Jr.), 105; Isabella, 105; Isabella (Jr.), 105; Thomas, 135.
Spring, Aaron, 61, 117, 134, 153, 172; Ann, 172; Ann (Jr.), 172; Avis, 61; Elizabeth, 153, 154; Elizabeth (Jr.), 154; John, 62, 153, 172; Martha, 172; Robert, 10, 61, 154, 172; Robert (Jr.), 62; Sarah, 153, 172; Moses, 61, 142, 143, 172; Moses (Jr.), 172.
Squire, John, 111.
Stafford, William, 85.
Starnell, Anne, 17; Elizabeth, 17; Richard, 15, 16; Richard (Jr.), 17.
Stanley, Elinor, 51.
Stenson, John, 31.
Stevens, Charles, 10; George, 34.
Stephens, Humphrey, 62.
Stone, Richard, 98.
Stoneham, Ann, 164.
Stratton, Henry, 63; John, 20; ———; 32.
Stringer, Daniel, 73.
Strong, John, 8.
Stubes, Morris, 94, 95.
Suellivant, John, 79.
Suggs, George, 194; Joseph, 159, 194; Joseph (Jr.), 194; Margaret, 194; Mary, 194; Moses, 194; Sarah, 194; Thomas, 194; William, 193; William (Jr.), 193, 194.
Sutton, John, 6.
Swaine, John, 24.
Syllivan, John, 40.

Tabor, John, 175; Mary, 175, 176; Rosamond, 176; Thomas, 175; Thomas (Jr.), 176.
Tanner Daniel, 11.
Tart, Alice, 181; Eleazer, 50, 82, 117, 146, 147, 154, 155, 161, 180, 181, 196; Elizabeth, 181, 196; Elnathan, 180; Enoch, 181; Joseph, 180, 181; Mary, 181; Theophilus, 180; Thomas, 180; William, 161.
Taylor, Ann, 158, 183, 186; Hester, 23; Jacob, 128; John, 65, 68; Judith, 186; Katherine, 91; Margaret (Jr.), 65, 68; Mary, 23, 65, 68; Richard, 65, 68; Richard (Jr.), 65; Rose, 128; Susanna, 65, 68; Theodore, 158, 183; Thomas, 68, 183; William, 182.
Thelaball, Dyer, 187; Elizabeth, 11, 41, 145, 146, 182; Frances, 28; Francis, 145, 167, 187; Francis (Jr.), 187; James, 117, 182, 187; James (Jr.), 145; John, 145; Lemuel, 145; Margaret, 187; Sarah, 187.
Thomas, Abraham, 16; Elizabeth, 131; Hester, 34; Mary, 34; William, 34.
Thorowgood, Adam, 96; Adam (Jr.), 96; Argoll, 96, 129; Dinah, 192; Frances, 96, 97; Francis, 96; John, 96, 97, 105; John (Jr.), 96; Robert, 96; Rose, 97.
Thraver, John, 46; John, 156.

Thruston, Elizabeth, 196; James, 170, 171; Jeane, 171; John, 159, 163, 170, 171, 196; Malachy, Malachi, 39, 87, 88, 96, 97, 102, 125, 134, 135, 157, 159, 161, 162, 163, 164, 165, 170, 171, 196; Malachi (Jr.), 170; Margaret, 196; Martha, 171, 196; Martha (Jr.), 171; Sarah, 171; ———, 131.
Tompkins, Thomas, 78.
Tomson, Richard, 17.
Toppin, Ann, 35; Arthur, 35.
Tooker, Thomas, 11.
Tottle, John, 80.
Townsend, Jean, 144; Jonah, 144; Joseph, 144; Joseph (Jr.), 144; Mary, 144.
Tranter, Edward, 136, 157.
Traucer, John 77.
Trevethan, Ann, 191.
Triggs, Elizabeth, 64; Elizabeth (Jr.), 64; Henry, 64; Mary, 64; Paul, 64; Thomas, 64.
Trustram, Barbery, 56.
Tucker, Edward, 53; Elinor, 199; Elizabeth, 53; John, 53; Robert, 53, 196; Thomas, 53; Thomas (Jr.), 53; William, 199.
Tull, Jane, 113; Thomas, 113.
Tully, John, 190; Mary, 190.
Turner, John, 23, 26, 73, 124; Mary, 124; Thomas, 124 Winford, 124; Winifred, 23.
Tutte, John, 10.
Tuttge, John, 30.
Twyst, William, 116, 115.

Valentine, Frances, 23; George, 23, 59, 169; John, 198.
Vaughan, Elizabeth, 125; William, 122, 124.
Veale, Elizabeth, 189; John, 190; Mary, 189; Morrice, 189; Morrice (Jr.), 190; William, 189.
Vincent, Elizabeth, 14; William, 14.

Waite, Ann, 32.
Wake, Henry, 9.
Wakefield, Dorothy, 193; Edward, 196; Elizabeth, 196; George, 32; John, 196; Joseph, 196; Sarah, 196; Thomas (Sr.), 196; Thomas, 196.
Wakling, Abraham, 47.
Walford, Joseph, 151.
Walke, Anthony, 147, 148; Margaret, 148; Mary, 148; Robert, 148; Thomas, 147, 148, 149; Thomas (Jr.), 147.
Walker, Elizabeth, 154, 155; George, 76; Samuel, 154, 155.
Wallis, Wallice, John, 59, 177; John (Jr.), 177; Martha, 177; Richard, 178; Thomas, 136, 178, 190; William (Sr.), 190; William, 178, 190.
Wallston, Walsten, Henry, 119; Samuel, 103.
Ward, Edward, 29, 40; Edward (Jr.), 29; Elizabeth, 29; Elizabeth (Jr.), 29; Frances, 29; John, 156, 196; Thomas, 6, 13, 109, 117.
Wardin, Alice, 127; James, 127, 183.
Warington, Marmaduke, 54.
Wasten, Francis, 33.
Waterman, Richard, 60.
Wattford, John, 137, 151.
Watkins, Frances, 5; John, 5; John (Jr.), 5.
Watson, Henry, 35, 103.
Wayburne, Michael, 31, 115.
Wayte, John, 120.
Webb, Thomas, 21, 131; William, 21, 76.
Weblin, Anna, 106; George, 106; Henry, 106; John, 106; John (Jr.), 106.
Webster, John, 65.
Wedicke, Mary, 30.
Weldbone, Joseph, 70.
Wenham, William, 153, 168.
Wesgate, Anne, 6, 18; Elizabeth, 18, 22; Ellen, 18; Henry, 6, 8, 18; Roger, 18.
Wesley, Nicholas, 67.
Weston, Ann, 173; Edward, 36, 37, 103, 135; Edwin, 173; John, 109, 152.
Whettinhall, John, 117.
Whidby, Elizabeth, 140, 160; George, 140, 160; George (Jr.), 160.
Whiddon, Augustine, 140; Augustine (Jr.), 140; John, 64, 140, 141; John (Jr.), 64; Sarah, 140; William, 140.

Whinfield, Winfell, Abigail, 66; Ann 166; George, 166; Katherine, 166, 168; Henry, 166, 189; John, 41, 43, 110, 153, 166; John (Jr.), 110; Juno, 168; Sarah, 166; Thomas, 166.
Whitbe, Richard, 103.
White, Francis, 85; John, 36, 76, 199; Jane, 91; Joseph, 91; Mary, 7; Robert, 34; Susanna, 91; William, 47, 91.
Whitehurst, Eleanor, 137; Elizabeth, 137; Ellen, 13; Ellen (Jr.), 13; Henry, 52, 62, 136, 137, 154; James, 52, 137, 138, 139, 179, 201; Jane, 179; John, 52, 63, 136; John (Jr.), 136, 137; Margaret, 51; Mary, 137, 201; Richard, 94, 178, 179; Richard (Jr.), 178; Robert, 62; Robert (Jr.), 63; Sarah, 138; Susan, 13; William, 94, 138, 178, 179.
Whitfield, John, 28.
Whitford, David, 76, 81, 82, 103, 104.
Whiten, John, 99.
Whitson, Joseph, 59; Joseph (Jr.), 59; Thomas, 59.
Wiblin, John, 101, 107.
Wickstead, Elizabeth, 9; Margery, 9.
Widdeike, Henry, 89.
Wildbore, Elizabeth, 139; John, 103, 104, 139.
Willbro, John, 104.
Wilder, Ann, 81; Edward, 49, 117; Henry, 117; Michael, 117.
Wilkerson, Arnall, 12.
Wilkins, William, 159, 195.
Williams, Edy, 155; Elizabeth, 122, 150; Elinor, 34; Elizabeth, 34; Evan, 34; Frances, 61; Jane, 61; John, 72; Mary, 44; Nicholas, 61; Richard, 72, 155; Roger, 7; Sarah, 7, 34; ———, 132.
Williamson, Bartholomew, 114, 140; Dorcas, 147; John (Sr.), 49; John, 50, 147; John (Jr.), 49; Mary, 58; Milborough, 49, 50; Milbough (Jr.), 49; Nicholas, 50; Richard, 58, 140.
Willette, Evan, 10.
Willis, Elizabeth, 44; John, 186, 189, 200.
Willoughby, Elizabeth, 41; Sarah, 41; Thomas, 41, 65, 133, 192, 194.
Wilson, Elizabeth, 150; Hugh, 129; James, 174, 183, 185, 195; John, 142, 143, 150, 158, 180; Lemuel, 194, 195; Sarah, 180; Thomas, 134, 142, 158, 166, 180; Thomas (Jr.), 142, 143, 180; Willis, 156, 195.
Windham, Edward, 8.
Winfeld, John, 154.
Windett, Edmond, 9; Elizabeth, 9.
Wishart, Elizabeth, 73; Francis, 74; James, 29, 46, 73, 74, 124, 130; John, 74; Joyce, 74; Mary, 124; Thomas, 74; William, 74.
Wittinghall, John, 100.
Wood, Thomas, 77.
Woodhouse, Elizabeth, 63, 101, 102; Henry, 17, 23, 67, 101, 109; Henry (Jr.), 17, 101, 102; Horatio, 17, 101; John, 17, 63; 101, 102; Luce, 101; Maria, 17; Ruth, 63; William, 18.
Woodward, Elizabeth, 67; Francis, 29, 40, 67; Henry, 67; John, 67; Mary, 67.
Woody, Robert, 9, 43.
Workman, John, 5, 13, 29, 45, 46; Thomas, 5, 12, 13, 46; Thomas (Jr.), 13; Mrs. ———, 13.
Worland, John, 23, 29.
Worley, Edward, 60.
Worsia, Mary, 172.
Worsle, Thomas, 144.
Worsley, Thomas, 62, 172.
Worsman, John, 11.
Wright, Ann, 153; Christian, 15, 33; Francis, 181; George, 8, 18, 23, 29; James, 15, 100, 120; Jane, 15; John, 120; Katherine, 100; Richard, 15; Tabitha, 100; Thomas, 9, 15, 32; Thomas (Jr.), 15; William, 15, 100, 198.
Wyatt, Anna, 166.
Wybord, Michael, 115.

Yates, Elizabeth, 24, 64; Faith, 64; Jane, 64; Jane (Jr.), 64; Joan, 23; Mary, 24, 64; Richard, 23, 27, 64; Richard (Jr.), 24, 64.
Yeardley, Francis, 7, 8; Sir George, 97; Mrs., 19.

MISCELLANEOUS INDEX

Accomac County, 37.
Amsterdam, 14.
Antigua, 133.
Arms, Coats of, 97, 171.
Back Creek, 159.
Baers St. Marys, near Colchester, Eng., 195.
Barbadoes, 148.
Barren Point, 24, 50.
Baytree Hole, 23.
Bear Point, 48.
Bear Quarter, 105.
Bedfordshire, Eng., 77.
Beech Ridge, 112.
Bermudas, 17.
Bigleswade, Bedfordshire, Eng., 77, 78.
Black Walnut Ridge, 87.
Blackwater in Coratock, 75.
Books, 17, 27, 28, 35, 80, 88, 100, 130, 146, 147, 154, 175, 198.
Broad Creek 103.
Broad Neck, 132, 187.
Brushy Neck, 134, 170.
Carolina, 90.
Chester Forrest, 80.
Church of Lynnhaven, 97.
Churches, 79, 97, 107.
Church Lane, St. Giles in the Fields, London, 90.
Clothing, etc., 21, 74, 50, 60, 88, 103, 109, 110, 114, 120, 126, 133, 172, 186.
Cockington, Eng., 167.
Codd Plantation, 83.
Colchester, Eng., 195.
Colonies Branch, 129.
Costin's Island, 151.
Craney Island Creek, 15.
Craney Point, 9.
Currituck, 171.
Curituck Bay, 147.

Dartsmouth, Eng., 80, 81, 167.
Deep Creek, 17, 64, 75.
Drum Point, 24.
Dublin, Ireland, 149.
Durham, Eng., 27.
Eaglescliffe, Durham, Eng., 27.
Education, 15, 28, 63, 87, 96, 102, 142, 164.
Elizabeth River Parish, 35, 56, 133, 134, 144, 145, 159, 192, 194, 197; Bequest to poor of, 28.
Elizabeth Town, 130.
Fancies Ridge, 172.
Fishing Creek, 146.
Francious (Fenchurch?) Street, London, Eng., 135.
Fresh Ponds, Lynnhaven Parish, 78.
Goose Hill, 50.
Gregorys Creek, 17.
Hague, The, Holland, 18.
Herefordshire, Eng., 90.
Hickory Branch, 197.
Hockes Ridge, 100.
Hog Island, 39.
Horse Bridge Run, 105.
Ireland, 149.
Isle of Wight County Town, 165; Lower parish of, 165; Upper parish of, 77.
Isle of Wight, England, 26.
James City, 111.
Jamaica, 26.
Jewelry, 15, 17, 18, 21, 35, 44, 47, 57, 76, 80, 87, 90, 92, 97, 98, 108, 112, 122, 133, 135, 148, 156, 176, 177, 186.
Little Creek, 18, 19, 20, 37, 46, 70, 73, 90, 101, 155.
London, Eng., 12, 90, 135, 149, 173.
London Bridge, Lower Norfolk Co., 86.
Long Island, N. Y., 37.
Long Point, 200.
Long Ridge, 108.
Lyons Quarter, 150.
Lynnhaven Church, 79, 97.
Lynnhaven Parish, 3, 8, 28, 37, 41, 52, 67, 70, 76, 78, 92, 95, 101, 110, 111; Bequest to poor of, 115.
Maryland, 90.
Matchepongo, 86.
Ministers, 3, 7, 90, 130, 194.
Modbury, Eng., 80, 81.
Mossy Neck, 200.
Mount Pleasant, 131.
Muddy Branch, 134.
Nansemond Co., 32, 181.
Nawnoys Creek, 105.
Newport, R. I., 156.
Negroes, 82, 97, 98, 112, 132, 145, 148, 152, 153, 162, 163, 174, 187, 191, 195, 196.
Norfolk County, Records of, 1.
Norfolk Town, 159, 163, 164, 165, 170, 176, 190, 196, 201; Bequest to poor of, 159.

Paradise Creek, 197.
Plate, 9, 32, 57, 78, 102, 145, 146, 171.
Plymouth, Eng., 80, 173.
Point Comfort, 90.
Poplar Ridge, 112.
Possum Neck, 147.
Possum Quarter, 104.
Possum Ridge, 112.
Princess Anne Co., 170, 171.
Reedy Branch, 190.
Richford Swamp, 149, 152.
Rolph's Ridge, 48.
Royden, Eng., 195.
St. Giles in the Fields, London, 90.
Scots Walk, London, Eng., 135.
Scotland, 106.
Servants, 4, 5, 8, 9, 10, 17, 18, 22, 49, 60, 61, 85, 92, 112, 135, 142, 164, 173.
Ships and Boats, 9, 12, 72, 133, 148, 165.
Southampton, Eng., 26.
Sowells Point, 74.
Surgeons, 3. 4. 136.
Tanners Creek, 43, 49, 77, 179; Bequest to poor of, 107.
Tanners Creek Church, 107.
Templemans Ridge, 109.
Three Runs, 63, 136.
Thames Quarter, 179.
Throop (Thorp?), England, 136.
Tobacco, 11, 18, 19, 28, 33, 71, 75, 101, 107, 135, 142, 159, 171, 172, 175, 179, 196.
Walnut Neck, 48.
Weapons, 7, 9, 17, 18, 23, 35, 38, 42, 43, 47, 48, 51, 61, 62, 63, 65, 66, 74, 75, 76, 78, 80, 86, 119, 120, 122, 123, 131, 137, 154, 166, 171, 188, 196, 200.
Wilderness, 180.
Wolfe's Neck, 37.
Wormleybury House, Wormley Parish, Herefordshire, Eng., 90.
Wormley Parish, Herefordshire, Eng., 90.

www.ingramcontent.com/pod-product-compliance
Lightning Source LLC
Chambersburg PA
CBHW050143170426
43197CB00011B/1947

* 9 7 8 1 5 8 5 4 9 2 6 4 0 *